FARRAR
STRAUS
GIROUX

JOHN BETJEMAN

Collected Poems

John Betjeman was born near Highgate, London, in 1906. After reading English literature at Magdalen College, Oxford, he worked in various jobs, including stints at the *Architectural Review*, as the British press attaché in Dublin during World War II, and as codeveloper of a series of British county guides. He published prolifically through the 1930s and 1940s, and achieved sudden fame in 1958 with the release of his *Collected Poems*. A hugely popular and influential national poet, he continued to work in radio and television and as a film critic. John Betjeman was knighted in 1969 and made poet laureate in 1972. He died in Trebetherick in 1984.

COLLECTED POEMS

COLLECTED

POEMS

JOHN BETJEMAN

FARRAR, STRAUS AND GIROUX

NEW YORK

Farrar, Straus and Giroux
19 Union Square West, New York 10003

Copyright © 2006 by The Estate of John Betjeman
Introduction copyright © 2006 by Andrew Motion
All rights reserved
Printed in the United States of America
Collected Poems *originally published in 1958 by John Murray (Publishers), a division*
of Hodder Headline, Great Britain
Summoned by Bells *originally published in 1960 by John Murray (Publishers), a*
division of Hodder Headline, Great Britain
This collected edition originally published in 2006 by John Murray (Publishers), a
division of Hodder Headline, Great Britain
Published in the United States by Farrar, Straus and Giroux
First American edition, 2006

Library of Congress Cataloging-in-Publication Data
Betjeman, John, 1906–1984.
Collected poems / John Betjeman. — *1st American ed.*
p. cm.
Includes the author's verse autobiography Summoned by bells.
ISBN-13: 978-0-374-12653-7 (pbk. : alk. paper)
ISBN-10: 0-374-12653-4 (pbk. : alk. paper)
I. Betjeman, John, 1906–1984. Summoned by bells. II. Title.

PR6003.E77A17 2006
821'.912—dc22

2006015898

www.fsgbooks.com

1 3 5 7 9 10 8 6 4 2

Contents

UNCOLLECTED POEMS (1982)

Acknowledgements

Grateful acknowledgement is made to the Editors of *Punch*, *The London Magazine*, *The New Yorker*, *Harper's Bazaar*, *The Saturday Book*, *The Cornhill*, *The Atlantic Monthly*, *Encounter*, *The Observer*, *Vogue*, *Weekend Telegraph* and *The Philbeach Quarterly*. "The Harvest Hymn" was published as a letter in *Farmers Weekly*.

The author is grateful to his friends John Hanbury Angus Sparrow, Lord Birkenhead and Thomas Edward Neil Driberg. The first made and introduced the original selection for *Selected Poems*; the second advised on the first edition of *Collected Poems*; and the third corrected grammar and punctuation, and changed some lines for the better.

Additional Acknowledgements
for UK 4th Edition

The author is grateful to H.R.H. The Prince of Wales for his gracious permission to print 'A Ballad of the Investiture' and to the late Thomas Edward Neil Driberg again for his consistent encouragement and constructive help. He thanks the editors of *The Architect*, *The Cornhill Magazine*, *Encounter*, *The London Magazine*, *The Saturday Book* and *The Sunday Express*, where some of the poems were first published.

Introduction

In the course of his long life (1906–1984), John Betjeman became the most popular British poet of the late twentieth century. He outsold his contemporaries (including W. H. Auden); several of his lines entered the national bloodstream (mainly from 'lighter' poems such as 'Slough', 'A Subaltern's Love-song', 'How to Get On in Society'); and he became a television celebrity before the term was invented. Furthermore, in a career which was at once separate from and entwined with his life as a poet, he spearheaded a movement to change public aversion to most things Victorian into general approval of that period's buildings and styles. As an example of a writer helping to create the taste by which he wished to be judged, it is an achievement to compare with T. S. Eliot's championing of modernism.

Yet Betjeman – who was briefly taught by Eliot at Highgate Junior School in north London – is widely regarded as modernism's great opposite; as the poet who managed, in Philip Larkin's words, to 'knock over the "No Road Through to Real Life" signs that this new tradition erected'. Even at the height of his fame, this created problems for Betjeman, and for his audience. It meant that readers who defended his use of traditional forms, his moments of music hall comedy, his accessibility and lack of writerly guile, were branded as reactionaries, while people who attacked him risked seeming doctrinaire, academy-bound, and interested in newness to the exclusion of everything else. No one wrote about this better than Larkin. In the longest of several essays on Betjeman – the

Introduction to a *Collected Poems* for a largely uninterested American audience – Larkin admitted: 'The quickest way to start a punch-up between two British literary critics is to ask them what they think of the poems of Sir John Betjeman. For while their author has attained nearly every honour open to a writer of verse in this country, his work and its reputation still evoke a remarkable variety of response here.'

Twenty-two years after Betjeman's death, and in the centenary of his birth, this 'variety' is still evident. On the one hand there is still a flourishing Betjeman Society, a sizeable (but ageing) audience, and evidence to suggest that some of the most popular contemporary British poets (Simon Armitage, Wendy Cope) appeal to the readership he attracted. On the other hand, there is still a lack of academic interest in his work (university English departments have generally voted with the modernists), and no properly edited edition of his poems or prose.

Inevitably, this creates a sense of unevenness, even of instability, in his reputation. But there is nothing new in this. Right from the beginning of his career (his first collection, *Mount Zion*, was published in 1932), Betjeman went to considerable lengths to complicate the question of how seriously his readers should take him. *Mount Zion* itself – elaborately designed by his friend Edward James – set the pattern. Were the fancy typefaces a joke or a serious act of homage to earlier ages? And what about the poems? Some were obviously skittish ('The 'Varsity Students' Rag'), some were obviously sombre ('Death in Leamington'), but many walked a fine line between the two types, or actually partook of both, in a way which confused categories. The subjects and titles of several poems compounded the problem – and its pleasures: 'An Eighteenth-

Century Calvinistic Hymn', 'For Nineteenth-Century Burials', 'The Sandemanian Meeting-House in Highbury Quadrant'. Nine years after *The Waste Land*, poetry-readers were used to seeing the old laws flouted – but Eliot and Pound and company did their flouting in the open, using broken forms which reflected the fragmented interior worlds of their poems. Betjeman's rebellion was to put his new wine in old bottles, to make the staid Victorians dance, to see the airiness as well as the pathos in fast-vanishing things, and to incorporate details into the tradition (all those place names and ecclesiastical sub-groups) while producing unofficial elegies for it.

There is a word for this: camp – meaning to make light of what is in fact taken seriously. And what *Mount Zion* did was to introduce into British poetry a voice that makes better use of the camp range, of its subtle opportunities, unexpected depths and defensive tendernesses, than any other modern poet. It is the single most significant quality of the early work in Betjeman's *Collected Poems*. But because the register of his camp is so readily mistaken for mere silliness, and because its texture has a delicacy which can easily be overlooked, it might also count as a drawback. So it is worth emphasizing that although Betjeman wrote a lot of funny poems, and said a lot of funny things, his camp (and the instinct for self-protection upon which it feeds) has its origin in very unfunny experience. It is this experience which forms the bedrock of his work, and guarantees its fundamental seriousness.

In his verse autobiography *Summoned by Bells* (1960), Betjeman admits to the embarrassments and difficulties of growing up in wartime England with a name that sounded German:

"Your name is German, John" —
But I had always thought that it was Dutch . . .
That tee-jay-ee, that fatal tee-jay-ee
Which I have watched the hesitating pens
Of Government clerks and cloakroom porters funk.
I asked my mother. "No," she said, "it's Dutch;
Thank God you're English on your mother's side."
O happy, happy Browns and Robinsons!

It wasn't just the 'tee-jay-ee' that was 'fatal'; there was the question of whether his name ended in '-n' or '-nn', too. And although Betjeman would have poo-poohed the idea of submitting the name-business to a thorough Freudian analysis, there is enough readily available evidence in the poems to prove that his upbringing was fraught with issues of belonging, identity, acceptance, and tradition. It helps to explain why, through his prep school, then Marlborough, and even more decisively at Oxford, he went out of his way to cultivate the cultivated — as well as the rich and titled. It also sheds light on why he preferred the old forms in his writing. He wanted to be himself, to maintain a watchful distance, but he also needed to develop contacts with the national past, and particularly with the Victorian period — which represented stability and prosperity — because his personal past was less than he wished it to be.

Around and beneath the formative name-drama lies an even more vitalizing difficulty: Betjeman's relationship with his father as both man and tradesman. Betjeman senior spent all his life in the family firm (founded 1820) making furniture — most of it for the luxury market ('Maharajahs' dressing-cases', 'the Tantalus / On which the family fortune had been made', 'The Alexandra Palace patent lock', 'The Betjemann trolley').

Although many of these objects were beautiful, and produced to a high standard, the young Betjeman spurned them, along with the idea that he should enter the family Works. He would have been the fourth generation to do so, but this was not the kind of tradition he wanted. It was trade, and therefore beneath him.

Betjeman senior was understandably upset by his son's decision, and by the feelings which informed it. (He might have felt a little baffled, too: weren't these Tantaluses and so on the domestic equivalent of much of the architecture that Betjeman spent his life defending?) Their relationship suffered accordingly – though Betjeman generally had the good grace to keep quiet about this, in print at least, during his father's life-time. But after his father died, he turned to writing about him at regular intervals, and what had once been a figure of fun and dislike became deeply touching – so touching, in fact, and so haunting, that Betjeman senior lives through the *Collected Poems*, let alone *Summoned by Bells*, as a quietly admonitory spirit: deaf, suffering, pathetic, and terminal:

> "Oh, little body, do not die.
>   You hold the soul that talks to me
> Although our conversation be
>   As wordless as the windy sky."

> So looked my father at the last
>   Right in my soul, before he died,
> Though words we spoke went heedless past
>   As London traffic-roar outside.

Poems such as this ('A Child Ill') appear to be a far cry from the facetiousness of *Mount Zion* – and indeed many of

Betjeman's best poems have the same compelling clarity of utterance and directness of gaze. Yet they spring from similar ground. The campery is a form of protection for Betjeman's deepest feelings – it converts them into forms and a diction that is entertaining and unthreatening. The poems about his father show deep feelings with the protective veil ripped away. They are studies of remorse and self-accusation, howls about death in general and the prospect of his own death in particular, and frettings about time. They prove his remarkable range as a poet, but they also show that its two opposite poles are connected.

Given this, it is not surprising to find Betjeman searching time and again for a mood or a place he can consider safe. The word 'safe', or 'safety', appears like a nervous tic in his poems – 'safe in bed', 'safety with old friends', 'safe in G. F. Bodley's greens and browns, / Safe in the surge of undogmatic hymns': there are at least ten uses of the word in the one hundred-odd pages of *Summoned by Bells*, and it connects with every one of his interests and allegiances: his passion for the seaside (especially Cornwall), which distils childhood memories of feeling coddled and secure; his enthusiasm for parish churches and their time-honoured reassurances; his addiction to Victoriana, with its elaborate manifestations of solidity. Even his snobbishness forms a part of the pattern: it wasn't greed or the wish for an easy life that drew him to posh people, it was his sense of their ancient rootedness. And there is a camp manifestation, too: Betjeman's notorious teddy bear Archibald, much mentioned in his poems, much filmed in his films, and evidently much loved, is an image of childhood security ('my safe old bear') that he worked hard to unite with his public persona.

It is only a short step from Betjeman's search for safety to his devotion to things – to objects that defy the passage of time, and accumulate significance as they do so. The few people to have written well about his work have often commented on this, enjoying the skill with which he uses hard facts and proper names to evoke time past. They are right to do so: he has a wonderfully sharp eye and a brilliant memory, and a sure sense of the pathos which lurks in half-forgotten or easily missed details. In this respect (and paradoxically) his work recalls James Joyce – a modernist who revelled in the everyday, but whose experimental forms seem entirely at odds with Betjeman's own styles.

It is not simply that, for Betjeman, things, and the names of things, are a source of nostalgic pleasure. Rather, they become for him a means of conveying strong feelings that he may well choose not to deliver directly – either because the subject is especially inaccessible or awkward, or because his poetics require him to deal with 'sensations' rather than 'thoughts'. One of his best poems, 'Devonshire Street W.1', is a good case in point. The street and consulting room, which we see at the beginning of the poem, act both as a background for the reticence which forms an important part of the poem's subject, and also as a way of dramatizing the unspoken fears of the two central characters – an elderly husband and wife. As readers, we are then allowed into the mind of the man, and hear him wondering, 'Why was I made / For the long and the painful deathbed coming to me?' It is a moment of shocking candour, from which Betjeman characteristically turns away in the final quatrain to concentrate on everyday things. But this re-focusing is not an evasion. It is a way for the wife simultaneously to accept her husband's reserve, find brief comfort in the familiar, and register a literally unspeakable sadness:

She puts her fingers in his as, loving and silly,
At long-past Kensington dances she used to do
"It's cheaper to take the tube to Piccadilly
And then we can catch a nineteen or a twenty-two."

Time and again in the *Collected Poems*, and throughout *Summoned by Bells*, things are trusted to carry the emotional burden. The process has the great advantage of making the poems feel intimate, and of allowing them to retain their impact in a way that would be impossible if their conclusions had been more obviously spelt-out. Think of 'that wide bedroom with its two branched lighting' in 'Oxford: Sudden Illness at the Bus-stop', or the hock and seltzer, the astrakhan coat, the morocco portmanteau, and the palms on the staircase in 'The Arrest of Oscar Wilde at the Cadogan Hotel'. They are adornments, of course, and often enjoyably actual and shrewdly positioned. But they are, more significantly, the means of conveying whatever fear, dread, desire, sorrow, delight is the poem's main subject.

There is another side to this. Things anchor Betjeman – they allow him to show his heart without speaking his mind – and to that extent they are a comfort and pleasure. But they can have the opposite effect too. Physical reminders of death terrify him (the crumbling teeth, failing limbs, deaf ears, and rotting corpses we find in some of his finest poems – 'On a Portrait of a Deaf Man', for instance, or 'I. M. Walter Ramsden'). And living bodies can shame him – either because they are trapped in a situation that he regrets (being 'that strange, rather common little boy'), or because they are repellent. The 'large behinds and jingling chains, / And riddled teeth and riddling brains' of an early poem like 'The City' manifests a discomfort that swells with time and eventually includes himself ('For I am bald and old and green').

This awkwardness gains a special edge in Betjeman's love poetry. Typically – and in line with his general tone of camp – he makes a joke of it by showing off about how much he likes big girls. He seems to be saying: look, these women are obviously slightly grotesque, so how could anyone believe I liked them *really*? Think of 'Pam, I adore you, Pam, you great big mountainous sports girl', or the 'Ringleader, tom-boy, and chum to the weak' that is 'Myfanwy' ('Were you a hockey girl, tennis or gym?'), or the 'golden hiking girl' of 'Senex', or Miss Joan Hunter Dunn with her 'speed of a swallow' and 'grace of a boy', or the 'sturdy' and 'flannel-slack'd' legs in 'The Licorice Fields at Pontefract', or the beefy racket-squeezing Amazon of 'The Olympic Girl'. In every case Betjeman seems to be letting himself off the charge of being taken seriously as a lover. Yet as the evidence accumulates, we realize the joke is on us. These big girls truly are desirable – and for reasons that chime tellingly with his other thoughts about safety. They are made unthreatening by recurring as a type. They are reassuringly familiar to the extent of being part-male (Betjeman always insisted that none of us is wholly straight or gay, but a variable percentage of both). And they take charge.

One of the highest accolades Larkin gave Betjeman was to call him 'an accepter, not a rejecter, of his time and the people he shares it with'. This quite properly emphasizes what is democratic in Betjeman, in spite of his reputation for being a snob preoccupied by the horrors of 'ghastly good taste'. But Larkin might have added that Betjeman accepted his own self, too – his flaws and fears and primitive needs, as well as his sociable gifts. This helps to explain why the nostalgia in his poems, and their instinct to run for cover, does not often turn into sentimentality. Betjeman is generally a tough-minded, as well as a tender-eyed, poet. That is reason enough for thinking that in the years following this centenary, his star will remain bright. But it will only attain its proper height if his readers can attune themselves to what is complex and unusual in his poems: their cultivation of comedy for serious ends, and their reliance on familiar things to express unusually intense feeling. 'I do not think that what is said or written matters, but what is felt. Often most "serious" feelings are expressed in a joke. I very rarely talk about what I really feel.' So Betjeman wrote to his father in 1929. He could equally well have said it every other day of his life.

Andrew Motion

COLLECTED POEMS

Death in Leamington

She died in the upstairs bedroom
    By the light of the ev'ning star
That shone through the plate glass window
    From over Leamington Spa.

Beside her the lonely crochet
    Lay patiently and unstirred,
But the fingers that would have work'd it
    Were dead as the spoken word.

And Nurse came in with the tea-things
    Breast high 'mid the stands and chairs—
But Nurse was alone with her own little soul,
    And the things were alone with theirs.

She bolted the big round window,
    She let the blinds unroll,
She set a match to the mantle,
    She covered the fire with coal.

And "Tea!" she said in a tiny voice
    "Wake up! It's nearly *five*."
Oh! Chintzy, chintzy cheeriness,
    Half dead and half alive!

Do you know that the stucco is peeling?
    Do you know that the heart will stop?

From those yellow Italianate arches
   Do you hear the plaster drop?

Nurse looked at the silent bedstead,
   At the gray, decaying face,
As the calm of a Leamington ev'ning
   Drifted into the place.

She moved the table of bottles
   Away from the bed to the wall;
And tiptoeing gently over the stairs
   Turned down the gas in the hall.

Hymn

The Church's Restoration
  In eighteen-eighty-three
Has left for contemplation
  Not what there used to be.
How well the ancient woodwork
  Looks round the Rect'ry hall,
Memorial of the good work
  Of him who plann'd it all.

He who took down the pew-ends
  And sold them anywhere
But kindly spared a few ends
  Work'd up into a chair.
O worthy persecution
  Of dust! O hue divine!
O cheerful substitution,
  Thou varnishéd pitch-pine!

Church furnishing! Church furnishing!
  Sing art and crafty praise!
He gave the brass for burnishing
  He gave the thick red baize,
He gave the new addition,
  Pull'd down the dull old aisle,
—To pave the sweet transition
  He gave th' encaustic tile.

Of marble brown and veinéd
   He did the pulpit make;
He order'd windows stainéd
   Light red and crimson lake.
Sing on, with hymns uproarious,
   Ye humble and aloof,
Look up! and oh how glorious
   He has restored the roof!

The 'Varsity Students' Rag

I'm afraid the fellows in Putney rather wish they had
The social ease and manners of a 'varsity undergrad,
For tho' they're awf'lly decent and up to a lark as a rule
You want to have the 'varsity touch after a public school.

CHORUS:

> *We* had a rag at Monico's. *We* had a rag at the Troc.,
> And the one we had at the Berkeley gave the customers
> quite a shock.
> *Then* we went to the Popular, and after that—oh my!
> I *wish* you'd seen the rag we had in the Grill Room at the
> Cri.

I started a rag in Putney at our Frothblower's Branch down
there;
We got in a damn'd old lorry and drove to Trafalgar Square;
And we each had a couple of toy balloons and made the hell of a
din,
And I saw a bobby at Parson's Green who looked like running
us in.

CHORUS: We, etc.

But that's nothing to the rag we had at the college the other
night;
We'd gallons and gallons of cider—and I got frightfully tight.

And then we smash'd up ev'rything, and what was the funniest
part
We smashed some rotten old pictures which were priceless works
of art.

CHORUS: We, etc.

There's something about a 'varsity man that distinguishes him
from a cad:
You can tell by his tie and blazer he's a 'varsity undergrad,
And you know that he's always ready and up to a bit of a lark,
With a toy balloon and a whistle and some cider after dark.

CHORUS: We, etc.

6

The City

Business men with awkward hips
And dirty jokes upon their lips,
And large behinds and jingling chains,
And riddled teeth and riddling brains,
And plump white fingers made to curl
Round some anaemic city girl,
And so lend colour to the lives
And old suspicions of their wives.

Young men who wear on office stools
The ties of minor public schools,
Each learning how to be a sinner
And tell "a good one" after dinner,
And so discover it is rather
Fun to go one more than father.
But father, son and clerk join up
To talk about the Football Cup.

An Eighteenth-Century
Calvinistic Hymn

———————

Thank God my Afflictions are such
    That I cannot lie down on my Bed,
And if I but take to my Couch
    I incessantly Vomit and Bleed.

I am not too sure of my Worth,
    Indeed it is tall as a Palm;
But what Fruits can it ever bring forth
    When Leprosy sits at the Helm?

Though Torment's the Soul's Goal's Rewards
    The contrary's Proof of my Guilt,
While Dancing, Backgammon and Cards,
    Are among the worst Symptoms I've felt.

Oh! I bless the good Lord for my Boils
    For my mental and bodily pains,
For without them my Faith all congeals
    And I'm doomed to HELL'S NE'ER-ENDING FLAMES.

For Nineteenth-Century Burials

This cold weather
Carries so many old people away.
Quavering voices and blankets and breath
Go silent together.
The gentle fingers are touching to pray
Which crumple and straighten for Death.
These cold breezes
Carry the bells away on the air,
Stuttering tales of Gothic, and pass,
Catching new grave flowers into their hair,
Beating the chapel and red-coloured glass.

Camberley

I wonder whether you would make
A friend of Mrs. Kittiwake?
Colonel Kittiwake, it's true,
Is not the sort of man for you.
I'll tell you how to get to know
Their cosy little bungalow.
When sunset gilds the Surrey pines
The fam'ly usually dines.
So later, in the Surrey dark,
Make for Poonah Punkah Park,
And by the monument to Clive
You'll come to Enniscorthy Drive,
Coolgreena is the last of all,
And mind the terrier when you call.

The drawing-room is done in pink
The other rooms are mauve, I think,
So when you see electric light
Behind pink curtains it's all right.
Knock gently, don't disturb the maid,
She's got to clear, and I'm afraid
That she is less inclined to take
The blame than Mrs. Kittiwake.

Croydon

In a house like that
    Your Uncle Dick was born;
Satchel on back he walked to Whitgift
    Every weekday morn.

Boys together in Coulsdon woodlands,
    Bramble-berried and steep,
He and his pals would look for spadgers
    Hidden deep.

The laurels are speckled in Marchmont Avenue
    Just as they were before,
But the steps are dusty that still lead up to
    Your Uncle Dick's front door.

Pear and apple in Croydon gardens
    Bud and blossom and fall,
But your Uncle Dick has left his Croydon
    Once for all.

Westgate-on-Sea

Hark, I hear the bells of Westgate,
  I will tell you what they sigh,
Where those minarets and steeples
  Prick the open Thanet sky.

Happy bells of eighteen-ninety,
  Bursting from your freestone tower!
Recalling laurel, shrubs and privet,
  Red geraniums in flower.

Feet that scamper on the asphalt
  Through the Borough Council grass,
Till they hide inside the shelter
  Bright with ironwork and glass,

Striving chains of ordered children
  Purple by the sea-breeze made,
Striving on to prunes and suet
  Past the shops on the Parade.

Some with wire around their glasses,
  Some with wire across their teeth,
Writhing frames for running noses
  And the drooping lip beneath.

Church of England bells of Westgate!
  On this balcony I stand,

White the woodwork wriggles round me,
    Clock towers rise on either hand.

For me in my timber arbour
    You have one more message yet,
"Plimsolls, plimsolls in the summer,
    Oh goloshes in the wet!"

The Wykehamist
(*To Randolph Churchill, but not about him.*)

———

Broad of Church and broad of mind,
Broad before and broad behind,
A keen ecclesiologist,
A rather dirty Wykehamist.
'Tis not for us to wonder why
He wears that curious knitted tie;
We should not cast reflections on
The very slightest kind of don.
We should not giggle as we like
At his appearance on his bike;
It's something to become a bore,
And more than that, at twenty-four.
It's something too to know your wants
And go full pelt for Norman fonts.
Just now the chestnut trees are dark
And full with shadow in the park,
And "six o'clock!" St. Mary calls
Above the mellow college walls.
The evening stretches arms to twist
And captivate her Wykehamist.
But not for him these autumn days,
He shuts them out with heavy baize;
He gives his Ovaltine a stir
And nibbles at a "petit beurre",
And, satisfying fleshy wants,
He settles down to Norman fonts.

The Sandemanian Meeting-House
in Highbury Quadrant

On roaring iron down the Holloway Road
  The red trams and the brown trams pour,
And little each yellow-faced jolted load
  Knows of the fast-shut grained oak door.

From Canonbury, Dalston and Mildmay Park
  The old North London shoots in a train
To the long black platform, gaslit and dark,
  Oh Highbury Station once and again.

Steam or electric, little they care,
  Yellow brick terrace or terra-cotta hall,
White-wood sweet shop or silent square,
  That the LORD OF THE SCRIPTURES IS LORD OF ALL.

Away from the barks and the shouts and the greetings,
  Psalm-singing over and love-lunch done,
Listening to the Bible in their room for meetings,
  Old Sandemanians are hidden from the sun.

The Arrest of Oscar Wilde at the
Cadogan Hotel

He sipped at a weak hock and seltzer
  As he gazed at the London skies
Through the Nottingham lace of the curtains
  Or was it his bees-winged eyes?

To the right and before him Pont Street
  Did tower in her new built red,
As hard as the morning gaslight
  That shone on his unmade bed,

"I want some more hock in my seltzer,
  And Robbie, please give me your hand—
Is this the end or beginning?
  How can I understand?

"So you've brought me the latest *Yellow Book*:
  And Buchan has got in it now:
Approval of what is approved of
  Is as false as a well-kept vow.

"More hock, Robbie—where is the seltzer?
  Dear boy, pull again at the bell!
They are all little better than *cretins*,
  Though this *is* the Cadogan Hotel.

"One astrakhan coat is at Willis's—
    Another one's at the Savoy:
Do fetch my morocco portmanteau,
    And bring them on later, dear boy."

A thump, and a murmur of voices—
    ("Oh why must they make such a din?")
As the door of the bedroom swung open
    And TWO PLAIN CLOTHES POLICEMEN came in:

"Mr. Woilde, we 'ave come for tew take yew
    Where felons and criminals dwell:
We must ask yew tew leave with us quoietly
    For this *is* the Cadogan Hotel."

He rose, and he put down *The Yellow Book*.
    He staggered—and, terrible-eyed,
He brushed past the palms on the staircase
    And was helped to a hansom outside.

Distant View of a Provincial Town

Beside those spires so spick and span
　　Against an unencumbered sky
The old Great Western Railway ran
　　When someone different was I.

St. Aidan's with the prickly nobs
　　And iron spikes and coloured tiles—
Where Auntie Maud devoutly bobs
　　In those enriched vermilion aisles:

St. George's where the mattins bell
　　But rarely drowned the trams for prayer—
No Popish sight or sound or smell
　　Disturbed that gas-invaded air:

St. Mary's where the Rector preached
　　In such a jolly friendly way
On cricket, football, things that reached
　　The simple life of every day:

And that United Benefice
　　With entrance permanently locked,—
How Gothic, grey and sad it is
　　Since Mr. Grogley was unfrocked!

The old Great Western Railway shakes
 The old Great Western Railway spins—
The old Great Western Railway makes
 Me very sorry for my sins.

Slough

———

Come, friendly bombs, and fall on Slough
It isn't fit for humans now,
There isn't grass to graze a cow
    Swarm over, Death!

Come, bombs, and blow to smithereens
Those air-conditioned, bright canteens,
Tinned fruit, tinned meat, tinned milk, tinned beans
    Tinned minds, tinned breath.

Mess up the mess they call a town—
A house for ninety-seven down
And once a week a half-a-crown
    For twenty years,

And get that man with double chin
Who'll always cheat and always win,
Who washes his repulsive skin
    In women's tears,

And smash his desk of polished oak
And smash his hands so used to stroke
And stop his boring dirty joke
    And make him yell.

But spare the bald young clerks who add
The profits of the stinking cad;

It's not their fault that they are mad,
    They've tasted Hell.

It's not their fault they do not know
The birdsong from the radio,
It's not their fault they often go
    To Maidenhead

And talk of sports and makes of cars
In various bogus Tudor bars
And daren't look up and see the stars
    But belch instead.

In labour-saving homes, with care
Their wives frizz out peroxide hair
And dry it in synthetic air
    And paint their nails.

Come, friendly bombs, and fall on Slough
To get it ready for the plough.
The cabbages are coming now;
    The earth exhales.

Clash went the Billiard Balls

Clash went the billiard balls in the Clerkenwell Social Saloon.
Shut up the shutters and turn down the gas they'll be calling
                                                          the coppers in soon.
Goodnight, Alf!
Goodnight, Bert!
Goodnight, Mrs. Gilligan!
Rain in the archway, no trams in the street.
COP COP
Cop on the cobbleway
Quick little ladylike feet
" 'Ard luck, ain't got a gentleman?"
"Not on a night like this, sweet"
"The Red Lion, Myddleton, all the 'ole lot of 'em
Shut but a light in The Star
Counting the coppers to see what they've got of 'em
Glistening wet in the bar
32, 34, 36, 38, Gaskin's not back with 'is tart
Left the 'all door open gives 'imself airs 'e does
Thinks 'imself too bloody smart
Gas on in the 'all and it's *we've* got to pay for it
Damn these old stairs and this bug-ridden panelling
See 'im to-morrow what *'e's* got to say for it
Get on the bed there and start."

Love in a Valley

Take me, Lieutenant, to that Surrey homestead!
   Red comes the winter and your rakish car,
Red among the hawthorns, redder than the hawberries
   And trails of old man's nuisance, and noisier far.
Far, far below me roll the Coulsdon woodlands,
   White down the valley curves the living rail,[1]
Tall, tall, above me, olive spike the pinewoods,
   Olive against blue-black, moving in the gale.

Deep down the drive go the cushioned rhododendrons,
   Deep down, sand deep, drives the heather root,
Deep the spliced timber barked around the summer-house,
   Light lies the tennis-court, plantain underfoot.
What a winter welcome to what a Surrey homestead!
   Oh! the metal lantern and white enamelled door!
Oh! the spread of orange from the gas-fire on the carpet!
   Oh! the tiny patter, sandalled footsteps on the floor!

Fling wide the curtains!—that's a Surrey sunset
   Low down the line sings the Addiscombe train,
Leaded are the windows lozenging the crimson,
   Drained dark the pines in resin-scented rain.
Portable Lieutenant! they carry you to China
   And me to lonely shopping in a brilliant arcade;
Firm hand, fond hand, switch the giddy engine!
   So for us a last time is bright light made.

               [1] Southern Electric 25 mins.

An Impoverished Irish Peer

Within that parsonage
There is a personage
Who owns a mortgage
    On his Lordship's land,
On his fine plantations,
Well speculated,
With groves of beeches
    On either hand—
On his ten ton schooner
Upon Loch Gowna,
And the silver birches
    Along the land—
Where the little pebbles
Do sing like trebles
As the waters bubble
    Upon the strand—

On his gateway olden
Of plaster moulded
And his splendid carriage way
    To Castle Grand,
(They've been aquatinted
For a book that's printed
And even wanted
    In far England)
His fine saloons there
Would make you swoon, sir,

And each surrounded
    By a gilded band—
And 'tis there Lord Ashtown
Lord Trimlestown and
Clonmore's Lord likewise
    Are entertained.

As many flunkeys
As Finnea has donkeys
Are there at all times
    At himself's command.
Though he doesn't pay them
They all obey him
And would sure die for him
    If he waved his hand;
Yet if His Lordship
Comes for to worship
At the Holy Table
    To take his stand,
Though humbly kneeling
There's no fair dealing
And no kind feeling
    In the parson's hand.
Preaching of Liberty
Also of Charity
In the grand high pulpit
    To see him stand,
You'ld think that personage
In that parsonage
Did own no mortgage
    On His Lordship's land.

Our Padre

Our padre is an old sky pilot,
  Severely now they've clipped his wings,
But still the flagstaff in the Rect'ry garden
  Points to Higher Things.

Still he has got a hearty handshake;
  Still he wears his medals and a stole;
His voice would reach to Heaven, *and* make
  The Rock of Ages Roll.

He's too sincere to join the high church
  Worshipping idols for the Lord,
And, though the lowest church is my church,
  Our padre's Broad.

Our padre is an old sky pilot,
  He's tied a reef knot round my heart,
We'll be rocked up to Heaven on a rare old tune—
  Come on—take part!

CHORUS
  (*Sung*) Pull for the shore, sailor, pull for the shore!
    Heed not the raging billow, bend to the oar!
  Bend to the oar before the padre!
    Proud, with the padre rowing stroke!
  Good old padre! God for the services!
    Row like smoke!

Exchange of Livings

Lines suggested by an advertisement in *The Guardian*
(the Broad Church newspaper).

———————

The church was locked, so I went to the incumbent—
the incumbent enjoying a supine incumbency—
a tennis court, a summerhouse, deckchairs by the walnut tree
and only the hum of the bees in the rockery.
"May I have the keys of the church, your incumbency?"
"Yes, my dear sir, as a moderate churchman,
I am willing to exchange: light Sunday duty:
                    nice district: pop 149: eight hundred per annum:
no extremes: A and M: bicyclist essential:
                                same income expected."
"I think I'm the man that you want, your incumbency.
Here's my address when I'm not on my bicycle, poking
                    about for recumbent stone effigies—
14, Mount Ephraim, Cheltenham, Glos:
Rector St. George-in-the-Rolling Pins, Cripplegate:
non resident pop in the City of London:
eight fifty per annum (but verger an asset):
willing to exchange (no extremes) for incumbency,
similar income, but closer to residence."

Undenominational

Undenominational
  But still the church of God
He stood in his conventicle
  And ruled it with a rod.

Undenominational
  The walls around him rose,
The lamps within their brackets shook
  To hear the hymns he chose.

"Glory" "Gopsal" "Russell Place"
  "Wrestling Jacob" "Rock"
"Saffron Walden" "Safe at Home"
  "Dorking" "Plymouth Dock"

I slipped about the chalky lane
  That runs without the park,
I saw the lone conventicle
  A beacon in the dark.

Revival ran along the hedge
  And made my spirit whole
When steam was on the window panes
  And glory in my soul.

City

___

When the great bell
BOOMS over the Portland stone urn, and
From the carved cedar wood
Rises the odour of incense,
I SIT DOWN
In St. Botolph Bishopsgate Churchyard
And wait for the spirit of my grandfather
Toddling along from the Barbican.

A Hike on the Downs

"Yes, rub some soap upon your feet!
   We'll hike round Winchester for weeks—
Like ancient Britons—just we two—
   Or more perhaps like ancient Greeks.

"You take your pipe—that will impress
   Your strength on anyone who passes;
I'll take my *Plautus* (*non purgatus*)
   And both my pairs of horn-rimmed glasses.

"I've got my first, and now I know
   What life is and what life contains—
For, being just a first year man
   You don't meet all the first-class brains.

"Objectively, our Common Room
   Is like a small Athenian State—
Except for Lewis: he's all right
   But do you think he's *quite* first rate?

Hampshire mentality is low,
   And that is why they stare at us.
Yes, here's the earthwork—but it's dark;
   We may as well return by bus."

Dorset

Rime Intrinsica, Fontmell Magna, Sturminster Newton and
Melbury Bubb,
Whist upon whist upon whist upon whist drive, in Institute,
Legion and Social Club.
Horny hands that hold the aces which this morning held the
plough—
While Tranter Reuben, T.S. Eliot, H.G. Wells and Edith Sitwell
lie in Mellstock Churchyard now.

Lord's Day bells from Bingham's Melcombe, Iwerne Minster,
Shroton, Plush,
Down the grass between the beeches, mellow in the evening
hush.
Gloved the hands that hold the hymn-book, which this morning
milked the cow—
While Tranter Reuben, Mary Borden, Brian Howard and
Harold Acton lie in Mellstock Churchyard now.

Light's abode, celestial Salem! Lamps of evening, smelling
strong,
Gleaming on the pitch-pine, waiting, almost empty evensong:
From the aisles each window smiles on grave and grass and
yew-tree bough—
While Tranter Reuben, Gordon Selfridge, Edna Best and
Thomas Hardy lie in Mellstock Churchyard now.

NOTE: *The names in the last lines of these stanzas are put in
not out of malice or satire but merely for their euphony.*

Calvinistic Evensong

The six bells stopped, and in the dark I heard
Cold silence wait the Calvinistic word;
For Calvin now the soft oil lamps are lit
Hands on their hymnals six old women sit.
Black gowned and sinister, he now appears
Curate-in-charge of aged parish fears.
Let, unaccompanied, that psalm begin
Which deals most harshly with the fruits of sin!
Boy! pump the organ! let the anthem flow
With promise for the chosen saints below!
Pregnant with warning the globed elm trees wait
Fresh coffin-wood beside the churchyard gate.
And that mauve hat three cherries decorate
Next week shall topple from its trembling perch
While wet fields reek like some long empty church.

Exeter

The doctor's intellectual wife
  Sat under the ilex tree
The Cathedral bells pealed over the wall
  But never a bell heard she
And the sun played shadowgraphs on her book
  Which was writ by A. Huxléy.

Once those bells, those Exeter bells
  Called her to praise and pray
By pink, acacia-shaded walls
  Several times a day
To Wulfric's altar and riddel posts
  While the choir sang Stanford in A.

The doctor jumps in his Morris car,
  The surgery door goes bang,
Clash and whirr down Colleton Crescent,
  Other cars all go hang
My little bus is enough for us—
  Till a tram-car bell went clang.

They brought him in by the big front door
  And a smiling corpse was he;
On the dining-room table they laid him out
  Where the *Bystanders* used to be—
The Tatler, The Sketch and *The Bystander*
  For the canons' wives to see.

Now those bells, those Exeter bells
    Call her to praise and pray
By pink, acacia-shaded walls
    Several times a day
To Wulfric's altar and riddel posts
    And the choir sings Stanford in A.

Death of King George V

"New King arrives in his capital by air . . ." *Daily Newspaper.*

————————

Spirits of well-shot woodcock, partridge, snipe
  Flutter and bear him up the Norfolk sky:
In that red house in a red mahogany book-case
  The stamp collection waits with mounts long dry.

The big blue eyes are shut which saw wrong clothing
  And favourite fields and coverts from a horse;
Old men in country houses hear clocks ticking
  Over thick carpets with a deadened force;

Old men who never cheated, never doubted,
  Communicated monthly, sit and stare
At the new suburb stretched beyond the run-way
  Where a young man lands hatless from the air.

The Heart of Thomas Hardy

The heart of Thomas Hardy flew out of Stinsford churchyard
A little thumping fig, it rocketed over the elm trees.
Lighter than air it flew straight to where its Creator
Waited in golden nimbus, just as in eighteen sixty,
Hardman and son of Brum had depicted Him in the chancel.
Slowly out of the grass, slitting the mounds in the centre
Riving apart the roots, rose the new covered corpses
Tess and Jude and His Worship, various unmarried mothers,
Woodmen, cutters of turf, adulterers, church restorers,
Turning aside the stones thump on the upturned churchyard.
Soaring over the elm trees slower than Thomas Hardy,
Weighted down with a Conscience, now for the first time fleshly
Taking form as a growth hung from the feet like a sponge-bag.
There, in the heart of the nimbus, twittered the heart of Hardy
There, on the edge of the nimbus, slowly revolved the corpses
Radiating around the twittering heart of Hardy,
Slowly started to turn in the light of their own Creator
Died away in the night as frost will blacken a dahlia.

Suicide on Junction Road Station after Abstention from Evening Communion in North London

With the roar of the gas my heart gives a shout—
  To Jehovah Tsidkenu the praise!
Bracket and bracket go blazon it out
  In this Evangelical haze!

Jehovah Jireh! the arches ring,
  The Mintons glisten, and grand
Are the surpliced boys as they sweetly sing
  On the threshold of glory land.

Jehovah Nisi! from Tufnell Park,
  Five minutes to Junction Road,
Through grey brick Gothic and London dark,
  And my sins, a fearful load.

Six on the upside! six on the down side!
  One gaslight in the Booking Hall
And a thousand sins on this lonely station—
  What shall I do with them all?

The Flight from Bootle

Lonely in the Regent Palace,
   Sipping her "Banana Blush",
Lilian lost sight of Alice
   In the honey-coloured rush.

Settled down at last from Bootle,
   Alice whispered, "Just a min,
While I pop upstairs and rootle
   For another safety pin."

Dreamy from the band pavilion
   Drops of the *Immortal Hour*
Fell around the lonely Lilian
   Like an ineffectual shower.

Half an hour she sat and waited
   In the honey-coloured lounge
Till she with herself debated,
   "Time for me to go and scrounge!"

Time enough! or not enough time!
   Lilian, you wait in vain;
Alice will not have a rough time,
   Nor be quite the same again.

Public House Drunk

<table>
<tr><td>*Bass*</td><td>Turn again, Higginson,</td></tr>
<tr><td>*Treble*</td><td>*thrice Mayor of London!*</td></tr>
<tr><td>*Bass*</td><td>Stretch the bow of your bells,</td></tr>
<tr><td>*Treble*</td><td>*St. Mary's steeple!*</td></tr>
<tr><td>*Bass*</td><td>Finsbury, Highbury,</td></tr>
<tr><td>*Treble*</td><td>*you are all undone!*</td></tr>
<tr><td>*Bass*</td><td>Moorfields and Cripplegate,</td></tr>
<tr><td>*Treble*</td><td>*wake up your people!*</td></tr>
</table>

<table>
<tr><td>*Bass*</td><td>Saint Andrew Undershaft,</td></tr>
<tr><td>*Treble*</td><td>*Saint Andrew Hubbard,*</td></tr>
<tr><td>*Bass*</td><td>Saint Catherine Coleman,</td></tr>
<tr><td>*Treble*</td><td>*Saint Botolph, Saint Bride's*</td></tr>
<tr><td>*Bass*</td><td>Where are your registers?</td></tr>
<tr><td>*Treble*</td><td>*In vestry cupboard*</td></tr>
<tr><td>*Bass*</td><td>Look him up, Higginson,</td></tr>
<tr><td>*Treble*</td><td>*find where he hides!*</td></tr>
</table>

<table>
<tr><td>*Bass*</td><td>Out of the Jew's Harp House</td></tr>
<tr><td>*Treble*</td><td>*Old Mother Redcap*</td></tr>
<tr><td>*Bass*</td><td>Turn down the gas again</td></tr>
<tr><td>*Treble*</td><td>*—gas again, Glory!*</td></tr>
<tr><td>*Bass*</td><td>Clean up the bar in the</td></tr>
<tr><td>*Treble*</td><td>*wake of that madcap*</td></tr>
<tr><td>*Bass*</td><td>Lord Mayor of London! Oh</td></tr>
<tr><td>*Treble*</td><td>*Lord what a story!*</td></tr>
</table>

Bass	Hold him down, Higginson!
Treble	*send for the beadles!*
Bass	"Fourteen, Macaulay street
Treble	*Bromley-by-Bow*
Bass	Represents pen-nibs
Treble	*steel holders and needles*
Bass	For the Office Equipment
Treble	*Efficiency Co.*"

Cheltenham

Floruit, floret, floreat!
  Cheltonia's children cry.
I composed those lines when a summer wind
  Was blowing the elm leaves dry,
And we were seventy-six for seven
  And they had C.B. Fry.

Shall I forget the warm marquee
  And the general's wife so soon,
When my son's colleger[1] acted as tray
  For an ice and a macaroon,
And distant carriages jingled through
  The stuccoed afternoon?

Floruit. Yes, the Empire Map
  Cheltonia's sons have starred.
Floret. Still the stream goes on
  Of soldier, brusher[2] and bard.
Floreat. While behind the limes
  Lengthens the Promenade.

[1] Mortar board.   [2] Schoolmaster.

A Shropshire Lad

N.B.—This should be recited with a Midland accent.
Captain Webb, the swimmer and a relation of Mary Webb
by marriage, was born at Dawley in an industrial district in
Salop.

———

The gas was on in the Institute,[1]
  The flare was up in the gym,
A man was running a mineral line,
  A lass was singing a hymn,
When Captain Webb the Dawley man,
  Captain Webb from Dawley,
Came swimming along the old canal
  That carried the bricks to Lawley.
    Swimming along—
    Swimming along—
    Swimming along from Severn,
And paying a call at Dawley Bank while swimming along to
                                    Heaven.

The sun shone low on the railway line
  And over the bricks and stacks,
And in at the upstairs windows
  Of the Dawley houses' backs,
When we saw the ghost of Captain Webb,
  Webb in a water sheeting,
Come dripping along in a bathing dress
  To the Saturday evening meeting.

[1] "The Institute was radiant with gas." Ch. XIX, *Boyhood.*
A novel in verse by Rev. E. E. Bradford, D.D.

Dripping along—
Dripping along—
To the Congregational Hall;
Dripping and still he rose over the sill and faded away in a wall.

There wasn't a man in Oakengates
  That hadn't got hold of the tale,
And over the valley in Ironbridge,
  And round by Coalbrookdale,
How Captain Webb the Dawley man,
  Captain Webb from Dawley,
Rose rigid and dead from the old canal
  That carries the bricks to Lawley.
    Rigid and dead—
    Rigid and dead—
    To the Saturday congregation,
Paying a call at Dawley Bank on his way to his destination.

Upper Lambourne

Up the ash-tree climbs the ivy,
  Up the ivy climbs the sun,
With a twenty-thousand pattering
  Has a valley breeze begun,
Feathery ash, neglected elder,
  Shift the shade and make it run—

Shift the shade toward the nettles,
  And the nettles set it free
To streak the stained Carrara headstone
  Where, in nineteen-twenty-three,
He who trained a hundred winners
  Paid the Final Entrance Fee.

Leathery limbs of Upper Lambourne,
  Leathery skin from sun and wind,
Leathery breeches, spreading stables,
  Shining saddles left behind—
To the down the string of horses
  Moving out of sight and mind.

Feathery ash in leathery Lambourne
  Waves above the sarsen stone,
And Edwardian plantations
  So coniferously moan
As to make the swelling downland,
  Far-surrounding, seem their own.

44

Pot Pourri from a Surrey Garden

Miles of pram in the wind and Pam in the gorse track,
  Coco-nut smell of the broom, and a packet of Weights
Press'd in the sand. The thud of a hoof on a horse-track—
    A horse-riding horse for a horse-track—
    Conifer county of Surrey approached
  Through remarkable wrought-iron gates.

Over your boundary now, I wash my face in a bird-bath,
  Then which path shall I take? that over there by the pram?
Down by the pond! or—yes, I will take the slippery third path,
    Trodden away with gym shoes,
    Beautiful fir-dry alley that leads
  To the bountiful body of Pam.

Pam, I adore you, Pam, you great big mountainous sports girl,
  Whizzing them over the net, full of the strength of five:
That old Malvernian brother, you zephyr and khaki shorts girl,
    Although he's playing for Woking,
    Can't stand up
  To your wonderful backhand drive.

See the strength of her arm, as firm and hairy as Hendren's;
  See the size of her thighs, the pout of her lips as, cross,
And full of a pent-up strength, she swipes at the rhododendrons,
    Lucky the rhododendrons,
    And flings her arrogant love-lock
  Back with a petulant toss.

Over the redolent pinewoods, in at the bathroom casement,
    One fine Saturday, Windlesham bells shall call:
Up the Butterfield aisle rich with Gothic enlacement,
        Licensed now for embracement,
        Pam and I, as the organ
    Thunders over you all.

Holy Trinity, Sloane Street
MCMVII

An Acolyte singeth
Light six white tapers with the Flame of Art,
Send incense wreathing to the lily flowers,
And, with your cool hands white,
Swing the warm censer round my bruised heart,
Drop, dove-grey eyes, your penitential showers
On this pale acolyte.

A cofirmandus continueth
The tall red house soars upward to the stars,
The doors are chased with sardonyx and gold,
And in the long white room
Thin drapery draws backward to unfold
Cadogan Square between the window-bars
And Whistler's mother knitting in the gloom.

The Priest endeth
How many hearts turn Motherward to-day?
(Red roses faint not on your twining stems!)
Bronze triptych doors unswing!
Wait, restive heart, wait, rounded lips, to pray,
Mid beaten copper interset with gems
Behold! Behold! your King!

On Seeing an Old Poet in the
Café Royal

———————

I saw him in the Café Royal.
   Very old and very grand.
Modernistic shone the lamplight
   There in London's fairyland.
"Devilled chicken. Devilled whitebait.
   Devil if I understand.

Where is Oscar? Where is Bosie?
   Have I seen that man before?
And the old one in the corner,
   Is it really Wratislaw?"
Scent of Tutti-Frutti-Sen-Sen
   And cheroots upon the floor.

An Incident in the Early Life of
Ebenezer Jones, Poet, 1828

"WE were together at a well-known boarding-school of that day (1828), situated at the foot of Highgate Hill, and presided over by a dissenting minister, the Rev. John Bickerdike. . . .

We were together, though not on the same form; and on a hot summer afternoon, with about fifty other boys, were listlessly conning our tasks in a large schoolroom built out from the house, which made a cover for us to play under when it was wet. Up the ladder-like stairs from the playground a lurcher dog had strayed into the schoolroom, panting with the heat, his tongue lolling out with thirst. The choleric usher who presided, and was detested by us for his tyranny, seeing this, advanced down the room. Enraged at our attention being distracted from our tasks, he dragged the dog to the top of the stairs, and there lifted him bodily up with the evident intention—and we had known him do similar things—of hurling the poor creature to the bottom.

'YOU SHALL NOT!' rang through the room, as little Ebby, so exclaiming at the top of his voice, rushed with kindling face to the spot from among all the boys—some of them twice his age.

· But even while the words passed his lips, the heavy fall was heard, and the sound seemed to travel through his listening form and face, as, with a strange look of anguish in one so young, he stood still, threw up his arms, and burst into an uncontrollable passion of tears.

With a coarse laugh at this, the usher led him back by his ear to the form; and there he sat, long after his sobbing had subsided, like one dazed and stunned." (*From an account of his brother by Sumner Jones in the 1879 re-issue of Ebenezer Jones's "Studies of Sensation and Event".*)

The lumber of a London-going dray,
The still-new stucco on the London clay,
Hot summer silence over Holloway.

Dissenting chapels, tea-bowers, lovers' lairs,
Neat new-built villas, ample Grecian squares,
Remaining orchards ripening Windsor pears.

Hot silence where the older mansions hide
On Highgate Hill's thick elm-encrusted side,
And Pancras, Hornsey, Islington divide.

June's hottest silence where the hard rays strike
Yon hill-foot house, window and wall alike,
School of the Reverend Mr. Bickerdike,

For sons of Saints, blest with this world's possessions
(Seceders from the Protestant Secessions),
Good grounding in the more genteel professions.

A lurcher dog, which draymen kick and pass
Tongue lolling, thirsty over shadeless grass,
Leapt up the playground ladder to the class.

The godly usher left his godly seat,
His skin was prickly in the ungodly heat,
The dog lay panting at his godly feet.

The milkman on the road stood staring in,
The playground nettles nodded "Now begin"—
And Evil waited, quivering, for sin.

He lifted it and not a word he spoke,
His big hand tightened. Could he make it choke
He trembled, sweated, and his temper broke.

"YOU SHALL NOT!" clear across to Highgate Hill
A boy's voice sounded. Creaking forms were still.
The cat jumped slowly from the window sill.

"YOU SHALL NOT!" flat against the summer sun,
Hard as the hard sky frowning over one,
Gloat, little boys! enjoy the coming fun!

"GOD DAMNS A CUR. I AM, I AM HIS WORD!"
He flung it, flung it and it never stirred,
"You shall not!—shall not!" ringing on unheard.

Blind desolation! bleeding, burning rod!
Big, bull-necked Minister of Calvin's God!
Exulting milkman, redfaced, shameless clod,

Look on and jeer! Not Satan's thunder-quake
Can cause the mighty walls of Heaven to shake
As now they do, to hear a boy's heart break.

Trebetherick

We used to picnic where the thrift
    Grew deep and tufted to the edge;
We saw the yellow foam-flakes drift
    In trembling sponges on the ledge
Below us, till the wind would lift
    Them up the cliff and o'er the hedge.
Sand in the sandwiches, wasps in the tea,
Sun on our bathing-dresses heavy with the wet,
Squelch of the bladder-wrack waiting for the sea,
Fleas round the tamarisk, an early cigarette.

From where the coastguard houses stood
    One used to see, below the hill,
The lichened branches of a wood
    In summer silver-cool and still;
And there the Shade of Evil could
    Stretch out at us from Shilla Mill.
Thick with sloe and blackberry, uneven in the light,
Lonely ran the hedge, the heavy meadow was remote,
The oldest part of Cornwall was the wood as black as night,
And the pheasant and the rabbit lay torn open at the throat.

But when a storm was at its height,
    And feathery slate was black in rain,
And tamarisks were hung with light
    And golden sand was brown again,
Spring tide and blizzard would unite

And sea came flooding up the lane.
Waves full of treasure then were roaring up the beach,
Ropes round our mackintoshes, waders warm and dry,
We waited for the wreckage to come swirling into reach,
Ralph, Vasey, Alastair, Biddy, John and I.

Then roller into roller curled
        And thundered down the rocky bay,
And we were in a water-world
        Of rain and blizzard, sea and spray,
And one against the other hurled
        We struggled round to Greenaway.
Blesséd be St. Enodoc, blesséd be the wave,
Blesséd be the springy turf, we pray, pray to thee,
Ask for our children all the happy days you gave
To Ralph, Vasey, Alastair, Biddy, John and me.

Oxford: Sudden Illness at the Bus-stop

At the time of evening when cars run sweetly,
  Syringas blossom by Oxford gates.
In her evening velvet with a rose pinned neatly
  By the distant bus-stop a don's wife waits.

From that wide bedroom with its two branched lighting
  Over her looking-glass, up or down,
When sugar was short and the world was fighting
  She first appeared in that velvet gown.

What forks since then have been slammed in places?
  What peas turned out from how many a tin?
From plate-glass windows how many faces
  Have watched professors come hobbling in?

Too much, too many! so fetch the doctor,
  This dress has grown such a heavier load
Since Jack was only a Junior Proctor,
  And rents were lower in Rawlinson Road.

Group Life: Letchworth

Tell me Pippididdledum,
  Tell me how the children are.
Working each for weal of all
  After what you said.
Barry's on the common far
  Pedalling the Kiddie Kar.
Ann has had a laxative
  And Alured is dead.
Sympathy is stencilling
  Her decorative leatherwork,
Wilfred's learned a folk-tune for
  The Morris Dancers' band.
I have my ex-Service man and
  Mamie's done a lino-cut.
And Charlie's in the *kinderbank*
  A-kicking up the sand.
Wittle-tittle, wittle-tittle
  Toodle-oodle ducky birds,
What a lot my dicky chicky
  Tiny tots have done.
Wouldn't it be jolly now,
  To take our Aertex panters off
And have a jolly tumble in
  The jolly, jolly sun?

Bristol and Clifton

———

"Yes, I was only sidesman here when last
You came to Evening Communion.
But now I have retired from the bank
I have more leisure time for church finance.
We moved into a somewhat larger house
Than when you knew us in Manilla Road.
This is the window to my lady wife.
You cannot see it now, but in the day
The greens and golds are truly wonderful."

"How very sad. I do not mean about
The window, but I mean about the death
Of Mrs. Battlecock. When did she die?"

"Two years ago when we had just moved in
To Pembroke Road. I rather fear the stairs
And basement kitchen were too much for her—
Not that, of course, she did the servants' work—
But supervising servants all the day
Meant quite a lot of climbing up and down."

"How very sad. Poor Mrs. Battlecock."
" 'The glory that men do lives after them,'[1]
And so I gave this window in her name.
It's executed by a Bristol firm;

[1] Shakespeare, of course.

The lady artist who designed it, made
The figure of the lady on the left
Something like Mrs. Battlecock."
"How nice."

        "Yes, was it not? We had
A stained glass window on the stairs at home,
In Pembroke Road. But not so good as this.
This window is the glory of the church
At least I think so—and the unstained oak
Looks very chaste beneath it. When I gave
The oak, that brass inscription on your right
Commemorates the fact, the Dorcas Club
Made these blue kneelers, though we do not kneel:
We leave that to the Roman Catholics."
"How very nice, indeed. How very nice."

"Seeing I have some knowledge of finance
Our kind Parochial Church Council made
Me People's Warden, and I'm glad to say
That our collections are still keeping up.
The chancel has been flood-lit, and the stove
Which used to heat the church was obsolete.
So now we've had some radiators fixed
Along the walls and eastward of the aisles;
This last I thought of lest at any time
A Ritualist should be inducted here
And want to put up altars. He would find
The radiators inconvenient.
Our only ritual here is with the Plate;
I think we make it dignified enough.

I take it up myself, and afterwards,
Count the Collection on the vestry safe."

"Forgive me, aren't we talking rather loud?
I think I see a woman praying there."
"Praying? The service is all over now
And here's the verger waiting to turn out
The lights and lock the church up. She cannot
Be Loyal Church of England. Well, good-bye.
Time flies. I must be going. Come again.
There are some pleasant people living here.
I know the Inskips very well indeed."

Sir John Piers

OH! BOLD BAD BARONET
YOU NEED NO CORONET
YOU SIGN YOUR WARRANT WITH
A BLOODY HAND.

INTRODUCTION

"In 1807, Sir John Piers, the last of the name who resided in Trister-
nagh, and who was a gambler, duellist, and spendthrift, was a school-
fellow of the patriot, Lord Cloncurry. Shortly after the marriage of that
nobleman, Piers, who shared his hospitality, and even received pecuni-
ary aid from him, made a diabolical wager to ruin for life the happiness
of the wedded pair. Mr. W. J. Fitzpatrick, the able biographer of Lord
Cloncurry, says: '. . . A more unlikely person than Lady Cloncurry to
prove unfaithful to him she had vowed to love, honour and obey, did not,
perhaps, exist in Christendom. Can it be believed that such was the
character which Sir John Piers resolved by every art of hell to wither and
destroy? A bet, or agreement, as we have heard, was entered into
between the monster and some kindred spirit, that in the event of the
utter and complete ruin of Lord and Lady Cloncurry's happiness, a sum
of money would be placed to the credit of his (Piers') account in a certain
Dublin Bank. In case of failure, the operation was, of course, to be
reversed. . . .'

"On the 19th of February, 1807, the celebrated trial, Cloncurry v.
Piers, for crim. con., commenced in the Court of King's Bench before
Lord Chief Justice Downes. Damages were laid at £100,000. The case
created great interest and resulted in a verdict for the plaintiff, £20,000
and costs. John Philpot Curran and Charles Kendal Bushe were the
leading Counsel for Lord Cloncurry, and their speeches were what
might be expected from such gifted advocates. Those who would wish to
read the speeches should consult *Curran and His Contemporaries*, by
Charles Philips. Piers put in no appearance at the trial. Haunted by the
near approach of retribution, he packed his portmanteau and fled to the
Isle of Man. By this proceeding his recognizances became, of course,
forfeited to the Crown. After a time the strong arm of the law secured
him; he gave what he could reluctantly enough, and his bond for the
remainder. Assailed on all sides by creditors, Sir John Piers had a cottage

built at Tristernagh, surrounded by a high wall, to protect himself from the minions of justice; but ruin and misfortune overtook him; his estates were sold out in the Encumbered Estates Court."

(*Annals of Westmeath, Ancient and Modern*, by James Woods.)

I. *The Fête Champêtre*

Oh, gay lapped the waves on the shores of Lough Ennel
And sweet smelt the breeze 'mid the garlic and fennel,
But sweeter and gayer than either of these
Were the songs of the birds in Lord Belvedere's trees.

The light skiff is push'd from the weed-waving shore,
The rowlocks creak evenly under the oar,
And a boatload of beauty darts over the tide,
The Baron Cloncurry and also his bride.

Lord Belvedere sits like a priest in the prow,
'Tis the Lady Mount Cashel sits next to him now.
And both the de Blacquieres to balance the boat,
Was so much nobility ever afloat?

The party's arranged on the opposite shore,
Lord Clonmore is present and one or two more,
But why has the Lady Cloncurry such fears?
Oh, one of the guests will be Baronet Piers.

The grotto is reached and the parties alight,
The feast is spread out, and begob! what a sight,
Pagodas of jelly in bowls of champagne,
And a tower of blancmange from the Baron Kilmaine.

In the shell-covered shelter the grotto affords
The meats and the pies are arranged on the boards,

The nobility laugh and are free from all worry
Excepting the bride of the Baron Cloncurry.

But his lordship is gayer than ever before,
He laughs like the ripples that lap the lake shore,
Nor thinks that his bride has the slightest of fears
Lest one of the guests be the Baronet Piers.

A curricle rolling along on the grass,
The servants make way to allow it to pass,
A high-stepping grey and the wheels flashing yellow
And Sir John in the seat, what a capital fellow!

Huzza for Sir John! and huzza for the fête,
For without his assistance no fête is complete;
Oh, gay is the garland the ladies will wreathe
For the handsomest blade in the County Westmeath.

The harness is off with a jingle of steel,
The grey in the grass crops an emerald meal,
Sir John saunters up with a smile and a bow
And the Lady Cloncurry is next to him now.

Her eyes on the landscape, she don't seem to hear
The passing remark he designs for her ear,
For smooth as a phantom and proud as a stork
The Lady Cloncurry continues her walk.

II. The Attempt

I love your brown curls, | black in rain, my colleen,
   I love your grey eyes, | by this verdant shore
Two Derravaraghs | to plunge into and drown me,
   Hold not those lakes of | light so near me more.

My hand lies yellow | and hairy in your pink hand,
   Fragilis rubra | of the bramble flower,
Yet soft and thornless, | cool and as caressing
   As grasses bending | heavy with a shower.

See how the clouds twist | over in the twilight,
   See how the gale is | ruffling up the lake;
Lie still for ever | on this little peninsula,
   Heart beat and heart beat | steady till we wake.

Hear how the beech trees | roar above Glencara,
   See how the fungus | circles in the shade,
Roar trees and moan, you | gliding royal daughters,
   Circle us with poison, | we are not afraid.

Gothic on Gothic | my abbey soars around me,
   I've walks and avenues | emerald from rain,
Plentiful timber | in a lake reflected,
   And creamy meadowsweet | scenting my demesne.

Press to your cheeks | my hand so hot and wasted,
   Smooth with my fingers | the freckles of your frown,

63

Take you my abbey, | it is yours for always,
    I am so full of | love that I shall drown.

> *I lie by the lake water*
>   *And you, Cloncurry, not near,*
> *I live in a girl's answer,*
>   *You, in a bawd's fear.*

III. The Exile

On Mannin's rough coast-line the twilight descending
    With its last dying rays on thy height, O Snaefell!
A refuge of dark to the Island is lending
    And to yon *cottage ornée* that lies in the dell.

Its helpless inhabitant dare not appear in
    The rain-weathered streets of adjacent Rumsaa,
But he sees in his dreams the green island of Erin
    And he sits in an orat'ry most of the day.

Yet sometimes, at night, when the waves in commotion
    Are tumbling about round the long point of Ayr,
He strides through the tamarisks down to the ocean
    Beyond the lush curraghs of sylvan Lezayre.

Alone with his thoughts when the wild waves are beating
    He walks round to Jurby along the wet sand,
And there, where the moon shows the waves are retreating,
    He too would retreat to his own native land.

IV. The Return

My speculated avenues are wasted,
   The artificial lake is choked and dry,
My old delight by other lips is tasted,
   Now I can only build my walls and die.

I'll nail the southern wall with Irish peaches,
   Portloman cuttings warmed in silver suns,
And eastwards to Lough Iron's reedy reaches
   I'll build against the vista and the duns.

To westward where the avenue approaches,
   Since they have felled the trees of my demesne,
And since I'll not be visited by coaches,
   I'll build a mighty wall against the rain.

And from the North, lest you, Malone, should spy me
   You, Sunderlin of Baronstown, the peer,
I'll fill your eye with all the stone that's by me
   And live four-square protected in my fear.

Blue dragonflies dart on and do not settle,
   Live things stay not; although my walls are high,
They keep not out the knapweed and the nettle,
   Stone are my coffin walls, waiting till I die.

V. Tristernagh To-day

In the ivy dusty is the old lock rusty
  That opens rasping on the place of graves,
'Tis no home for mortals behind those portals
  Where the shining dock grows and the nettle waves.
Of the walls so ferny, near Tristernagh churchyard,
  Often the learned historians write,
And the Abbey splendificent, most magnificent,
  Ribbed and springing in ancient night.

Kyrie eleison! blessed St. Bison!
  Holy Piran! Veronica's Veil!
SS. Columb, Colman and St. Attracta,
  Likewise St. Hector, please aid my tale!
Holy Virgin! What's that emergin'?
  I daren't go down in the place of graves,
Head of a dragonfly, twenty times magnified,
  Creeping diagonal, out of the caves!

Dockleaves lapping it, maidenhair flapping it,
  Blue veins mapping it, skin of the moon,
Suck of the bog in it, cold of the frog in it,
  Keep it away from me, shrouded cocoon.
The worms are moving this soft and smooth thing
  And I'm the creature for foolish fears,

There's not a feature that's super nature
'Tis only rational, 'tis
　　SIR
　　　　JOHN
　　　　　　PIERS.

Myfanwy

Kind o'er the *kinderbank* leans my Myfanwy,
    White o'er the play-pen the sheen of her dress,
Fresh from the bathroom and soft in the nursery
    Soap-scented fingers I long to caress.

Were you a prefect and head of your dormit'ry?
    Were you a hockey girl, tennis or gym?
Who was your favourite? Who had a crush on you?
    Which were the baths where they taught you to swim?

Smooth down the Avenue glitters the bicycle,
    Black-stockinged legs under navy-blue serge,
Home and Colonial, Star, International,
    Balancing bicycle leant on the verge.

Trace me your wheel-tracks, you fortunate bicycle,
    Out of the shopping and into the dark,
Back down the Avenue, back to the pottingshed,
    Back to the house on the fringe of the park.

Golden the light on the locks of Myfanwy,
    Golden the light on the book on her knee,
Finger-marked pages of Rackham's Hans Andersen,
    Time for the children to come down to tea.

Oh! Fuller's angel-cake, Robertson's marmalade,
    Liberty lampshade, come, shine on us all,

My! what a spread for the friends of Myfanwy
  Some in the alcove and some in the hall.

Then what sardines in the half-lighted passages!
  Locking of fingers in long hide-and-seek.
You will protect me, my silken Myfanwy,
  Ringleader, tom-boy, and chum to the weak.

Myfanwy at Oxford

Pink may, double may, dead laburnum
  Shedding an Anglo-Jackson shade,
Shall we ever, my staunch Myfanwy,
  Bicycle down to North Parade?
Kant on the handle-bars, Marx in the saddlebag,
  Light my touch on your shoulder-blade.

Sancta Hilda, Myfanwyatia
  Evansensis—I hold your heart,
Willowy banks of a willowy Cherwell a
  Willowy figure with lips apart,
Strong and willowy, strong to pillow me,
  Gold Myfanwy, kisses and art.

Tubular bells of tall St. Barnabas,
  Single clatter above St. Paul,
Chasuble, acolyte, incense-offering,
  Spectacled faces held in thrall.
There in the nimbus and Comper tracery
  Gold Myfanwy blesses us all.

Gleam of gas upon Oxford station,
  Gleam of gas on her straight gold hair,
Hair flung back with an ostentation,
  Waiting alone for a girl friend there.
Second in Mods and a Third in Theology
  Come to breathe again Oxford air.

Her Myfanwy as in Cadena days,
　　Her Myfanwy, a schoolgirl voice,
Tentative brush of a cheek in a cocoa crush,
　　Coffee and Ulysses, Tennyson, Joyce,
Alpha-minded and other dimensional,
　　Freud or Calvary? Take your choice.

Her Myfanwy? *My* Myfanwy.
　　Bicycle bells in a Boar's Hill Pine,
Stedman Triple from All Saints' steeple,
　　Tom and his hundred and one at nine,
Bells of Butterfield, caught in Keble,
　　Sally and backstroke answer "*Mine!*"

Lake District

"On their way back they found the girls at Easedale, sitting beside the cottage where they sell ginger beer in August." (*Peer and Heiress*, Walter Besant.)

———————

I pass the cruet and I see the lake
    Running with light, beyond the garden pine,
      That lake whose waters make me dream her mine.
Up to the top board mounting for my sake,
For me she breathes, for me each soft intake,
    For me the plunge, the lake and limbs combine.
    I pledge her in non-alcoholic wine
And give the H.P. Sauce another shake.

Spirit of Grasmere, bells of Ambleside,
    Sing you and ring you, water bells, for me;
      You water-colour waterfalls may froth.
Long hiking holidays will yet provide
    Long stony lanes and back at six to tea
      And Heinz's ketchup on the tablecloth.

In Westminster Abbey

Let me take this other glove off
   As the *vox humana* swells,
And the beauteous fields of Eden
   Bask beneath the Abbey bells.
Here, where England's statesmen lie,
Listen to a lady's cry.

Gracious Lord, oh bomb the Germans.
   Spare their women for Thy Sake,
And if that is not too easy
   We will pardon Thy Mistake.
But, gracious Lord, whate'er shall be,
Don't let anyone bomb me.

Keep our Empire undismembered
   Guide our Forces by Thy Hand,
Gallant blacks from far Jamaica,
   Honduras and Togoland;
Protect them Lord in all their fights,
And, even more, protect the whites.

Think of what our Nation stands for,
   Books from Boots' and country lanes,
Free speech, free passes, class distinction,
   Democracy and proper drains.
Lord, put beneath Thy special care
One-eighty-nine Cadogan Square.

Although dear Lord I am a sinner,
　　I have done no major crime;
Now I'll come to Evening Service
　　Whensoever I have the time.
So, Lord, reserve for me a crown,
And do not let my shares go down.

I will labour for Thy Kingdom,
　　Help our lads to win the war,
Send white feathers to the cowards
　　Join the Women's Army Corps,
Then wash the Steps around Thy Throne
In the Eternal Safety Zone.

Now I feel a little better,
　　What a treat to hear Thy Word,
Where the bones of leading statesmen,
　　Have so often been interr'd.
And now, dear Lord, I cannot wait
Because I have a luncheon date.

Senex

Oh would I could subdue the flesh
   Which sadly troubles me!
And then perhaps could view the flesh
As though I never knew the flesh
   And merry misery.

To see the golden hiking girl
   With wind about her hair,
The tennis-playing, biking girl,
The wholly-to-my-liking girl,
   To see and not to care.

At sundown on my tricycle
   I tour the Borough's edge,
And icy as an icicle
See bicycle by bicycle
   Stacked waiting in the hedge.

Get down from me! I thunder there,
   You spaniels! Shut your jaws!
Your teeth are stuffed with underwear,
Suspenders torn asunder there
   And buttocks in your paws!

Oh whip the dogs away my Lord,
  They make me ill with lust.
Bend bare knees down to pray, my Lord,
Teach sulky lips to say, my Lord,
  That flaxen hair is dust.

Olney Hymns

Oh God the Olney Hymns abound
　　With words of Grace which Thou didst choose,
And wet the elm above the hedge
　　Reflected in the winding Ouse.

Pour in my soul unemptied floods
　　That stand between the slopes of clay,
Till deep beyond a deeper depth
　　This Olney day is any day.

On a Portrait of a Deaf Man

The kind old face, the egg-shaped head,
　　The tie, discreetly loud,
The loosely fitting shooting clothes,
　　A closely fitting shroud.

He liked old City dining-rooms,
　　Potatoes in their skin,
But now his mouth is wide to let
　　The London clay come in.

He took me on long silent walks
　　In country lanes when young,
He knew the name of ev'ry bird
　　But not the song it sung.

And when he could not hear me speak
　　He smiled and looked so wise
That now I do not like to think
　　Of maggots in his eyes.

He liked the rain-washed Cornish air
　　And smell of ploughed-up soil,
He liked a landscape big and bare
　　And painted it in oil.

But least of all he liked that place
　　Which hangs on Highgate Hill

Of soaked Carrara-covered earth
   For Londoners to fill.

He would have liked to say good-bye,
   Shake hands with many friends,
In Highgate now his finger-bones
   Stick through his finger-ends.

You, God, who treat him thus and thus,
   Say "Save his soul and pray."
You ask me to believe You and
   I only see decay.

Saint Cadoc

A flame of rushlight in the cell
On holy walls and holy well
And to the west the thundering bay
With soaking seaweed, sand and spray,
    Oh good St. Cadoc pray for me
    Here in your cell beside the sea.

Somewhere the tree, the yellowing oak,
Is waiting for the woodman's stroke,
Waits for the chisel saw and plane
To prime it for the earth again
    And in the earth, for me inside,
    The generous oak tree will have died.

St. Cadoc blest the woods of ash
Bent landwards by the Western lash,
He loved the veinéd threshold stones
Where sun might sometime bleach his bones
    He had no cowering fear of death
    For breath of God was Cadoc's breath.

Some cavern generates the germs
To send my body to the worms,
To-day some red hands make the shell
To blow my soul away to Hell
    To-day a pair walks newly married
    Along the path where I'll be carried.

St. Cadoc, when the wind was high,
Saw angels in the Cornish sky
As ocean rollers curled and poured
Their loud Hosannas to the Lord,
   His little cell was not too small
   For that great Lord who made them all.

Here where St. Cadoc sheltered God
The archaeologist has trod,
Yet death is now the gentle shore
With Land upon the cliffs before
   And in his cell beside the sea
   The Celtic saint has prayed for me.

Blackfriars

By the shot tower near the chimneys,
    Off the road to Waterloo,
Stands the cottage of "The Agéd"
    As in eighteen-forty-two.
Over brickwork, brownish brickwork,
    Lilac hangs in London sun
And by light fantastic clockwork
    Moves the drawbridge, sounds the gun.
When the sunset in the side streets
    Brought the breezes up the tide,
Floated bits of daily journals,
    Stable smells and silverside.
And the gaslight, yellow gaslight,
    Flaring in its wiry cage,
Like the Prison Scene in *Norval*
    On the old Olympic stage,
Lit the archway as the thunder,
    And the rumble and the roll,
Heralded a little handcart,
    And "The Agéd" selling coal.

Henley-on-Thames

I see the winding water make
A short and then a shorter lake
    As here stand I,
    And house-boat high
Survey the Upper Thames.
    By sun the mud is amber-dyed
    In ripples slow and flat and wide,
    That flap against the house-boat side
And flop away in gems.

In mud and elder-scented shade
A reach away the breach is made
    By dive and shout
    That circles out
To Henley tower and town;
    And "Boats for Hire" the rafters ring,
    And pink on white the roses cling,
    And red the bright geraniums swing
In baskets dangling down.

When shall I see the Thames again?
The prow-promoted gems again,
    As beefy ATS
    Without their hats
Come shooting through the bridge?
    And "cheerioh" and "cheeri-bye"
    Across the waste of waters die,
    And low the mists of evening lie
And lightly skims the midge.

Parliament Hill Fields

Rumbling under blackened girders, Midland, bound for
Cricklewood,
Puffed its sulphur to the sunset where that Land of Laundries
stood.
Rumble under, thunder over, train and tram alternate go,
Shake the floor and smudge the ledger, Charrington, Sells,
Dale and Co.,
Nuts and nuggets in the window, trucks along the lines below.

When the Bon Marché was shuttered, when the feet were hot
and tired,
Outside Charrington's we waited, by the "STOP HERE IF
REQUIRED",
Launched aboard the shopping basket, sat precipitately down,
Rocked past Zwanziger the baker's, and the terrace blackish
brown,
And the curious Anglo-Norman parish church of Kentish Town.

Till the tram went over thirty, sighting terminus again,
Past municipal lawn tennis and the bobble-hanging plane;
Soft the light suburban evening caught our ashlar-speckled spire,
Eighteen-sixty Early English, as the mighty elms retire
Either side of Brookfield Mansions flashing fine French-window
fire.

Oh the after-tram-ride quiet, when we heard a mile beyond,
Silver music from the bandstand, barking dogs by Highgate
Pond;

Up the hill where stucco houses in Virginia creeper drown—
And my childish wave of pity, seeing children carrying down
Sheaves of drooping dandelions to the courts of Kentish Town.

A Subaltern's Love-song

Miss J. Hunter Dunn, Miss J. Hunter Dunn,
Furnish'd and burnish'd by Aldershot sun,
What strenuous singles we played after tea,
We in the tournament—you against me!

Love-thirty, love-forty, oh! weakness of joy,
The speed of a swallow, the grace of a boy,
With carefullest carelessness, gaily you won,
I am weak from your loveliness, Joan Hunter Dunn.

Miss Joan Hunter Dunn, Miss Joan Hunter Dunn,
How mad I am, sad I am, glad that you won.
The warm-handled racket is back in its press,
But my shock-headed victor, she loves me no less.

Her father's euonymus shines as we walk,
And swing past the summer-house, buried in talk,
And cool the verandah that welcomes us in
To the six-o'clock news and a lime-juice and gin.

The scent of the conifers, sound of the bath,
The view from my bedroom of moss-dappled path,
As I struggle with double-end evening tie,
For we dance at the Golf Club, my victor and I.

On the floor of her bedroom lie blazer and shorts
And the cream-coloured walls are be-trophied with sports,

And westering, questioning settles the sun
On your low-leaded window, Miss Joan Hunter Dunn.

The Hillman is waiting, the light's in the hall,
The pictures of Egypt are bright on the wall,
My sweet, I am standing beside the oak stair
And there on the landing's the light on your hair.

By roads "not adopted", by woodlanded ways,
She drove to the club in the late summer haze,
Into nine-o'clock Camberley, heavy with bells
And mushroomy, pine-woody, evergreen smells.

Miss Joan Hunter Dunn, Miss Joan Hunter Dunn,
I can hear from the car-park the dance has begun.
Oh! full Surrey twilight! importunate band!
Oh! strongly adorable tennis-girl's hand!

Around us are Rovers and Austins afar,
Above us, the intimate roof of the car,
And here on my right is the girl of my choice,
With the tilt of her nose and the chime of her voice,

And the scent of her wrap, and the words never said,
And the ominous, ominous dancing ahead.
We sat in the car park till twenty to one
And now I'm engaged to Miss Joan Hunter Dunn.

Bristol

Green upon the flooded Avon shone the after-storm-wet-sky
Quick the struggling withy branches let the leaves of autumn fly
And a star shone over Bristol, wonderfully far and high.

Ringers in an oil-lit belfry—Bitton? Kelston? who shall say?—
Smoothly practising a plain course, caverned out the dying day
As their melancholy music flooded up and ebbed away.

Then all Somerset was round me and I saw the clippers ride,
High above the moonlit houses, triple-masted on the tide,
By the tall embattled church-towers of the Bristol waterside.

And an undersong to branches dripping into pools and wells
Out of multitudes of elm trees over leagues of hills and dells
Was the mathematic pattern of a plain course on the bells.*

*1 2 2 4 4 5 5 3 3 1 1
 2 1 4 2 5 4 3 5 1 3 2
 3 4 1 5 2 3 4 1 5 2 3
 4 3 5 1 3 2 1 4 2 5 4
 5 5 3 3 1 1 2 2 4 4 5

On an Old-Fashioned Water-Colour of Oxford
(*Early Twentieth-Century Date*)

———

Shines, billowing cold and gold from Cumnor Hurst,
   A winter sunset on wet cobbles, where
   By Canterbury Gate the fishtails flare.
Someone in Corpus reading for a first
Pulls down red blinds and flounders on, immers'd
   In Hegel, heedless of the yellow glare
   On porch and pinnacle and window square,
The brown stone crumbling where the skin has burst.

A late, last luncheon staggers out of Peck
   And hires a hansom: from half-flooded grass
     Returning athletes bark at what they see.
But we will mount the horse-tram's upper deck
   And wave salute to Buols', as we pass
     Bound for the Banbury Road in time for tea.

A Lincolnshire Tale

Kirkby with Muckby-cum-Sparrowby-cum-Spinx
Is down a long lane in the county of Lincs,
And often on Wednesdays, well-harnessed and spruce,
I would drive into Wiss over Winderby Sluice.

A whacking great sunset bathed level and drain
From Kirkby with Muckby to Beckby-on-Bain,
And I saw, as I journeyed, my marketing done
Old Caistorby tower take the last of the sun.

The night air grew nippy. An autumn mist roll'd
(In a scent of dead cabbages) down from the wold,
In the ocean of silence that flooded me round
The crunch of the wheels was a comforting sound.

The lane lengthened narrowly into the night
With the Bain on its left bank, the drain on its right,
And feebly the carriage-lamps glimmered ahead
When all of a sudden *the pony fell dead*.

The remoteness was awful, the stillness intense,
Of invisible fenland, around and immense;
And out of the dark, with a roar and a swell,
Swung, hollowly thundering, Speckleby bell.

Though myself the Archdeacon for many a year,
I had not summoned courage for visiting here;

Our incumbents were mostly eccentric or sad
But—*the Speckleby Rector was said to be mad.*

Oh cold was the ev'ning and tall was the tower
And strangely compelling the tenor bell's power!
As loud on the reed-beds and strong through the dark
It toll'd from the church in the tenantless park.

The mansion was ruined, the empty demesne
Was slowly reverting to marshland again—
Marsh where the village was, grass in the Hall,
And the church and the Rectory waiting to fall.

And even in springtime with kingcups about
And stumps of old oak-trees attempting to sprout,
'Twas a sinister place, neither fenland nor wold,
And doubly forbidding in darkness and cold.

As down swung the tenor, a beacon of sound,
Over listening acres of waterlogged ground
I stood by the tombs to see pass and repass
The gleam of a taper, through clear leaded glass,

And such lighting of lights in the thunderous roar
That heart summoned courage to hand at the door;
I grated it open on scents I knew well,
The dry smell of damp rot, the hassocky smell.

What a forest of woodwork in ochres and grains
Unevenly doubled in diamonded panes,

And over the plaster, so textured with time,
Sweet discoloration of umber and lime.

The candles ensconced on each high pannelled pew
Brought the caverns of brass-studded baize into view,
But the roof and its rafters were lost to the sight
As they soared to the dark of the Lincolnshire night:

And high from the chancel arch paused to look down
A sign-painter's beasts in their fight for the Crown,
While massive, impressive, and still as the grave
A three-decker pulpit frowned over the nave.

Shall I ever forget what a stillness was there
When the bell ceased its tolling and thinned on the air?
Then an opening door showed a long pair of hands
And the Rector himself in his gown and his bands.

 *   *   *   *   *

Such a fell Visitation I shall not forget,
Such a rush through the dark, that I rush through it yet,
And I pray, as the bells ring o'er fenland and hill,
That the Speckleby acres be tenantless still.

St. Barnabas, Oxford

How long was the peril, how breathless the day,
In topaz and beryl, the sun dies away,
His rays lying static at quarter to six
On polychromatical lacing of bricks.
Good Lord, as the angelus floats down the road,
Byzantine St. Barnabas, be Thine Abode.

Where once the fritillaries hung in the grass
A baldachin pillar is guarding the Mass.
Farewell to blue meadows we loved not enough,
And elms in whose shadows were Glanville and Clough
Not poets but clergymen hastened to meet
Thy redden'd remorselessness, Cardigan Street.

An Archaeological Picnic

In this high pasturage, this Blunden time,
  With Lady's Finger, Smokewort, Lovers' Loss,
And lin-lan-lone a Tennysonian chime
    Stirring the sorrel and the gold-starred moss,
    Cool is the chancel, bright the altar cross.

Drink, Mary, drink your fizzy lemonade
  And leave the king-cups; take your grey felt hat;
Here, where the low-side window lends a shade,
    There, where the key lies underneath the mat,
    The rude forefathers of the hamlet sat.

Sweet smell of cerements and of cold wet stones,
  Hassock and cassock, paraffin and pew;
Green in a light which that sublime Burne-Jones
    White-hot and wondering from the glass-kiln drew,
    Gleams and re-gleams this Trans arcade anew.

So stand you waiting, freckled innocence!
  For me the squinch and squint and Trans arcade;
For you, where meadow grass is evidence,
    With flattened pattern, of our picnic made,
    One bottle more of fizzy lemonade.

May-Day Song for North Oxford
(*Annie Laurie Tune*)

Belbroughton Road is bonny, and pinkly bursts the spray
Of prunus and forsythia across the public way,
For a full spring-tide of blossom seethed and departed hence,
Leaving land-locked pools of jonquils by sunny garden fence.

And a constant sound of flushing runneth from windows where
The toothbrush too is airing in this new North Oxford air
From Summerfields to Lynam's, the thirsty tarmac dries,
And a Cherwell mist dissolveth on elm-discovering skies.

Oh! well-bound Wells and Bridges! Oh! earnest ethical search
For the wide high-table λογος of St. C.S. Lewis's Church.
This diamond-eyed Spring morning my soul soars up the slope
Of a right good rough-cast buttress on the housewall of my hope.

And open-necked and freckled, where once there grazed the cows,
Emancipated children swing on old apple boughs,
And pastel-shaded book rooms bring New Ideas to birth
As the whitening hawthorn only hears the heart beat of the earth.

Before Invasion, 1940

Still heavy with may, and the sky ready to fall,
Meadows buttercup high, shed and chicken and wire?
And here where the wind leans on a sycamore silver wall,
Are you still taller than sycamores, gallant Victorian spire?

Still, fairly intact, and demolishing squads about,
Bracketed station lamp with your oil-light taken away?
Weep flowering currant, while your bitter cascades are out,
Born in an age of railways, for flowering into to-day!

Ireland with Emily

Bells are booming down the bohreens,
   White the mist along the grass.
Now the Julias, Maeves and Maureens
   Move between the fields to Mass.
Twisted trees of small green apple
Guard the decent whitewashed chapel,
Gilded gates and doorway grained
Pointed windows richly stained
   With many-coloured Munich glass.

See the black-shawled congregations
   On the broidered vestment gaze
Murmur past the painted stations
   As Thy Sacred Heart displays
Lush Kildare of scented meadows,
Roscommon, thin in ash-tree shadows,
And Westmeath the lake-reflected,
Spreading Leix the hill-protected,
   Kneeling all in silver haze?

In yews and woodbine, walls and guelder,
   Nettle-deep the faithful rest,
Winding leagues of flowering elder,
   Sycamore with ivy dressed,
Ruins in demesnes deserted,
Bog-surrounded bramble-skirted—
Townlands rich or townlands mean as

These, oh, counties of them screen us
    In the Kingdom of the West.

Stony seaboard, far and foreign,
    Stony hills poured over space,
Stony outcrop of the Burren,
    Stones in every fertile place,
Little fields with boulders dotted,
Grey-stone shoulders saffron-spotted,
Stone-walled cabins thatched with reeds,
Where a Stone Age people breeds
    The last of Europe's stone age race.

Has it held, the warm June weather?
    Draining shallow sea-pools dry,
When we bicycled together
    Down the bohreens fuchsia-high.
Till there rose, abrupt and lonely,
A ruined abbey, chancel only,
Lichen-crusted, time-befriended,
Soared the arches, splayed and splendid,
    Romanesque against the sky.

There in pinnacled protection,
    One extinguished family waits
A Church of Ireland resurrection
    By the broken, rusty gates.
Sheepswool, straw and droppings cover,
Graves of spinster, rake and lover,
Whose fantastic mausoleum
Sings its own seablown Te Deum,
    In and out the slipping slates.

Margate, 1940

From out the Queen's Highcliffe for weeks at a stretch
I watched how the mower evaded the vetch,
So that over the putting-course rashes were seen
Of pink and of yellow among the burnt green.

How restful to putt, when the strains of a band
Announced a *thé dansant* was on at the Grand,
While over the privet, comminglingly clear,
I heard lesser "Co-Optimists" down by the pier.

How lightly municipal, meltingly tarr'd,
Were the walks through the Laws by the Queen's Promenade
As soft over Cliftonville languished the light
Down Harold Road, Norfolk Road, into the night.

Oh! then what a pleasure to see the ground floor
With tables for two laid as tables for four,
And bottles of sauce and Kia-Ora[1] and squash
Awaiting their owners who'd gone up to wash—

Who had gone up to wash the ozone from their skins
The sand from their legs and the Rock from their chins,
To prepare for an evening of dancing and cards
And forget the sea-breeze on the dry promenades.

[1] Pronounced "Kee-ora".

From third floor and fourth floor the children looked down
Upon ribbons of light in the salt-scented town;
And drowning the trams roared the sound of the sea
As it washed in the shingle the scraps of their tea.

*   *   *   *   *

Beside the Queen's Highcliffe now rank grows the vetch,
Now dark is the terrace, a storm-battered stretch;
And I think, as the fairy-lit sights I recall,
It is those we are fighting for, foremost of all.

Invasion Exercise on the Poultry Farm

Softly croons the radiogram, loudly hoot the owls,
Judy gives the door a slam and goes to feed the fowls.
Marty rolls a Craven A around her ruby lips
And runs her yellow fingers down her corduroyded hips,
Shuts her mouth and screws her eyes and puffs her fag alight
And hears some most peculiar cries that echo through the night.
Ting-a-ling the telephone, to-whit to-whoo the owls,
Judy, Judy, Judy girl, and have you fed the fowls?
No answer as the poultry gate is swinging there ajar.
Boom the bombers overhead, between the clouds a star,
And just outside, among the arks, in a shadowy sheltered place
Lie Judy and a paratroop in horrible embrace.
Ting-a-ling the telephone. "Yes, this is Marty Hayne."
"Have you seen a paratroop come walking down your lane?
He may be on your premises, he may be somewhere near,
And if he is report the fact to Major Maxton-Weir."
Marty moves in dread towards the window—standing there
Draws the curtain—sees the guilty movement of the pair.[1]
White with rage and lined with age but strong and sturdy still
Marty now co-ordinates her passions and her will,
She will teach that Judy girl to trifle with the heart
And go and kiss a paratroop like any common tart.
She switches up the radiogram and covered by the blare
She goes and gets a riding whip and whirls it in the air,
She fetches down a length of rope and rushes, breathing hard
To let the couple have it for embracing in the yard.

[1] These lines in italic are by Henry Oscar.

Crack! the pair are paralysed. Click! they cannot stir.
Zip! she's trussed the paratroop. There's no embracing *her*.
"Hullo, hullo, hullo, hullo. . . Major Maxton-Weir?
I've trussed your missing paratroop. He's waiting for you here."

The Planster's Vision

Cut down that timber! Bells, too many and strong,
   Pouring their music through the branches bare,
   From moon-white church-towers down the windy air
Have pealed the centuries out with Evensong.
Remove those cottages, a huddled throng!
   Too many babies have been born in there,
   Too many coffins, bumping down the stair,
Carried the old their garden paths along.

I have a Vision of The Future, chum,
   The workers' flats in fields of soya beans
     Tower up like silver pencils, score on score:
And Surging Millions hear the Challenge come
   From microphones in communal canteens
     "No Right! No Wrong! All's perfect, evermore."

In a Bath Teashop

"Let us not speak, for the love we bear one another—
  Let us hold hands and look."
She, such a very ordinary little woman;
  He, such a thumping crook;
But both, for a moment, little lower than the angels
  In the teashop's ingle-nook.

Before the Anaesthetic,
or
A Real Fright

———————

Intolerably sad, profound
St. Giles's bells are ringing round,
They bring the slanting summer rain
To tap the chestnut boughs again
Whose shadowy cave of rainy leaves
The gusty belfry-song receives.
Intolerably sad and true,
Victorian red and jewel* blue,
The mellow bells are ringing round
And charge the evening light with sound,
And I look motionless from bed
On heavy trees and purple red
And hear the midland bricks and tiles
Throw back the bells of stone St. Giles,
Bells, ancient now as castle walls,
Now hard and new as pitchpine stalls,
Now full with help from ages past,
Now dull with death and hell at last.
Swing up! and give me hope of life,
Swing down! and plunge the surgeon's knife.
I, breathing for a moment, see
Death wing himself away from me
And think, as on this bed I lie,
Is it extinction when I die?

        * Adjective from Rumer Godden.

I move my limbs and use my sight;
Not yet, thank God, not yet the Night.
Oh better far those echoing hells
Half-threaten'd in the pealing bells
Than that this "I" should cease to be—
Come quickly, Lord, come quick to me.
St. Giles's bells are asking now
"And hast thou known the Lord, hast thou?"
St. Giles's bells, they richly ring
"And was that Lord our Christ the King?"
St. Giles's bells they hear me call
I never knew the Lord at all.
Oh not in me your Saviour dwells
You ancient, rich St. Giles's bells.
Illuminated missals—spires—
Wide screens and decorated quires—
All these I loved, and on my knees
I thanked myself for knowing these
And watched the morning sunlight pass
Through richly stained Victorian glass
And in the colour-shafted air
I, kneeling, thought the Lord was there.
Now, lying in the gathering mist
I know that Lord did not exist;
Now, lest this "I" should cease to be,
Come, real Lord, come quick to me.
With every gust the chestnut sighs,
With every breath, a mortal dies;
The man who smiled alone, alone,
And went his journey on his own
With "Will you give my wife this letter,

In case, of course, I don't get better?"
Waits for his coffin lid to close
On waxen head and yellow toes.
Almighty Saviour, had I Faith
There'd be no fight with kindly Death.
Intolerably long and deep
St. Giles's bells swing on in sleep:
"But still you go from here alone"
Say all the bells about the Throne.

On Hearing the Full Peal of Ten Bells
from Christ Church, Swindon, Wilts.

———

Your peal of ten ring over then this town,
Ring on my men nor ever ring them down.
This winter chill, let sunset spill cold fire
On villa'd hill and on Sir Gilbert's spire,
So new, so high, so pure, so broach'd, so tall.
Long run the thunder of the bells through all!

Oh still white headstones on these fields of sound
Hear you the wedding joybells wheeling round?
Oh brick-built breeding boxes of new souls,
Hear how the pealing through the louvres rolls!
Now birth and death-reminding bells ring clear,
Loud under 'planes and over changing gear.

Youth and Age on Beaulieu River, Hants

Early sun on Beaulieu water
　　Lights the undersides of oaks,
Clumps of leaves it floods and blanches,
All transparent glow the branches
　　Which the double sunlight soaks;
　　To her craft on Beaulieu water
　　Clemency the General's daughter
　　　Pulls across with even strokes.

Schoolboy-sure she is this morning;
　　Soon her sharpie's rigg'd and free.
Cool beneath a garden awning
　　Mrs. Fairclough, sipping tea
And raising large long-distance glasses
As the little sharpie passes,
　　Sighs our sailor girl to see:

Tulip figure, so appealing,
　　Oval face, so serious-eyed,
Tree-roots pass'd and muddy beaches.
On to huge and lake-like reaches,
　　Soft and sun-warm, see her glide—
　　Slacks the slim young limbs revealing,
　　Sun-brown arm the tiller feeling—
　　　With the wind and with the tide.

Evening light will bring the water,
Day-long sun will burst the bud,
Clemency, the General's daughter,
Will return upon the flood.
But the older woman only
Knows the ebb-tide leaves her lonely
With the shining fields of mud.

East Anglian Bathe

Oh when the early morning at the seaside
    Took us with hurrying steps from Horsey Mere
To see the whistling bent-grass on the leeside
    And then the tumbled breaker-line appear,
On high, the clouds with mighty adumbration
    Sailed over us to seaward fast and clear
And jellyfish in quivering isolation
    Lay silted in the dry sand of the breeze
And we, along the table-land of beach blown
    Went gooseflesh from our shoulders to our knees
And ran to catch the football, each to each thrown,
    In the soft and swirling music of the seas.

There splashed about our ankles as we waded
    Those intersecting wavelets morning-cold,
And sudden dark a patch of sea was shaded,
    And sudden light, another patch would hold
The warmth of whirling atoms in a sun-shot
    And underwater sandstorm green and gold.
So in we dived and louder than a gunshot
    Sea-water broke in fountains down the ear.
How cold the bathe, how chattering cold the drying,
    How welcoming the inland reeds appear,
The wood-smoke and the breakfast and the frying,
    And your warm freshwater ripples, Horsey Mere.

Sunday Afternoon Service in
St. Enodoc Church, Cornwall

Come on! come on! This hillock hides the spire,
Now that one and now none. As winds about
The burnished path through lady's finger, thyme
And bright varieties of saxifrage,
So grows the tinny tenor faint or loud
And all things draw towards St. Enodoc.

Come on! come on! and it is five to three.

Paths, unfamiliar to golfers' brogues,
Cross the eleventh fairway broadside on
And leave the fourteenth tee for thirteenth green,
Ignoring Royal and Ancient, bound for God.
   Come on! come on! no longer bare of foot,
The sole grows hot in London shoes again.
Jack Lambourne in his Sunday navy-blue
Wears tie and collar, all from Selfridge's.
There's Enid with a silly parasol,
And Graham in gray flannel with a crease
Across the middle of his coat which lay
Pressed 'neath the box of his Meccano set,
Sunday to Sunday.
            Still, Come on! come on!
The tinny tenor. Hover-flies remain
More than a moment on a ragwort bunch,
And people's passing shadows don't disturb

Red Admirals basking with their wings apart.
    A mile of sunny, empty sand away,
A mile of shallow pools and lugworm casts,
Safe, faint and surfy, laps the lowest tide.
    Even the villas have a Sunday look.
The Ransom mower's locked into the shed.
"I have a splitting headache from the sun,"
And bedroom windows flutter cheerful chintz
Where, double-aspirined, a mother sleeps;
While father in the loggia reads a book,
Large, desultory, birthday-present size,
Published with coloured plates by *Country Life*,
A Bernard Darwin on *The English Links*
Or Braid and Taylor on *The Mashie Shot*.
Come on! come on! he thinks of Monday's round—
Come on! come on! that interlocking grip!
Come on! come on! he drops into a doze—
Come on! come on! more far and far away
The children climb a final stile to church;
Electoral Roll still flapping in the porch—
Then the cool silence of St. Enodoc.

My eyes, recovering in the sudden shade,
Discern the long-known little things within—
A map of France in damp above my pew,
Grey-blue of granite in the small arcade
(Late Perp: and not a Parker specimen
But roughly hewn on windy Bodmin Moor),
The modest windows palely glazed with green,
The smooth slate floor, the rounded wooden roof,
The Norman arch, the cable-moulded font—

All have a humble and West Country look.
Oh "drastic restoration" of the guide!
Oh three-light window by a Plymouth firm!
Absurd, truncated screen! oh sticky pews!
Embroidered altar-cloth! untended lamps!
So soaked in worship you are loved too well
For that dispassionate and critic stare
That I would use beyond the parish bounds
Biking in high-banked lanes from tower to tower
On sunny, antiquarian afternoons.

   Come on! come on! a final pull. Tom Blake
Stalks over from the bell-rope to his pew
Just as he slopes about the windy cliffs
Looking for wreckage in a likely tide,
Nor gives the Holy Table glance or nod.
A rattle as red baize is drawn aside,
Miss Rhoda Poulden pulls the tremolo,
The oboe, flute and vox humana stops;
A Village Voluntary fills the air
And ceases suddenly as it began,
Save for one oboe faintly humming on,
As slow the weary clergyman subsides
Tired with his bike-ride from the parish church.
He runs his hands once, twice, across his face
"Dearly beloved . . . " and a bumble-bee
Zooms itself free into the churchyard sun
And so my thoughts this happy Sabbathtide.

   Where deep cliffs loom enormous, where cascade
Mesembryanthemum and stone-crop down,
Where the gull looks no larger than a lark
Hung midway twixt the cliff-top and the sand,

Sun-shadowed valleys roll along the sea.
Forced by the backwash, see the nearest wave
Rise to a wall of huge, translucent green
And crumble into spray along the top
Blown seaward by the land-breeze. Now she breaks
And in an arch of thunder plunges down
To burst and tumble, foam on top of foam,
Criss-crossing, baffled, sucked and shot again,
A waterfall of whiteness, down a rock,
Without a source but roller's furthest reach:
And tufts of sea-pink, high and dry for years,
Are flooded out of ledges, boulders seem
No bigger than a pebble washed about
In this tremendous tide. Oh kindly slate!
To give me shelter in this crevice dry.
These shivering stalks of bent-grass, lucky plant,
Have better chance than I to last the storm.
Oh kindly slate of these unaltered cliffs,
Firm, barren substrate of our windy fields!
Oh lichened slate in walls, they knew your worth
Who raised you up to make this House of God
What faith was his, that dim, that Cornish saint,
Small rushlight of a long-forgotten church,
Who lived with God on this unfriendly shore,
Who knew He made the Atlantic and the stones
And destined seamen here to end their lives
Dashed on a rock, rolled over in the surf,
And not one hair forgotten. Now they lie
In centuries of sand beside the church.
Less pitiable are they than the corpse
Of a large golfer, only four weeks dead,

This sunlit and sea-distant afternoon.
"Praise ye the Lord!" and in another key
The Lord's name by harmonium be praised.
"The Second Evening and the Fourteenth Psalm."

The Irish Unionist's Farewell to Greta Hellstrom in 1922

Golden haired and golden hearted
  I would ever have you be,
As you were when last we parted
  Smiling slow and sad at me.
Oh! the fighting down of passion!
  Oh! the century-seeming pain—
Parting in this off-hand fashion
  In Dungarvan in the rain.

Slanting eyes of blue, unweeping,
  Stands my Swedish beauty where
Gusts of Irish rain are sweeping
  Round the statue in the square;
Corner boys against the walling
  Watch us furtively in vain,
And the Angelus is calling
  Through Dungarvan in the rain.

Gales along the Commeragh Mountains,
  Beating sleet on creaking signs,
Iron gutters turned to fountains,
  And the windscreen laced with lines,
And the evening getting later,
  And the ache—increased again,
As the distance grows the greater
  From Dungarvan in the rain.

118

There is no one now to wonder
    What eccentric sits in state
While the beech trees rock and thunder
    Round his gate-lodge and his gate.
Gone—the ornamental plaster,
    Gone—the overgrown demesne
And the car goes fast, and faster,
    From Dungarvan in the rain.

Had I kissed and drawn you to me,
    Had you yielded warm for cold,
What a power had pounded through me
    As I stroked your streaming gold!
You were right to keep us parted:
    Bound and parted we remain,
Aching, if unbroken hearted—
    Oh! Dungarvan in the rain.

In Memory of Basil, Marquess of Dufferin and Ava

———

On such a morning as this
   with the birds ricocheting their music
Out of the whelming elms
   to a copper beech's embrace
And a sifting sound of leaves
   from multitudinous branches
Running across the park
   to a chequer of light on the lake,
On such a morning as this
   with *The Times* for June the eleventh
Left with coffee and toast
   you opened the breakfast-room window
And, sprawled on the southward terrace,
   Said: "That means war in September."

Friend of my youth, you are dead!
   and the long peal pours from the steeple
Over this sunlit quad
   in our University city
And soaks in Headington stone.
   Motionless stand the pinnacles.
Under a flying sky
   as though they too listened and waited
Like me for your dear return
   with a Bullingdon noise of an evening
In a Sports-Bugatti from Thame

that belonged to a man in Magdalen.
Friend of my youth, you are dead!
   and the quads are empty without you.

Then there were people about.
   Each hour, like an Oxford archway,
Opened on long green lawns
   and distant unvisited buildings
And you my friend were explorer
   and so you remained to me always
Humorous, reckless, loyal—
   my kind, heavy-lidded companion.
Stop, oh many bells, stop
   pouring on roses and creeper
Your unremembering peal
   this hollow, unhallowed V.E. day,—
I am deaf to your notes and dead
   by a soldier's body in Burma.

South London Sketch, 1944

From Bermondsey to Wandsworth
   So many churches are,
Some with apsidal chancels,
   Some Perpendicular
And schools by E.R. Robson
   In the style of Norman Shaw
Where blue-serged adolescence learn'd
   To model and to draw.

Oh, in among the houses,
   The viaduct below,
Stood the Coffee Essence Factory
   Of Robinson and Co.
Burnt and brown and tumbled down
   And done with years ago
Where the waters of the Wandle do
   Lugubriously flow.

From dust of dead explosions,
   From scarlet-hearted fires,
All unconcerned this train draws in
   And smoothly that retires
And calmly rise on smoky skies
   Of intersected wires
The Nonconformist spirelets
   And the Church of England spires.

South London Sketch, 1844

Lavender Sweep is drowned in Wandsworth,
  Drowned in jessamine up to the neck,
Beetles sway upon bending grass leagues
  Shoulder-level to Tooting Bec.
Rich as Middlesex, rich in signboards,
  Lie the lover-trod lanes between,
Red Man, Green Man, Horse and Waggoner,
  Elms and sycamores round a green.
Burst, good June, with a rush this morning,
  Bindweed weave me an emerald rope
Sun, shine bright on the blossoming trellises,
  June and lavender, bring me hope.

Indoor Games near Newbury

In among the silver birches winding ways of tarmac wander
 And the signs to Bussock Bottom, Tussock Wood and
                                                    Windy Brake,
Gabled lodges, tile-hung churches, catch the lights of our Lagonda
 As we drive to Wendy's party, lemon curd and Christmas cake.
      Rich the makes of motor whirring,
      Past the pine-plantation purring
           Come up, Hupmobile, Delage!
      Short the way your chauffeurs travel,
      Crunching over private gravel
           Each from out his warm garáge.

Oh but Wendy, when the carpet yielded to my indoor pumps
      There you stood, your gold hair streaming,
      Handsome in the hall-light gleaming
There you looked and there you led me off into the game of clumps
      Then the new Victrola playing
      And your funny uncle saying
"Choose your partners for a fox-trot! Dance until it's *tea* o'clock!
      "Come on, young 'uns, foot it featly!"
      Was it chance that paired us neatly,
      I, who loved you so completely,
You, who pressed me closely to you, hard against your party
                                                    frock?

"Meet me when you've finished eating!" So we met and no one
found us.
Oh that dark and furry cupboard while the rest played hide
and seek!
Holding hands our two hearts beating in the bedroom silence
round us,
Holding hands and hardly hearing sudden footstep, thud and
shriek.
Love that lay too deep for kissing—
"Where *is* Wendy? Wendy's missing!"
Love so pure it *had* to end,
Love so strong that I was frighten'd
When you gripped my fingers tight and
Hugging, whispered "I'm your friend."

Goodbye Wendy! Send the fairies, pinewood elf and larch tree
gnome,
Spingle-spangled stars are peeping
At the lush Lagonda creeping
Down the winding ways of tarmac to the leaded lights of home.
There, among the silver birches,
All the bells of all the churches
Sounded in the bath-waste running out into the frosty air.
Wendy speeded my undressing,
Wendy is the sheet's caressing
Wendy bending gives a blessing,
Holds me as I drift to dreamland, safe inside my slumber-wear.

St. Saviour's, Aberdeen Park,
Highbury, London, N.

With oh such peculiar branching and over-reaching of wire
    Trolley-bus standards pick their threads from the London sky
Diminishing up the perspective, Highbury-bound retire
    Threads and buses and standards with plane trees volleying by
And, more peculiar still, that ever-increasing spire
    Bulges over the housetops, polychromatic and high.

Stop the trolley-bus, stop! And here, where the roads unite
    Of weariest worn-out London—no cigarettes, no beer,
No repairs undertaken, nothing in stock—alight;
    For over the waste of willow-herb, look at her, sailing clear,
A great Victorian church, tall, unbroken and bright
    In a sun that's setting in Willesden and saturating us here.

These were the streets my parents knew when they loved and
                                 won—
    The brougham that crunched the gravel, the laurel-girt paths
                                 that wind,
Geranium-beds for the lawn, Venetian blinds for the sun,
    A separate tradesman's entrance, straw in the mews behind,
Just in the four-mile radius where hackney carriages run,
    Solid Italianate houses for the solid commercial mind.

These were the streets they knew; and I, by descent, belong
    To these tall neglected houses divided into flats.
Only the church remains, where carriages used to throng

And my mother stepped out in flounces and my father stepped
out in spats
To shadowy stained-glass matins or gas-lit evensong
And back in a country quiet with doffing of chimney hats.

Great red church of my parents, cruciform crossing they knew—
Over these same encaustics they and their parents trod
Bound through a red-brick transept for a once familiar pew
Where the organ set them singing and the sermon let them nod
And up this coloured brickwork the same long shadows grew
As these in the stencilled chancel where I kneel in the presence
of God.

Wonder beyond Time's wonders, that Bread so white and small
Veiled in golden curtains, too mighty for men to see,
Is the Power which sends the shadows up this polychrome wall,
Is God who created the present, the chain-smoking millions and
me;
Beyond the throb of the engines is the throbbing heart of all—
Christ, at this Highbury altar, I offer myself To Thee.

Beside the Seaside

Green Shutters, shut your shutters! Windyridge,
Let winds unnoticed whistle round your hill!
High Dormers, draw your curtains! Slam the door,
And pack the family in the Morris eight.
Lock up the garage. Put her in reverse,
Back out with care, now, forward, off—away!
The richer people living farther out
O'ertake us in their Rovers. We, in turn,
Pass poorer families hurrying on foot
Towards the station. Very soon the town
Will echo to the groan of empty trams
And sweetshops advertise Ice Cream in vain.
Solihull, Headingley and Golders Green.
Preston and Swindon, Manchester and Leeds,
Braintree and Bocking, hear the sea! the sea!
The smack of breakers upon windy rocks,
Spray blowing backwards from their curling walls
Of green translucent water. England leaves
Her centre for her tide-line. Father's toes,
Though now encased in coloured socks and shoes
And pressing the accelerator hard,
Ache for the feel of sand and little shrimps
To tickle in between them. Mother vows
To be more patient with the family:
Just for its sake she will be young again.
And, at that moment, Jennifer is sick
(Over-excitement must have brought it on,

The hurried breakfast and the early start)
And Michael's rather pale, and as for Anne . . .
"Please stop a moment, Hubert, anywhere."
   So evening sunlight shows us Sandy Cove
The same as last year and the year before.
Still on the brick front of the Baptist Church
SIX-THIRTY. PREACHER:—*Mr. Pentecost—*
All visitors are welcomed. Still the quartz
Glitters along the tops of garden walls.
Those macrocarpa still survive the gales
They must have had last winter. Still the shops
Remain unaltered on the Esplanade—
The Circulating Library, the Stores,
Jill's Pantry, Cynthia's Ditty Box (Antiques),
Trecarrow (Maps and Souvenirs and Guides).
Still on the terrace of the big hotel
Pale pink hydrangeas turn a rusty brown
Where sea winds catch them, and yet do not die.
The bumpy lane between the tamarisks,
The escallonia hedge, and still it's there—
Our lodging-house, ten minutes from the shore.
Still unprepared to make a picnic lunch
Except by notice on the previous day.
Still nowhere for the children when it's wet
Except that smelly, overcrowded lounge.
And still no garage for the motor-car.
Still on the bedroom wall, the list of rules:
Don't waste the water. It is pumped by hand.
Don't throw old blades into the W.C.
Don't keep the bathroom long and don't be late
For meals and don't hang swim-suits out on sills

(A line has been provided at the back).
Don't empty children's sand-shoes in the hall.
Don't this, Don't that. Ah, still the same, the same
As it was last year and the year before—
But rather more expensive, now, of course.
"Anne, Jennifer and Michael—run along
Down to the sands and find yourselves some friends
While Dad and I unpack." The sea! the sea!

   On a secluded corner of the beach
A game of rounders has been organized
By Mr. Pedder, schoolmaster and friend
Of boys and girls—particularly girls.
And here it was the tragedy began,
That life-long tragedy to Jennifer
Which ate into her soul and made her take
To secretarial work in later life
In a department of the Board of Trade.
See boys and girls assembled for the game.
Reflected in the rock pools, freckled legs
Hop, skip and jump in coltish ecstasy.
Ah! parted lips and little pearly teeth,
Wide eyes, snub noses, shorts, divided skirts!
And last year's queen of them was Jennifer.
The snubbiest, cheekiest, lissomest of all.
One smile from her sent Mr. Pedder back
Contented to his lodgings. She could wave
Her little finger and the elder boys
Came at her bidding. Even tiny Ruth,
Old Lady D'Erncourt's grandchild, pet of all,
Would bring her shells as timid offerings.
So now with Anne and Michael see her stand,

Our Jennifer, our own, our last year's queen,
For this year's *début* fully confident.
"Get in your places." Heard above the waves
Are Mr. Pedder's organizing shouts.
"Come on. Look sharp. The tide is coming in!"
"He hasn't seen me yet," thinks Jennifer.
"Line up your team behind you, Christabel!"
On the wet sea-sand waiting to be seen
She stands with Anne and Michael. Let him turn
And then he'll see me. Let him only turn.
Smack went the tennis ball. The bare feet ran.
And smack again. "He's out! Well caught, Delphine!"
Shrieks, cartwheels, tumbling joyance of the waves.
Oh Mr. Pedder, look! Oh here I am!
And there the three of them forlornly stood.
"You ask him, Jennifer." "No—Michael?—Anne?"
"I'd rather not." "Fains I." "It's up to you."
"Oh, very well, then." Timidly she goes,
Timid and proud, for the last time a child.
"Can *we* play, Mr. Pedder?" But his eyes
Are out to where, among the tousled heads,
He sees the golden curls of Christabel.
"Can *we* play, Mr. Pedder?" So he turns.
"*Who* have we here?" The jolly, jolly voice,
The same but not the same. "*Who* have we here?
The Rawlings children! Yes, of course, you may,
Join that side, children, under Christabel."
No friendly wallop on the B.T.M.
No loving arm-squeeze and no special look.
Oh darting heart-burn, *under Christabel!*
So all those holidays the bitter truth

Sank into Jennifer. No longer queen,
She had outgrown her strength, as Mummy said,
And Mummy made her wear these spectacles.
Because of Mummy she had lost her looks.
Had lost her looks? Still she was Jennifer.
The sands were still the same, the rocks the same,
The seaweed-waving pools, the bathing-cove,
The outline of the cliffs, the times of tide.
And I'm the same, of course I'm always ME.
But all that August those terrific waves
Thundered defeat along the rocky coast,
And ginger-beery surf hissed 'Christabel!'

   Enough of tragedy! Let wail of gulls,
The sunbows in the breakers and the breeze
Which blows the sand into the sandwiches,
Let castles crumbling in the rise of tide,
Let cool dank caves and dark interstices
Where, underneath the squelching bladderwrack,
Lurk stinging fin and sharp, marauding claw
Ready to pierce the rope-soled bathing-shoe,
Let darting prawn and helpless jelly-fish
Spell joy or misery to youth. For we,
We older ones, have thoughts of higher things.
Whether we like to sit with Penguin books
In sheltered alcoves farther up the cliff,
Or to eat winkles on the Esplanade,
Or to play golf along the crowded course,
Or on a twopenny borough council chair
To doze away the strains of *Humoresque*,
Adapted for the cornet and the drums
By the conductor of the Silver Band,

Whether we own a tandem or a Rolls,
Whether we Rudge it or we trudge it, still
A single topic occupies our minds.
'Tis hinted at or boldly blazoned in
Our accents, clothes and ways of eating fish,
And being introduced and taking leave,
'Farewell,' 'So long,' 'Bunghosky,' 'Cheeribye'—
That topic all-absorbing, as it was,
Is now and ever shall be, to us—CLASS.

   Mr. and Mrs. Stephen Grosvenor-Smith
(He manages a Bank in Nottingham)
Have come to Sandy Cove for thirty years
And now they think the place is going down.
   "Not what it was, I'm very much afraid.
Look at that little mite with *Attaboy*
Printed across her paper sailor hat.
Disgusting, isn't it? Who *can* they be,
Her parents, to allow such forwardness?"

   The Browns, who thus are commented upon,
Have certainly done very well indeed.
The elder children bringing money in,
Father still working; with allowances
For this and that and little income-tax,
They probably earn seven times as much
As poor old Grosvenor-Smith. But who will grudge
Them this, their wild, spontaneous holiday?
The morning paddle, then the mystery tour
By motor-coach inland this afternoon.
For that old mother what a happy time!
At last past bearing children, she can sit
Reposeful on a crowded bit of beach.

A week of idleness, the salty winds
Play in her greying hair; the summer sun
Puts back her freckles so that Alfred Brown
Remembers courting days in Gospel Oak
And takes her to the Flannel Dance to-night.
But all the same they think the place 'Stuck up'
And Blackpool, next year—if there *is* a next.
    And all the time the waves, the waves, the waves
Chase, intersect and flatten on the sand
As they have done for centuries, as they will
For centuries to come, when not a soul
Is left to picnic on the blazing rocks,
When England is not England, when mankind
Has blown himself to pieces. Still the sea,
Consolingly disastrous, will return
While the strange starfish, hugely magnified,
Waits in the jewelled basin of a pool.

North Coast Recollections

No people on the golf-links, not a crack
Of well-swung driver from the fourteenth tee,
No sailing bounding ball across the turf
And lady's slipper of the fairway. Black
Rises Bray Hill and, Stepper-wards, the sun
Sends Bray Hill's phantom stretching to the church.
The lane, the links, the beach, the cliffs are bare
The neighbourhood is dressing for a dance
And lamps are being lit in bungalows.
   O! thymy time of evening: clover scent
And feathery tamarisk round the churchyard wall
And shrivelled sea-pinks and this foreshore pale
With silver sand and sharpened quartz and slate
And brittle twigs, bleached, salted and prepared
For kindling blue-flamed fires on winter nights.
   Here Petroc landed, here I stand to-day;
The same Atlantic surges roll for me
As rolled for Parson Hawker and for him,
And spent their gathering thunder on the rocks
Crashing with pebbly backwash, burst again
And strewed the nibbled fields along the cliffs.

   When low tides drain the estuary gold
Small intersecting breakers far away
Ripple about a bar of shifting sand
Where centuries ago were waving woods
Where centuries hence, there will be woods again.

135

Within the bungalow of Mrs. Hanks
Her daughter Phoebe now French-chalks the floor.
Norman and Gordon in their dancing pumps
Slide up and down, but can't make concrete smooth.
"My Sweet Hortense . . ."
Sings louder down the garden than the sea.
"A practice record, Phoebe. Mummykins,
Gordon and I will do the washing-up."
"We picnic here; we scrounge and help ourselves,"
Says Mrs. Hanks, and visitors will smile
To see them all turn to it. Boys and girls
Weed in the sterile garden, mostly sand
And dead tomato-plants and chicken-runs.
To-day they cleaned the dulled Benares ware
(Dulled by the sea-mist), early made the beds,
And Phoebe twirled the icing round the cake
And Gordon tinkered with the gramophone
While into an immense enamel jug
Norman poured "Eiffel Tower" for lemonade.

O! healthy bodies, bursting into 'teens
And bursting out of last year's summer clothes,
Fluff barking and French windows banging to
Till the asbestos walling of the place
Shakes with the life it shelters, and with all
The preparations for this evening's dance.

Now drains the colour from the convolvulus,
The windows of Trenain are flashing fire,
Black sways the tamarisk against the West,
And bathing things are taken in from sills.
One child still zig-zags homewards up the lane,

Cold on bare feet he feels the dew-wet sand.
Behind him, from a walk along the cliff,
Come pater and the mater and the dogs.

Four macrocarpa hide the tennis club.
Two children of a chartered actuary
(Beaworthy, Trouncer, Heppelwhite and Co.),
Harold and Bonzo Trouncer are engaged
In semi-finals for the tournament.
"Love thirty!" Pang! across the evening air
Twangs Harold's racquet. Plung! the ball returns.
Experience at Budleigh Salterton
Keeps Bonzo steady at the net. "Well done!"
"Love forty!" Captain Mycroft, midst applause,
Pronounces for the Trouncers, to be sure
He can't be certain Bonzo didn't reach
A shade across the net, but Demon Sex,
That tulip figure in white cotton dress,
Bare legs, wide eyes and so tip-tilted nose
Quite overset him. Harold serves again
And Mrs. Pardon says it's getting cold,
Miss Myatt shivers, Lady Lambourn thinks
These English evenings are a little damp
And dreams herself again in fair Shanghai.
"Game . . . AND! and thank you!"; so the pair from Rock
(A neighbouring and less exclusive place)
Defeated, climb into their Morris Ten.
"The final is to-morrow! Well, good night!"
 He lay in wait, he lay in wait, he did,
John Lambourn, curly-headed; dewy grass
Dampened his flannels, but he still remained.

The sunset drained the colours black and gold,
From his all-glorious First Eleven scarf.
But still he waited by the twilit hedge.
Only his eyes blazed blue with early love,
Blue blazing in the darkness of the lane,
Blue blazer, less incalculably blue,
Dark scarf, white flannels, supple body still,
First love, first light, first life. A heartbeat noise!
His heart or little feet? A snap of twigs
Dry, dead and brown the under branches part
And Bonzo scrambles by their secret way.
First love so deep, John Lambourn cannot speak,
So deep, he feels a tightening in his throat,
So tender, he could brush away the sand
Dried up in patches on her freckled legs,
Could hold her gently till the stars went down,
And if she cut herself would staunch the wound,
Yes, even with this First Eleven scarf,
And hold it there for hours.
So happy, and so deep he loves the world,
Could worship God and rocks and stones and trees,
Be nicer to his mother, kill himself
If that would make him pure enough for her.
And so at last he manages to say
"You going to the Hanks's hop to-night?"
"Well, I'm not sure. Are you?" "I think I may—
"It's pretty dud though,—only lemonade."
   Sir Gawaint was a right and goodly knight
Nor ever wist he to uncurtis be.
So old, so lovely, and so very true!
Then Mrs. Wilder shut the Walter Crane

And tied the tapes and tucked her youngest in
What time without amidst the lavender
At late last 'He' played Primula and Prue
With new-found liveliness, for bed was soon.
And in the garage, serious seventeen
Harvey, the eldest, hammered on, content,
Fixing a mizzen to his model boat.
"Coo-ee! Coo-ee!" across the lavender,
Across the mist of pale gypsophila
And lolling purple poppies, Mumsie called,
A splendid sunset lit the rocking-horse
And Morris pattern of the nursery walls.
"Coo-ee!" the slate-hung, goodly-builded house
And sunset-sodden garden fell to quiet.
"Prue! Primsie! Mumsie wants you. Sleepi-byes!"
Prue jumped the marigolds and hid herself,
Her sister scampered to the Wendy Hut
And Harvey, glancing at his Ingersoll,
Thought "Damn! I must get ready for the dance."

So on this after-storm-lit evening
To Jim the raindrops in the tamarisk,
The fuchsia bells, the sodden matchbox lid
That checked a tiny torrent in the lane
Were magnified and shining clear with life.
Then pealing out across the estuary
The Padstow bells rang up for practice-night
An undersong to birds and dripping shrubs.
The full Atlantic at September spring
Flooded a final tide-mark up the sand,
And ocean sank to silence under bells,

And the next breaker was a lesser one
Then lesser still. Atlantic, bells and birds
Were layer on interchanging layers of sound.

A Lincolnshire Church

Greyly tremendous the thunder
Hung over the width of the wold
But here the green marsh was alight
In a huge cloud cavern of gold,
And there, on a gentle eminence,
Topping some ash trees, a tower
Silver and brown in the sunlight,
Worn by sea-wind and shower,
Lincolnshire Middle Pointed.
And around it, turning their backs,
The usual sprinkle of villas;
The usual woman in slacks,
Cigarette in her mouth,
Regretting Americans, stands
As a wireless croons in the kitchen
Manicuring her hands.
Dear old, bloody old England
Of telegraph poles and tin,
Seemingly so indifferent
And with so little soul to win.
What sort of church, I wonder?
The path is a grassy mat,
And grass is drowning the headstones
Sloping this way and that.
"Cathedral Glass" in the windows,
A roof of unsuitable slate—
Restored with a vengeance, for certain,

About eighteen-eighty-eight.
The door swung easily open
(Unlocked, for these parts, is odd)
And there on the South aisle altar
Is the tabernacle of God.
There where the white light flickers
By the white and silver veil,
A wafer dipped in a wine-drop
Is the Presence the angels hail,
Is God who created the Heavens
And the wide green marsh as well
Who sings in the sky with the skylark
Who calls in the evening bell,
Is God who prepared His coming
With fruit of the earth for his food
With stone for building His churches
And trees for making His rood.
There where the white light flickers,
Our Creator is with us yet,
To be worshipped by you and the woman
Of the slacks and the cigarette.

                *   *   *   *   *

The great door shuts, and lessens
That roar of churchyard trees
And the Presence of God Incarnate
Has brought me to my knees.
"I acknowledge my transgressions"
The well-known phrases rolled
With thunder sailing over

From the heavily clouded wold.
"And my sin is ever before me."
There in the lighted East
He stood in that lowering sunlight,
An Indian Christian priest.
And why he was here in Lincolnshire
I neither asked nor knew,
Nor whether his flock was many
Nor whether his flock was few
I thought of the heaving waters
That bore him from sun glare harsh
Of some Indian Anglican Mission
To this green enormous marsh.
There where the white light flickers,
Here, as the rains descend,
The same mysterious Godhead
Is welcoming His friend.

The Town Clerk's Views

"Yes, the Town Clerk will see you." In I went.
He was, like all Town Clerks, from north of Trent;
A man with bye-laws busy in his head
Whose Mayor and Council followed where he led.
His most capacious brain will make us cower,
His only weakness is a lust for power—
And that is not a weakness, people think,
When unaccompanied by bribes or drink.
So let us hear this cool careerist tell
His plans to turn our country into hell.
"I cannot say how shock'd I am to see
The *variations* in our scenery.
Just take for instance, at a casual glance,
Our muddled coastline opposite to France:
Dickensian houses by the Channel tides
With old hipp'd roofs and weather-boarded sides.
I blush to think one corner of our isle
Lacks concrete villas in the modern style.
Straight lines of hops in pale brown earth of Kent,
Yeomen's square houses once, no doubt, content
With willow-bordered horse-pond, oast-house, shed,
Wide orchard, garden walls of browny-red—
All useless now, but what fine sites they'ld be
For workers' flats and some light industry.
Those lumpy church towers, unadorned with spires,
And wavy roofs that burn like smouldering fires
In sharp spring sunlight over ashen flint

144

Are out of date as some old aquatint.
Then glance below the line of Sussex downs
To stucco terraces of seaside towns
Turn'd into flats and residential clubs
Above the wind-slashed Corporation shrubs.
Such Georgian relics should by now, I feel,
Be all rebuilt in glass and polished steel.
Bournemouth is looking up. I'm glad to say
That modernistic there has come to stay.
I walk the asphalt paths of Branksome Chine
In resin-scented air like strong Greek wine
And dream of cliffs of flats along those heights,
Floodlit at night with green electric lights.
But as for Dorset's flint and Purbeck stone,
Its old thatched farms in dips of down alone—
It should be merged with Hants and made to be
A self-contained and plann'd community.
Like Flint and Rutland, it is much too small
And has no reason to exist at all.
Of Devon one can hardly say the same,
But "South-West Area One" 's a better name
For those red sandstone cliffs that stain the sea
By mid-Victoria's Italy—Torquay.
And "South-West Area Two" could well include
The whole of Cornwall from Land's End to Bude.
Need I retrace my steps through other shires?
Pinnacled Somerset? Northampton's spires?
Burford's broad High Street is descending still
Stone-roofed and golden-walled her elmy hill
To meet the river Windrush. What a shame
Her houses are not brick and all the same.

Oxford is growing up to date at last.
Cambridge, I fear, is living in the past.
She needs more factories, not useless things
Like that great chapel which they keep at King's.
As for remote East Anglia, he who searches
Finds only thatch and vast, redundant churches.
But that's the dark side. I can safely say
A beauteous England's really on the way.
Already our hotels are pretty good
For those who're fond of *very simple food*—
Cod and two veg., free pepper, salt and mustard,
Followed by nice hard plums and lumpy custard,
A pint of bitter beer for one-and-four,
Then coffee in the lounge a shilling more.
In a few years this country will be looking
As uniform and tasty as its cooking.
Hamlets which fail to pass the planners' test
Will be demolished. We'll rebuild the rest
To look like Welwyn mixed with Middle West.
All fields we'll turn to sports grounds, lit at night
From concrete standards by fluorescent light:
And over all the land, instead of trees,
Clean poles and wire will whisper in the breeze.
We'll keep one ancient village just to show
What England once was when the times were slow—
Broadway for me. But here I know I must
Ask the opinion of our National Trust.
And ev'ry old cathedral that you enter
By then will be an Area Culture Centre.
Instead of nonsense about Death and Heaven
Lectures on civic duty will be given;

146

Eurhythmic classes dancing round the spire,
And economics courses in the choir.
So don't encourage tourists. Stay your hand
Until we've really got the country plann'd."

Harrow-on-the-Hill

When melancholy Autumn comes to Wembley
  And electric trains are lighted after tea
The poplars near the Stadium are trembly
  With their tap and tap and whispering to me,
      Like the sound of little breakers
      Spreading out along the surf-line
When the estuary's filling
      With the sea.

Then Harrow-on-the-Hill's a rocky island
  And Harrow churchyard full of sailors' graves
And the constant click and kissing of the trolley buses
                         hissing
  Is the level to the Wealdstone turned to waves
      And the rumble of the railway
      Is the thunder of the rollers
As they gather up for plunging
      Into caves.

There's a storm cloud to the westward over Kenton,
  There's a line of harbour lights at Perivale,
Is it rounding rough Pentire in a flood of sunset fire
  The little fleet of trawlers under sail?
      Can those boats be only roof tops
      As they stream along the skyline
In a race for port and Padstow
      With the gale?

in aid of A Public Subscription (1952)
towards the restoration of the
Church of St. Katherine
Chiselhampton, Oxon

Across the wet November night
The church is bright with candlelight
  And waiting Evensong.
A single bell with plaintive strokes
Pleads louder than the stirring oaks
  The leafless lanes along.

It calls the choirboys from their tea
And villagers, the two or three,
  Damp down the kitchen fire,
Let out the cat, and up the lane
Go paddling through the gentle rain
  Of misty Oxfordshire.

How warm the many candles shine
On SAMUEL DOWBIGGIN's design
  For this interior neat,
These high box pews of Georgian days
Which screen us from the public gaze
  When we make answer meet;

How gracefully their shadow falls
On bold pilasters down the walls
    And on the pulpit high.
The chandeliers would twinkle gold
As pre-Tractarian sermons roll'd
    Doctrinal, sound and dry.

From that west gallery no doubt
The viol and serpent tooted out
    The Tallis tune to Ken,
And firmly at the end of prayers
The clerk below the pulpit stairs
    Would thunder out "Amen."

But every wand'ring thought will cease
Before the noble altarpiece
    With carven swags array'd,
For there in letters all may read
The Lord's Commandments, Prayer and Creed,
    And decently display'd.

On country mornings sharp and clear
The penitent in faith draw near
    And kneeling here below
Partake the Heavenly Banquet spread
Of Sacramental Wine and Bread
    And JESUS' presence know.

And must that plaintive bell in vain
Plead loud along the dripping lane?
    And must the building fall?

Not while we love the Church and live
And of our charity will give
  Our much, our more, our all.

Sunday Morning, King's Cambridge

File into yellow candle light, fair choristers of King's
  Lost in the shadowy silence of canopied Renaissance stalls
In blazing glass above the dark glow skies and thrones and wings
  Blue, ruby, gold and green between the whiteness of the walls
And with what rich precision the stonework soars and springs
  To fountain out a spreading vault—a shower that never falls.

The white of windy Cambridge courts, the cobbles brown and dry,
  The gold of plaster Gothic with ivy overgrown,
The apple-red, the silver fronts, the wide green flats and high,
  The yellowing elm-trees circled out on islands of their own—
Oh, here behold all colours change that catch the flying sky
  To waves of pearly light that heave along the shafted stone.

In far East Anglian churches, the clasped hands lying long
  Recumbent on sepulchral slabs or effigied in brass
Buttress with prayer this vaulted roof so white and light and
                                                            strong
  And countless congregations as the generations pass
Join choir and great crowned organ case, in centuries of song
  To praise Eternity contained in Time and coloured glass.

Christmas

The bells of waiting Advent ring,
    The Tortoise stove is lit again
And lamp-oil light across the night
    Has caught the streaks of winter rain
In many a stained-glass window sheen
From Crimson Lake to Hooker's Green.

The holly in the windy hedge
    And round the Manor House the yew
Will soon be stripped to deck the ledge,
    The altar, font and arch and pew,
So that the villagers can say
"The church looks nice" on Christmas Day.

Provincial public houses blaze
    And Corporation tramcars clang,
On lighted tenements I gaze
    Where paper decorations hang,
And bunting in the red Town Hall
Says "Merry Christmas to you all."

And London shops on Christmas Eve
    Are strung with silver bells and flowers
As hurrying clerks the City leave
    To pigeon-haunted classic towers,
And marbled clouds go scudding by
The many-steepled London sky.

And girls in slacks remember Dad,
    And oafish louts remember Mum,
And sleepless children's hearts are glad,
    And Christmas-morning bells say "Come!"
Even to shining ones who dwell
Safe in the Dorchester Hotel.

And is it true? And is it true,
    This most tremendous tale of all,
Seen in a stained-glass window's hue,
    A Baby in an ox's stall?
The Maker of the stars and sea
Become a Child on earth for me?

And is it true? For if it is,
    No loving fingers tying strings
Around those tissued fripperies,
    The sweet and silly Christmas things,
Bath salts and inexpensive scent
And hideous tie so kindly meant,

No love that in a family dwells,
    No carolling in frosty air,
Nor all the steeple-shaking bells
    Can with this single Truth compare—
That God was Man in Palestine
And lives to-day in Bread and Wine.

The Licorice Fields at Pontefract

In the licorice fields at Pontefract
  My love and I did meet
And many a burdened licorice bush
  Was blooming round our feet;
Red hair she had and golden skin,
Her sulky lips were shaped for sin,
Her sturdy legs were flannel-slack'd,
The strongest legs in Pontefract.

The light and dangling licorice flowers
  Gave off the sweetest smells;
From various black Victorian towers
  The Sunday evening bells
Came pealing over dales and hills
And tanneries and silent mills
And lowly streets where country stops
And little shuttered corner shops.

She cast her blazing eyes on me
  And plucked a licorice leaf;
I was her captive slave and she
  My red-haired robber chief.
Oh love! for love I could not speak,
It left me winded, wilting, weak
And held in brown arms strong and bare
And wound with flaming ropes of hair.

Church of England thoughts
occasioned by hearing the bells
of Magdalen Tower
from the Botanic Garden, Oxford
on St. Mary Magdalen's Day

———————

I see the urn against the yew,
  The sunlit urn of sculptured stone,
I see its shapely shadow fall
On this enormous garden wall
  Which makes a kingdom of its own.

A grassy kingdom sweet to view
  With tiger lilies still in flower
And beds of umbelliferae
Ranged in Linnaean symmetry,
  All in the sound of Magdalen Tower.

A multiplicity of bells,
  A changing cadence, rich and deep
Swung from those pinnacles on high
To fill the trees and flood the sky
  And rock the sailing clouds to sleep.

A Church of England sound, it tells
  Of "moderate" worship, God and State,
Where matins congregations go
Conservative and good and slow
  To elevations of the plate.

And loud through resin-scented chines
    And purple rhododendrons roll'd,
I hear the bells for Eucharist
From churches blue with incense mist
    Where reredoses twinkle gold.

Chapels-of-ease by railway lines
    And humble streets and smells of gas
I hear your plaintive ting-tangs call
From many a gabled western wall
    To Morning Prayer or Holy Mass.

In country churches old and pale
    I hear the changes smoothly rung
And watch the coloured sallies fly
From rugged hands to rafters high
    As round and back the bells are swung.

Before the spell begin to fail,
    Before the bells have lost their power,
Before the grassy kingdom fade
And Oxford traffic roar invade,
    I thank the bells of Magdalen Tower.

Essex

"The vagrant visitor erstwhile,"
 My colour-plate book says to me,
"Could wend by hedgerow-side and stile,
 From Benfleet down to Leigh-on-Sea."

And as I turn the colour-plates
 Edwardian Essex opens wide,
Mirrored in ponds and seen through gates,
 Sweet uneventful countryside.

Like streams the little by-roads run
 Through oats and barley round a hill
To where blue willows catch the sun
 By some white weather-boarded mill.

"A Summer Idyll Matching Tye"
 "At Havering-atte-Bower, the Stocks"
And cobbled pathways lead the eye
 To cottage doors and hollyhocks.

Far Essex,—fifty miles away
 The level wastes of sucking mud
Where distant barges high with hay
 Come sailing in upon the flood.

Near Essex of the River Lea
 And anglers out with hook and worm

And Epping Forest glades where we
   Had beanfeasts with my father's firm.

At huge and convoluted pubs
   They used to set us down from brakes
In that half-land of football clubs
   Which London near the Forest makes.

The deepest Essex few explore
   Where steepest thatch is sunk in flowers
And out of elm and sycamore
   Rise flinty fifteenth-century towers.

I see the little branch line go
   By white farms roofed in red and brown,
The old Great Eastern winding slow
   To some forgotten country town.

Now yarrow chokes the railway track,
   Brambles obliterate the stile,
No motor coach can take me back
   To that Edwardian "erstwhile".

Huxley Hall

In the Garden City Café with its murals on the wall
Before a talk on "Sex and Civics" I meditated on the Fall.

Deep depression settled on me under that electric glare
While outside the lightsome poplars flanked the rose-beds in the
                                                      square.

While outside the carefree children sported in the summer haze
And released their inhibitions in a hundred different ways.

She who eats her greasy crumpets snugly in the inglenook
Of some birch-enshrouded homestead, dropping butter on her
                                                      book

Can she know the deep depression of this bright, hygienic hell?
And her husband, stout free-thinker, can he share in it as well?

Not the folk-museum's charting of man's Progress out of slime
Can release me from the painful seeming accident of Time.

Barry smashes Shirley's dolly, Shirley's eyes are crossed with
                                                      hate,
Comrades plot a Comrade's downfall "in the interests of the
                                                      State".

Not my vegetarian dinner, not my lime-juice minus gin,
Quite can drown a faint conviction that we may be born in Sin.

House of Rest

Now all the world she knew is dead
   In this small room she lives her days
The wash-hand stand and single bed
   Screened from the public gaze.

The horse-brass shines, the kettle sings,
   The cup of China tea
Is tasted among cared-for things
   Ranged round for me to see—

Lincoln, by Valentine and Co.,
   Now yellowish brown and stained,
But there some fifty years ago
   Her Harry was ordained;

Outside the Church at Woodhall Spa
   The smiling groom and bride,
And here's his old tobacco jar
   Dried lavender inside.

I do not like to ask if he
   Was "High" or "Low" or "Broad"
Lest such a question seem to be
   A mockery of Our Lord.

Her full grey eyes look far beyond
   The little room and me

To village church and village pond
   And ample rectory.

She sees her children each in place
   Eyes downcast as they wait,
She hears her Harry murmur Grace,
   Then heaps the porridge plate.

Aroused at seven, to bed by ten,
   They fully lived each day,
Dead sons, so motor-bike-mad then,
   And daughters far away.

Now when the bells for Eucharist
   Sound in the Market Square,
With sunshine struggling through the mist
   And Sunday in the air,

The veil between her and her dead
   Dissolves and shows them clear,
The Consecration Prayer is said
   And all of them are near.

Middlesex

Gaily into Ruislip Gardens
    Runs the red electric train,
With a thousand Ta's and Pardon's
    Daintily alights Elaine;
Hurries down the concrete station
With a frown of concentration,
Out into the outskirt's edges
Where a few surviving hedges
Keep alive our lost Elysium—rural Middlesex again.

Well cut Windsmoor flapping lightly,
    Jacqmar scarf of mauve and green
Hiding hair which, Friday nightly,
    Delicately drowns in Drene;
Fair Elaine the bobby-soxer,
Fresh-complexioned with Innoxa,
Gains the garden—father's hobby—
Hangs her Windsmoor in the lobby,
Settles down to sandwich supper and the television screen.

Gentle Brent, I used to know you
    Wandering Wembley-wards at will,
Now what change your waters show you
    In the meadowlands you fill!
Recollect the elm-trees misty
And the footpaths climbing twisty
Under cedar-shaded palings,

Low laburnum-leaned-on railings,
Out of Northolt on and upward to the heights of Harrow hill.

Parish of enormous hayfields
    Perivale stood all alone,
And from Greenford scent of mayfields
    Most enticingly was blown
Over market gardens tidy,
Taverns for the *bona fide*,
Cockney anglers, cockney shooters,
Murray Poshes, Lupin Pooters
Long in Kensal Green and Highgate silent under soot and stone.

Seaside Golf

How straight it flew, how long it flew,
    It clear'd the rutty track
And soaring, disappeared from view
    Beyond the bunker's back—
A glorious, sailing, bounding drive
That made me glad I was alive.

And down the fairway, far along
    It glowed a lonely white;
I played an iron sure and strong
    And clipp'd it out of sight,
And spite of grassy banks between
I knew I'd find it on the green.

And so I did. It lay content
    Two paces from the pin;
A steady putt and then it went
    Oh, most securely in.
The very turf rejoiced to see
That quite unprecedented three.

Ah! seaweed smells from sandy caves
    And thyme and mist in whiffs,
In-coming tide, Atlantic waves
    Slapping the sunny cliffs,
Lark song and sea sounds in the air
And splendour, splendour everywhere.

Walter Ramsden
ob. March 26, 1947
Pembroke College, Oxford

Dr. Ramsden cannot read *The Times* obituary to-day
  He's dead.
Let monographs on silk worms by other people be
  Thrown away
  Unread
For he who best could understand and criticize them, he
  Lies clay
  In bed.

The body waits in Pembroke College where the ivy taps the
                               panes
  All night;
That old head so full of knowledge, that good heart that kept the
                               brains
  All right,
Those old cheeks that faintly flushed as the port suffused the
                               veins,
  Drain'd white.

Crocus in the Fellows' Garden, winter jasmine up the wall
  Gleam gold.
Shadows of Victorian chimneys on the sunny grassplot fall
  Long, cold.
Master, Bursar, Senior Tutor, these, his three survivors, all
  Feel old.

They remember, as the coffin to its final obsequations
    Leaves the gates,
Buzz of bees in window boxes on their summer ministrations,
    Kitchen din,
    Cups and plates,
And the getting of bump suppers for the long-dead generations
    Coming in,
    From Eights.

Norfolk

How did the Devil come? When first attack?
   These Norfolk lanes recall lost innocence,
The years fall off and find me walking back
   Dragging a stick along the wooden fence
Down this same path, where, forty years ago,
My father strolled behind me, calm and slow.

I used to fill my hand with sorrel seeds
   And shower him with them from the tops of stiles,
I used to butt my head into his tweeds
   To make him hurry down those languorous miles
Of ash and alder-shaded lanes, till here
Our moorings and the masthead would appear.

There after supper lit by lantern light
   Warm in the cabin I could lie secure
And hear against the polished sides at night
   The lap lap lapping of the weedy Bure,
A whispering and watery Norfolk sound
Telling of all the moonlit reeds around.

How did the Devil come? When first attack?
   The church is just the same, though now I know
Fowler of Louth restored it. Time, bring back
   The rapturous ignorance of long ago,
The peace, before the dreadful daylight starts,
Of unkept promises and broken hearts.

The Metropolitan Railway
BAKER STREET STATION BUFFET

———

Early Electric! With what radiant hope
    Men formed this many-branched electrolier,
Twisted the flex around the iron rope
    And let the dazzling vacuum globes hang clear,
And then with hearts the rich contrivance fill'd
Of copper, beaten by the Bromsgrove Guild.

Early Electric! Sit you down and see,
    'Mid this fine woodwork and a smell of dinner,
A stained-glass windmill and a pot of tea,
    And sepia views of leafy lanes in PINNER,—
Then visualize, far down the shining lines,
Your parents' homestead set in murmuring pines.

Smoothly from HARROW, passing PRESTON ROAD,
    They saw the last green fields and misty sky,
At NEASDEN watched a workmen's train unload,
    And, with the morning villas sliding by,
They felt so sure on their electric trip
That Youth and Progress were in partnership.

And all that day in murky London Wall
    The thought of RUISLIP kept him warm inside;
At FARRINGDON that lunch hour at a stall
    He bought a dozen plants of London Pride;

While she, in arc-lit Oxford Street adrift,
Soared through the sales by safe hydraulic lift.

Early Electric! Maybe even here
    They met that evening at six-fifteen
Beneath the hearts of this electrolier
    And caught the first non-stop to WILLESDEN GREEN,
Then out and on, through rural RAYNER'S LANE
To autumn-scented Middlesex again.

Cancer has killed him. Heart is killing her.
    The trees are down. An Odeon flashes fire
Where stood their villa by the murmuring fir
    When "they would for their children's good
                                            conspire."
Of their loves and hopes on hurrying feet
Thou art the worn memorial, Baker Street.

Late-Flowering Lust

My head is bald, my breath is bad,
  Unshaven is my chin,
I have not now the joys I had
  When I was young in sin.

I run my fingers down your dress
  With brandy-certain aim
And you respond to my caress
  And maybe feel the same.

But I've a picture of my own
  On this reunion night,
Wherein two skeletons are shewn
  To hold each other tight;

Dark sockets look on emptiness
  Which once was loving-eyed,
The mouth that opens for a kiss
  Has got no tongue inside.

I cling to you inflamed with fear
  As now you cling to me,
I feel how frail you are my dear
  And wonder what will be—

A week? or twenty years remain?
  And then—what kind of death?

A losing fight with frightful pain
    Or a gasping fight for breath?

Too long we let our bodies cling,
    We cannot hide disgust
At all the thoughts that in us spring
    From this late-flowering lust.

Sun and Fun
SONG OF A NIGHT-CLUB PROPRIETRESS

I walked into the night-club in the morning;
   There was kummel on the handle of the door.
The ashtrays were unemptied,
The cleaning unattempted,
   And a squashed tomato sandwich on the floor.

I pulled aside the thick magenta curtains
   —So Regency, so Regency, my dear—
And a host of little spiders
Ran a race across the ciders
   To a box of baby 'pollies by the beer.

Oh sun upon the summer-going by-pass
   Where ev'rything is speeding to the sea,
And wonder beyond wonder
That here where lorries thunder
   The sun should ever percolate to me.

When Boris used to call in his Sedanca,
   When Teddy took me down to his estate
When my nose excited passion,
When my clothes were in the fashion,
   When my beaux were never cross if I was late,

There was sun enough for lazing upon beaches,
   There was fun enough for far into the night.

173

But I'm dying now and done for,
What on earth was all the fun for?
   For I'm old and ill and terrified and tight.

Original Sin on the Sussex Coast

Now on this out of season afternoon
Day schools which cater for the sort of boy
Whose parents go by Pullman once a month
To do a show in town, pour out their young
Into the sharply red October light.
Here where The Drive and Buckhurst Road converge
I watch the rival gangs and am myself
A schoolboy once again in shivering shorts.
I see the dust of sherbet on the chin
Of Andrew Knox well-dress'd, well-born, well-fed,
Even at nine a perfect gentleman,
Willie Buchanan waiting at his side—
Another Scot, eruptions on his skin.
I hear Jack Drayton whistling from the fence
Which hides the copper domes of "Cooch Behar".
That was the signal. So there's no escape.
A race for Willow Way and jump the hedge
Behind the Granville Bowling Club? Too late.
They'll catch me coming out in Seapink Lane.
Across the Garden of Remembrance? No,
That would be blasphemy and bring bad luck.
Well then, I'm *for* it. Andrew's at me first,
He pinions me in that especial grip
His brother learned in Kobë from a Jap
(No chance for me against the Japanese).
Willie arrives and winds me with a punch
Plum in the tummy, grips the other arm.

175

"You're to be booted. Hold him steady, chaps!"
A wait for taking aim. Oh trees and sky!
Then crack against the column of my spine,
Blackness and breathlessness and sick with pain
I stumble on the asphalt. Off they go
Away, away, thank God, and out of sight
So that I lie quite still and climb to sense
Too out of breath and strength to make a sound.

Now over Polegate vastly sets the sun;
Dark rise the Downs from darker looking elms,
And out of Southern railway trains to tea
Run happy boys down various Station Roads,
Satchels of homework jogging on their backs,
So trivial and so healthy in the shade
Of these enormous Downs. And when they're home,
When the Post-Toasties mixed with Golden Shred
Make for the kiddies such a scrumptious feast,
Does Mum, the Persil-user, still believe
That there's no Devil and that youth is bliss?
As certain as the sun behind the Downs
And quite as plain to see, the Devil walks.

Devonshire Street W.1

The heavy mahogany door with its wrought-iron screen
    Shuts. And the sound is rich, sympathetic, discreet.
The sun still shines on this eighteenth-century scene
    With Edwardian faience adornments—Devonshire Street.

No hope. And the X-ray photographs under his arm
    Confirm the message. His wife stands timidly by.
The opposite brick-built house looks lofty and calm
    Its chimneys steady against a mackerel sky.

No hope. And the iron nob of this palisade
    So cold to the touch, is luckier now than he
"Oh merciless, hurrying Londoners! Why was I made
    For the long and the painful deathbed coming to me?"

She puts her fingers in his as, loving and silly,
    At long-past Kensington dances she used to do
"It's cheaper to take the tube to Piccadilly
    And then we can catch a nineteen or a twenty-two."

The Cottage Hospital

At the end of a long-walled garden
    in a red provincial town,
A brick path led to a mulberry—
    scanty grass at its feet.
I lay under blackening branches
    where the mulberry leaves hung down
Sheltering ruby fruit globes
    from a Sunday-tea-time heat.
Apple and plum espaliers
    basked upon bricks of brown;
The air was swimming with insects,
    and children played in the street.

Out of this bright intentness
    into the mulberry shade
Musca domestica (housefly)
    swung from the August light
Slap into slithery rigging
    by the waiting spider made
Which spun the lithe elastic
    till the fly was shrouded tight.
Down came the hairy talons
    and horrible poison blade
And none of the garden noticed
    that fizzing, hopeless fight.

178

Say in what Cottage Hospital
   whose pale green walls resound
With the tap upon polished parquet
   of inflexible nurses' feet
Shall I myself be lying
   when they range the screens around?
And say shall I groan in dying,
   as I twist the sweaty sheet?
Or gasp for breath uncrying,
   as I feel my senses drown'd
While the air is swimming with insects
   and children play in the street?

A Child Ill

Oh, little body, do not die.
　　The soul looks out through wide blue eyes
So questioningly into mine,
　　That my tormented soul replies:

"Oh, little body, do not die.
　　You hold the soul that talks to me
Although our conversation be
　　As wordless as the windy sky."

So looked my father at the last
　　Right in my soul, before he died,
Though words we spoke went heedless past
　　As London traffic-roar outside.

And now the same blue eyes I see
　　Look through me from a little son,
So questioning, so searchingly
　　That youthfulness and age are one.

My father looked at me and died
　　Before my soul made full reply.
Lord, leave this other Light alight—
　　Oh, little body, do not die.

Business Girls

From the geyser ventilators
   Autumn winds are blowing down
On a thousand business women
   Having baths in Camden Town.

Waste pipes chuckle into runnels,
   Steam's escaping here and there,
Morning trains through Camden cutting
   Shake the Crescent and the Square.

Early nip of changeful autumn,
   Dahlias glimpsed through garden doors,
At the back precarious bathrooms
   Jutting out from upper floors;

And behind their frail partitions
   Business women lie and soak,
Seeing through the draughty skylight
   Flying clouds and railway smoke.

Rest you there, poor unbelov'd ones,
   Lap your loneliness in heat.
All too soon the tiny breakfast,
   Trolley-bus and windy street!

Remorse

———————

The lungs draw in the air and rattle it out again;
  The eyes revolve in their sockets and upwards stare;
No more worry and waiting and troublesome doubt again—
  She whom I loved and left is no longer there.

The nurse puts down her knitting and walks across to her,
  With quick professional eye she surveys the dead.
Just one patient the less and little the loss to her,
  Distantly tender she settles the shrunken head.

Protestant claims and Catholic, the wrong and the right of
                                                    them,
  Unimportant they seem in the face of death—
But my neglect and unkindness—to lose the sight of them
  I would listen even again to that labouring breath.

The Old Liberals

Pale green of the *English Hymnal*! Yattendon hymns
   Played on the *hautbois* by a lady dress'd in blue
   Her white-hair'd father accompanying her thereto
On tenor or bass-recorder. Daylight swims
   On sectional bookcase, delicate cup and plate
   And William de Morgan tiles around the grate
And many the silver birches the pearly light shines through.

I think such a running together of woodwind sound,
   Such painstaking piping high on a Berkshire hill,
   Is sad as an English autumn heavy and still,
Sad as a country silence, tractor-drowned;
For deep in the hearts of the man and the woman playing
   The rose of a world that was not has withered away.
Where are the wains with garlanded swathes a-swaying?
Where are the swains to wend through the lanes a-maying?
   Where are the blithe and jocund to ted the hay?
   Where are the free folk of England? Where are they?

Ask of the Abingdon bus with full load creeping
   Down into denser suburbs. The birch lets go
   But one brown leaf upon browner bracken below.
Ask of the cinema manager. Night airs die
To still, ripe scent of the fungus and wet woods weeping.
   Ask at the fish and chips in the Market Square.
   Here amid firs and a final sunset flare
Recorder and *hautbois* only moan at a mouldering sky.

Greenaway

I know so well this turfy mile,
    These clumps of sea-pink withered brown,
The breezy cliff, the awkward stile,
    The sandy path that takes me down

To crackling layers of broken slate
    Where black and flat sea-woodlice crawl
And isolated rock pools wait
    Wash from the highest tides of all.

I know the roughly blasted track
    That skirts a small and smelly bay
And over squelching bladderwrack
    Leads to the beach at Greenaway.

Down on the shingle safe at last
    I hear the slowly dragging roar
As mighty rollers mount to cast
    Small coal and seaweed on the shore,

And spurting far as it can reach
    The shooting surf comes hissing round
To heave a line along the beach
    Of cowries waiting to be found

Tide after tide by night and day
    The breakers battle with the land

And rounded smooth along the bay
  The faithful rocks protecting stand.

But in a dream the other night
  I saw this coastline from the sea
And felt the breakers plunging white
  Their weight of waters over me.

There were the stile, the turf, the shore,
  The safety line of shingle beach
With every stroke I struck the more
  The backwash sucked me out of reach.

Back into what a water-world
  Of waving weed and waiting claws?
Of writhing tentacles uncurled
  To drag me to what dreadful jaws?

The Olympic Girl

The sort of girl I like to see
Smiles down from her great height at me.
She stands in strong, athletic pose
And wrinkles her *retroussé* nose.
Is it distaste that makes her frown,
So furious and freckled, down
On an unhealthy worm like me?
Or am I what she likes to see?
I do not know, though much I care.
εἴθε γενηίην . . . would I were
(Forgive me, shade of Rupert Brooke)
An object fit to claim her look.
Oh! would I were her racket press'd
With hard excitement to her breast
And swished into the sunlit air
Arm-high above her tousled hair,
And banged against the bounding ball
"Oh! Plung!" my tauten'd strings would call,
"Oh! Plung! my darling, break my strings
For you I will do brilliant things."
And when the match is over, I
Would flop beside you, hear you sigh;
And then, with what supreme caress,
You'ld tuck me up into my press.
Fair tigress of the tennis courts,
So short in sleeve and strong in shorts,
Little, alas, to you I mean,
For I am bald and old and green.

The Dear Old Village

The dear old village! *Lin-lan-lone* the bells
(Which should be six) ring over hills and dells,
But since the row about the ringers' tea
It's *lin-lan-lone.* They're only ringing three.
The elm leaves patter like a summer shower
As *lin-lan-lone* pours through them from the tower.
From that embattled, lichen-crusted fane
Which scoops the sun into each western pane,
The bells ring over hills and dells in vain.
For we are free to-day. No need to praise
The Unseen Author of our nights and days;
No need to hymn the rich uncurling spring
For DYKES is nowhere half so good as BING.
Nature is out of date and GOD is too;
Think what atomic energy can do!
　　Farmers have wired the public rights-of-way
Should any wish to walk to church to pray.
Along the village street the sunset strikes
On young men tuning up their motor-bikes,
And country girls with lips and nails vermilion
Wait, nylon-legged, to straddle on the pillion.
Off to the roadhouse and the Tudor Bar
And then the Sunday-opened cinema.
While to the church's iron-studded door
Go two old ladies and a child of four.
　　This is the age of progress. Let us meet
The new progressives of the village street.

Hear not the water lapsing down the rills,
Lift not your eyes to the surrounding hills,
While spring recalls the miracle of birth
Let us, for heaven's sake, keep down to earth.

See that square house, late Georgian and smart,
Two fields away it proudly stands apart,
Dutch barn and concrete cow-sheds have replaced
The old thatched roofs which once the yard disgraced.
Here wallows Farmer WHISTLE in his riches,
His ample stomach heaved above his breeches.
You'd never think that in such honest beef
Lurk'd an adulterous braggart, liar and thief.
His wife brought with her thirty-thousand down:
He keeps his doxy in the nearest town.
No man more anxious on the R.D.C.
For better rural cottages than he,
Especially when he had some land to sell
Which, as a site, would suit the Council well.
So three times what he gave for it he got,
For one undrainable and useless plot
Where now the hideous Council houses stand.
Unworked on and unworkable their land,
The wind blows under each unseason'd door,
The floods pour over every kitchen floor,
And country wit, which likes to laugh at sin,
Christens the Council houses "Whistle's Win."
Woe to some lesser farmer who may try
To call his bluff or to expose his lie.
Remorseless as a shark in London's City,
He gets at them through the War Ag. Committee.

See he takes no part in village life beyond

Throwing his refuse in a neighbour's pond
And closing footpaths, not repairing walls,
Leaving a cottage till at last it falls.
People protest. A law-suit then begins,
But as he's on the Bench, he always wins.
  Behind rank elders, shadowing a pool,
And near the Church, behold the Village School,
Its gable rising out of ivy thick
Shows "Eighteen-Sixty" worked in coloured brick.
By nineteen-forty-seven, hurrah! hooray
This institution has outlived its day.
In the bad times of old feudality
The villagers were ruled by masters three—
Squire, parson, schoolmaster. Of these, the last
Knew best the village present and its past.
Now, I am glad to say, the man is dead,
The children have a motor-bus instead,
And in a town eleven miles away
We train them to be "Citizens of To-day."
And many a cultivated hour they pass
In a fine school with walls of vita-glass.
Civics, eurhythmics, economics, Marx,
How-to-respect-wild-life-in-National-Parks;
Plastics, gymnastics—thus they learn to scorn
The old thatch'd cottages where they were born.
The girls, ambitious to begin their lives
Serving in WOOLWORTH'S, rather than as wives;
The boys, who cannot yet escape the land,
At driving tractors lend a clumsy hand.
An eight-hour day for all, and more than three
Of these are occupied in making tea

189

And talking over what we all agree—
Though "Music while you work" is now our wont,
It's not so nice as "Music while you don't."
Squire, parson, schoolmaster turn in their graves.
And *let* them turn. We are no longer slaves.

   So much for youth. I fear we older folk
Must be dash'd off with a more hurried stroke.
Old Mrs. SPEAK has cut, for fifteen years,
Her husband's widowed sister Mrs. SHEARS,
Though how she's managed it, I cannot say,
Sharing a cottage with her night and day.
What caused the quarrel fifteen years ago
And how BERT SPEAK gets on, I do not know,
There the three live in that old dwelling quaint
Which water-colourists delight to paint.
Of the large brood round Mrs. COKER's door,
Coker has definitely fathered four
And two are Farmer Whistle's: two they say
Have coloured fathers in the U.S.A.
I learn'd all this and more from Mrs. FREE,
Pride of the Women's Institute is she,
Says "Sir" or "Madam" to you, knows her station
And how to make a quiet insinuation.
The unrespectable must well know why
They fear her lantern jaw and leaden eye.

    There is no space to tell about the chaps—
Which pinch, which don't, which beat their wives with
                                  straps.

Go to the Inn on any Friday night
And listen to them while they're getting tight
At the expense of him who stands them drinks,

The Mass-Observer with the Hillman Minx.
(Unwitting he of all the knowing winks)
The more he circulates the bitter ales
The longer and the taller grow the tales.
"Ah! this is England," thinks he, "rich and pure
As tilth and loam and wains and horse-manure,
Slow—yes. But sociologically sound."
"Landlord!" he cries, "the same again all round!"

The Village Inn

"The village inn, the dear old inn,
So ancient, clean and free from sin,
True centre of our rural life
Where Hodge sits down beside his wife
And talks of Marx and nuclear fission
With all a rustic's intuition.
Ah, more than church or school or hall,
The village inn's the heart of all."
So spake the brewer's P.R.O.,
A man who really ought to know,
For he is paid for saying so.
And then he kindly gave to me
A lovely coloured booklet free.
'Twas full of prose that sang the praise
Of coaching inns in Georgian days,
Showing how public-houses are
More modern than the motor-car,
More English than the weald or wold
And almost equally as old,
And run for love and not for gold
Until I felt a filthy swine
For loathing beer and liking wine,
And rotten to the very core
For thinking village inns a bore,
And village bores more sure to roam
To village inns than stay at home.
And then I thought I *must* be wrong,

So up I rose and went along
To that old village alehouse where
In neon lights is written "Bear".

Ah, where's the inn that once I knew
    With brick and chalky wall
Up which the knobbly pear-tree grew
    For fear the place would fall?

Oh, that old pot-house isn't there,
    It wasn't worth our while;
You'll find we have rebuilt "The Bear"
    In Early Georgian style.

But winter jasmine used to cling
    With golden stars a-shine
Where rain and wind would wash and swing
    The crudely painted sign.

And where's the roof of golden thatch?
    The chimney-stack of stone?
The crown-glass panes that used to match
    Each sunset with their own?

Oh now the walls are red and smart,
    The roof has emerald tiles.
The neon sign's a work of art
    And visible for miles.

The bar inside was papered green,
    The settles grained like oak,

The only light was paraffin,
   The woodfire used to smoke.

And photographs from far and wide
   Were hung around the room:
The hunt, the church, the football side,
   And Kitchener of Khartoum.

Our air-conditioned bars are lined
   With washable material,
The stools are steel, the taste refined,
   Hygienic and ethereal.

Hurrah, hurrah, for hearts of oak!
   Away with inhibitions!
For here's a place to sit and soak
   In sanit'ry conditions.

Station Syren

She sat with a Warwick Deeping,
   Her legs curl'd round in a ring,
Like a beautiful panther sleeping,
   Yet always ready to spring.

Tweed on her well-knit torso,
   Silk on each big strong leg,
An officer's lady—and more so
   Than those who buy off the peg.

More cash than she knew of for spending
   As a Southgate girl at home,
For there's crooning and clinging unending
   For the queen of the girls at the 'drome.

Beautiful brown eyes burning
   Deep on the Deeping page,
Beautiful dark hair learning
   Coiffuring tricks of the age.

Negligent hand for holding
   A Flight-Lieutenant at bay,
Petulant lips for scolding
   And kissing the trouble away.

But she isn't exactly partial
   To any of that sort of thing,

So maybe the Air Vice-Marshal
Will buy her a Bravington ring.

Hunter Trials

It's awf'lly bad luck on Diana,
  Her ponies have swallowed their bits;
She fished down their throats with a spanner
  And frightened them all into fits.

So now she's attempting to borrow.
  Do lend her some bits, Mummy, *do*;
I'll lend her my own for to-morrow,
  But to-day *I*'ll be wanting them too.

Just look at Prunella on Guzzle,
  The wizardest pony on earth;
Why doesn't she slacken his muzzle
  And tighten the breech in his girth?

I say, Mummy, there's Mrs. Geyser
  And doesn't she look pretty sick?
I bet it's because Mona Lisa
  Was hit on the hock with a brick.

Miss Blewitt says Monica threw it,
  But Monica says it was Joan,
And Joan's very thick with Miss Blewitt,
  So Monica's sulking alone.

And Margaret failed in her paces,
  Her withers got tied in a noose,

So her coronets caught in the traces
   And now all her fetlocks are loose.

Oh, it's me now. I'm terribly nervous.
   I wonder if Smudges will shy.
She's practically certain to swerve as
   Her Pelham is over one eye.

*   *   *   *   *

Oh wasn't it naughty of Smudges?
   Oh, Mummy, I'm sick with disgust.
She threw me in front of the Judges,
   And my silly old collarbone's bust.

A Literary Discovery

Sent to the Editor of *Time and Tide*, Dec. 1952

———————

Dear Sir,

I was lately in a second-hand bookshop in East Grinstead and bought for fourpence a green cloth and gilt-edged edition of Longfellow's poems (Crown octavo, Ward Lock & Co., London, 1875). Witness my surprise when I found inside it a piece of yellowish cream-laid paper (water-mark Mudie's Libraries—Swedenborg Bond) with a manuscript poem. There was no surname in the flyleaf of the book, but an inscription read, "To Ellen from her loving husband." The poem was certainly in the same hand as the inscription, a sloping rather clerkly fist suggesting long hours practising pothooks. Seeing that the verses refer to the celebrated novelist Mrs. Henry Wood (1814–1887) whose Christian name was Ellen, I hazard the guess that it is the work of her husband Henry Wood whom she married in 1836. The poem was placed in the leaves where "The Belfry at Bruges" appeared whose famous opening line requires Bruges to be pronounced as two syllables, American style, to obtain full beauty.

'In the market place of Bruges stands the belfry old and brown.'

Not far off is a similar poem "Nüremberg", imparting factual information of a most inspiring kind from the guide-book. I quote a few stanzas from "Nüremberg" for it seems to have influenced the poet of the verses I have found:

In the Courtyard of the castle, bound with many an iron band,
Stands the mighty linden planted by Queen Cunigunde's hand, . . .

Here, when Art was still religion, with a simple reverent heart,
Lived and laboured Albrecht Dürer, the Evangelist of Art;

Here Hans Sachs, the cobbler-poet, laureate of the gentle craft,
Wisest of the Twelve Wise Masters, in huge folios sang and laughed.

I am hoping that some readers, as scholarly as I am, will be able to throw some light on the verses that follow. Important questions are raised. Did the Henry Woods ever live at Gomshall? When did Longfellow visit them? Did Henry Wood survive his visit? Was the house renamed? With the idea of helping other scholars, I have annotated the verses. I may say that, if you do not see fit to print this, I shall send it to *The Times Literary Supplement* where it will, no doubt, be published on that interesting back page.

*   *   *

Where yon crenellated mansion on the hill surmounts the pines,
Many a long-departed merchant[1] in the cellar stored his wines,

Hock for fish,[2] for pheasant claret, as the sun sloped slowly down
Over ambient lawns and pinewoods backed beyond by Guildford
town.

Once the railway out of London over twenty years ago[3]
To that crenellated mansion brought the poet Longfellow.
There were footmen to receive him, and a butler, stern as doom
Led him by the beetling antlers[4] to the large withdrawing room.

[1] The Woods then did not build the house but rented or bought it from city friends.
[2] A wine authority tells me that hock with fish is a late innovation. How late?
[3] He would have come either to Guildford (L. & S.W.R., L.B. & S.C.R., S.E. & C.R.) or Redhill (S.E. & C.R., L.B. & S.C.R.) and changed on to the beautiful bit of line which runs under Box Hill. Did he also call on Meredith and Tupper? It is a key line (in the poem, I mean, not the railway system) for it helps to date the verses.
[4] I do not think this refers to the poet's bushy eyebrows but to the decoration of the hall.

She was waiting to receive him, by her side her husband stood
Who alive would see the husband?[1] this was MRS. Henry Wood.

"Mr. Longfellow, delighted to receive you in our bowers!
Welcome and a thousand welcomes! Rest you here in Gomshall
                                                    Towers!"[2]
Calmly in his Yankee accent, cultured, carefully and slow
To the greeting of his hostess answered Mr. Longfellow:

"Ma'am, your fine historic mansion[3] is a dream of mine come true.
'Tis, amid its pines and hemlocks,[4] some Helvetian rendezvous."

In his ivy-mantled bedroom, dirty as he was from town,[5]
'Ere he touched the wash-hand basin[6] did he write a poem down.

"Little Switzerland in England." What could please a lady more
Than to find her Surrey mansion had inspired "Excelsior"?

"Little Switzerland in England," still the name rings in my ears
When around the bend from Gomshall erstwhile Gomshall
                                                    Towers appears.[7]

[1] If it is Henry Wood writing, one can well understand the
sad implication.
[2] There is no "Gomshall Towers" on the ordnance map to-
day. Sheet 170 London S.W. 1 inch. Ordnance Survey Office,
Chessington, 1945.
[3] The poet must be in error. There is no *old* mansion at
Gomshall. But he may well have thought Gomshall Towers
old because of the crenellations, and historic because of its
hostess.
[4] Mr. C. E. Cherry, Parks Superintendent of the London
Borough of Sutton, kindly pointed out (March 1967) informa-
tion which calls for my original note to be amended. He
suggests with very sound evidence and wide knowledge that
the poet must have been referring to the hemlock spruces
which belong to the *genus Tsuga*. These are elegant ever-

green coniferous trees with leaves like those of a yew, usually with horizontal branches and drooping branchlets. He is inclined to specify the *Tsuga canadensis* because it succeeds in chalk soil such as is to be found in the Gomshall district. This *genus* is represented also on both sides of North America.

[5] The word "town" for London was in fashionable use until this century.

[6] There would not, of course, have been running water in the bedroom. We are to envisage a brass can with a face-towel over it. The water may have been cold and the poet therefore wrote the poem while waiting for a fresh can to be brought. We must not lightly accuse him of uncleanliness.

[7] Though the road bends here, I think the railway is intended, for it is more elevated and commands a view of the larger houses.

How to Get On in Society

Originally set as a competition in "Time and Tide"

———————

Phone for the fish-knives, Norman
 As Cook is a little unnerved;
You kiddies have crumpled the serviettes
 And I must have things daintily served.

Are the requisites all in the toilet?
 The frills round the cutlets can wait
Till the girl has replenished the cruets
 And switched on the logs in the grate.

It's ever so close in the lounge, dear,
 But the vestibule's comfy for tea
And Howard is out riding on horseback
 So do come and take some with me.

Now here is a fork for your pastries
 And do use the couch for your feet;
I know what I wanted to ask you—
 Is trifle sufficient for sweet?

Milk and then just as it comes dear?
 I'm afraid the preserve's full of stones;
Beg pardon, I'm soiling the doileys
 With afternoon tea-cakes and scones.

Variation on a Theme by
T. W. Rolleston

Under the ground, on a Saturday afternoon in winter
　　Lies a mother of five,
And frost has bitten the purple November rose flowers
　　Which budded when *she* was alive.

They have switched on the street lamps here by the cemet'ry
　　　　　　　　　　　　　　　　　railing;
　　In the dying afternoon
Men from football, and women from Timothy White's and
　　　　　　　　　　　　　　　　　McIlroy's
　　Will be coming teawards soon.

But her place is empty in the queue at the International,
　　The greengrocer's queue lacks one,
So does the crowd at MacFisheries. There's no one to go to
　　　　　　　　　　　　　　　　　Freeman's
　　To ask if the shoes are done.

Will she, who was so particular, be glad to know that after
　　The tears, the prayers and the priest,
Her clothing coupons and ration book were handed in at the
　　　　　　　　　　　　　　　　　Food Office
　　For the files marked "deceased"?

Diary of a Church Mouse

(Lines, written to order on a set subject, to be spoken on the wireless.)

———

Here among long-discarded cassocks,
Damp stools, and half-split open hassocks,
Here where the Vicar never looks
I nibble through old service books.
Lean and alone I spend my days
Behind this Church of England baize.
I share my dark forgotten room
With two oil-lamps and half a broom.
The cleaner never bothers me,
So here I eat my frugal tea.
My bread is sawdust mixed with straw;
My jam is polish for the floor.

Christmas and Easter may be feasts
For congregations and for priests,
And so may Whitsun. All the same,
They do not fill my meagre frame.
For me the only feast at all
Is Autumn's Harvest Festival,
When I can satisfy my want
With ears of corn around the font.
I climb the eagle's brazen head
To burrow through a loaf of bread.
I scramble up the pulpit stair
And gnaw the marrows hanging there.

It is enjoyable to taste

205

These items ere they go to waste,
But how annoying when one finds
That other mice with pagan minds
Come into church my food to share
Who have no proper business there.
Two field mice who have no desire
To be baptized, invade the choir.
A large and most unfriendly rat
Comes in to see what we are at.
He says he thinks there is no God
And yet he comes . . . it's rather odd.
This year he stole a sheaf of wheat
(It screened our special preacher's seat),
And prosperous mice from fields away
Come in to hear the organ play,
And under cover of its notes
Ate through the altar's sheaf of oats.
A Low Church mouse, who thinks that I
Am too papistical, and High,
Yet somehow doesn't think it wrong
To munch through Harvest Evensong,
While I, who starve the whole year through,
Must share my food with rodents who
Except at this time of the year
Not once inside the church appear.

Within the human world I know
Such goings-on could not be so,
For human beings only do
What their religion tells them to.
They read the Bible every day
And always, night and morning, pray,

And just like me, the good church mouse,
Worship each week in God's own house,
   But all the same it's strange to me
How very full the church can be
With people I don't see at all
Except at Harvest Festival.

Wantage Bells

Now with the bells through the apple bloom
  Sunday-ly sounding
And the prayers of the nuns in their chapel gloom
  Us all surrounding,
  Where the brook flows
  Brick walls of rose
Send on the motionless meadow the bell notes rebounding.

Wall flowers are bright in their beds
  And their scent all pervading,
Withered are primroses heads
  And the hyacinth fading
  But flowers by the score
  Multitudes more
Weed flowers and seed flowers and mead flowers our paths are
             invading.

Where are the words to express
  Such a reckless bestowing?
The voices of birds utter less
  Than the thanks we are owing,
  Bell notes alone
  Ring praise of their own
As clear as the weed-waving brook and as evenly flowing.

Winthrop Mackworth Redivivus

It's for Regency now I'm enthusing
  So we've Regency stripes on the wall
And—my dear, really frightf'lly amusing—
  A dome of wax fruit in the hall.
We've put the Van Gogh in the bathroom,
  Those sunflowers looked *so* out of date,
But instead, as there's plenty of hearth room,
  Real ivy grows out of the grate.

And plants for indoors are the fashion—
  Or so the *News Chronicle* said—
So I've ventured some housekeeping cash on
  A cactus which seems to be dead.
An artist with whom we're acquainted
  Has stippled the dining-room stove
And the walls are alternately painted
  Off-yellow and festival mauve.

The Minister's made the decision
  That Cedric's department must stay
So an O.B.E. (Civil Division)
  Will shortly be coming his way.
To you, dear, and also to me, dear,
  It's nothing, for you are a friend,
Not even if you and I see, dear,
  A knighthood, perhaps, in the end.

But it wasn't for this that I fill'd a
　　Whole page up with gossip of course.
No: I'm dreadf'lly concerned for Matilda
　　Who seems to believe she's a horse.
She neighs when we're sitting at table
　　And clutches a make-believe rein.
Her playroom she fancies a stable.
　　Do you think she is going insane?

I know I would not let them christen her—
　　Such an old superstition's absurd—
But when Cedric was reading *The Listener*
　　Before he tuned in to the Third,
She walked on all fours like a dumb thing
　　And nibbled my plants, I'm afraid.
Do you think we could exorcize something
　　If we called in the Church to our aid?

Ex-horse-ize—that's rather funny—
　　But it's not very funny to me
For I've spent all her grandmother's money
　　On analysis since she was three.
And just when we'd freed her libido
　　We went off to Venice and Rome
(You'll remember we met on the Lido)
　　And left dear Matilda at home.

I'm afraid that that Riding School did it,
　　The one where we sent her to stay;
Were she horse-mad before, then she hid it
　　Or her analyst kept it at bay.

But that capable woman in Surrey
Who seemed so reliable too,
Said "Leave her to me and don't worry,
This place is as good as the Zoo.

When she's not on a horse she's not idle;
She can muck out the stables and clean
Her snaffle and saddle and bridle
Till bed-time at seven-fifteen."
Twenty guineas a week was the price, dear,
For Matilda it may have been bliss,
But for us it is not very nice, dear,
To find it has left her like this.

False Security

I remember the dread with which I at a quarter past four
Let go with a bang behind me our house front door
And, clutching a present for my dear little hostess tight,
Sailed out for the children's party into the night
Or rather the gathering night. For still some boys
In the near municipal acres were making a noise
Shuffling in fallen leaves and shouting and whistling
And running past hedges of hawthorn, spikey and bristling.
And black in the oncoming darkness stood out the trees
And pink shone the ponds in the sunset ready to freeze
And all was still and ominous waiting for dark
And the keeper was ringing his closing bell in the park
And the arc lights started to fizzle and burst into mauve
As I climbed West Hill to the great big house in The Grove,
Where the children's party was and the dear little hostess.
But halfway up stood the empty house where the ghost is
I crossed to the other side and under the arc
Made a rush for the next kind lamp-post out of the dark
And so to the next and the next till I reached the top
Where the Grove branched off to the left. Then ready to drop
I ran to the ironwork gateway of number seven
Secure at last on the lamplit fringe of Heaven.
Oh who can say how subtle and safe one feels
Shod in one's children's sandals from Daniel Neal's,
Clad in one's party clothes made of stuff from Heal's?
And who can still one's thrill at the candle shine
On cakes and ices and jelly and blackcurrant wine,

And the warm little feel of my hostess's hand in mine?
Can I forget my delight at the conjuring show?
And wasn't I proud that I was the last to go?
Too overexcited and pleased with myself to know
That the words I heard my hostess's mother employ
To a guest departing, would ever diminish my joy,
I WONDER WHERE JULIA FOUND THAT STRANGE, RATHER COMMON
LITTLE BOY?

Eunice

With her latest roses happily encumbered
    Tunbridge Wells Central takes her from the night,
Sweet second bloomings frost has faintly umbered
    And some double dahlias waxy red and white.

Shut again till April stands her little hutment
    Peeping over daisies Michaelmas and mauve,
Lock'd is the Elsan in its brick abutment
    Lock'd the little pantry, dead the little stove.

Keys with Mr. Groombridge, but nobody will take them
    To her lonely cottage by the lonely oak,
Potatoes in the garden but nobody to bake them,
    Fungus in the living room and water in the coke.

I can see her waiting on this chilly Sunday
    For the five forty (twenty minutes late),
One of many hundreds to dread the coming Monday
    To fight with influenza and battle with her weight.

Tweed coat and skirt that with such anticipation
    On a merry spring time a friend had trimm'd with fur,
Now the friend is married and, oh desolation,
    Married to the man who might have married *her*.

High in Onslow Gardens where the soot flakes settle
    An empty flat is waiting her struggle up the stair

And when she puts the wireless on, the heater and the kettle
  It's cream and green and cosy, but home is never there.

Home's here in Kent and how many morning coffees
  And hurried little lunch hours of planning will be spent
Through the busy months of typing in the office
  Until the days are warm enough to take her back to Kent.

Monody on the Death of
Aldersgate Street Station

———

Snow falls in the buffet of Aldersgate station,
  Soot hangs in the tunnel in clouds of steam.
City of London! before the next desecration
  Let your steepled forest of churches be my theme.

Sunday Silence! with every street a dead street,
  Alley and courtyard empty and cobbled mews,
Till "tingle tang" the bell of St. Mildred's Bread Street
  Summoned the sermon taster to high box pews,

And neighbouring towers and spirelets joined the ringing
  With answering echoes from heavy commercial walls
Till all were drowned as the sailing clouds went singing
  On the roaring flood of a twelve-voiced peal from Paul's.

Then would the years fall off and Thames run slowly;
  Out into marshy meadow-land flowed the Fleet:
And the walled-in City of London, smelly and holy,
  Had a tinkling mass house in every cavernous street.

The bells rang down and St. Michael Paternoster
  Would take me into its darkness from College Hill,
Or Christ Church Newgate Street (with St. Leonard Foster)
  Would be late for Mattins and ringing insistent still.

Last of the east wall sculpture, a cherub gazes
   On broken arches, rosebay, bracken and dock,
Where once I heard the roll of the Prayer Book phrases
   And the sumptuous tick of the old west gallery clock.

Snow falls in the buffet of Aldersgate station,
   Toiling and doomed from Moorgate Street puffs the train,
For us of the steam and the gas-light, the lost generation,
   The new white cliffs of the City are built in vain.

Thoughts on "*The Diary of a Nobody*"

The Pooters walked to Watney Lodge
    One Sunday morning hot and still
Where public footpaths used to dodge
    Round elms and oaks to Muswell Hill.

That burning buttercuppy day
    The local dogs were curled in sleep,
The writhing trunks of flowery May
    Were polished by the sides of sheep.

And only footsteps in a lane
    And birdsong broke the silence round
And chuffs of the Great Northern train
    For Alexandra Palace bound.

The Watney Lodge I seem to see
    Is gabled gothic hard and red,
With here a monkey puzzle tree
    And there a round geranium bed.

Each mansion, each new-planted pine,
    Each short and ostentatious drive
Meant Morning Prayer and beef and wine
    And Queen Victoria alive.

Dear Charles and Carrie, I am sure,
    Despite that awkward Sunday dinner,

Your lives were good and more secure
Than ours at cocktail time in Pinner.

Longfellow's Visit to Venice
(To be read in a quiet New England accent)

———————

Near the celebrated Lido where the breeze is fresh and free
Stands the ancient port of Venice called the City of the Sea.

All its streets are made of water, all its homes are brick and stone,
Yet it has a picturesqueness which is justly all its own.

Here for centuries have artists come to see the vistas quaint,
Here Bellini set his easel, here he taught his School to paint.

Here the youthful Giorgione gazed upon the domes and towers,
And interpreted his era in a way which pleases ours.

A later artist, Tintoretto, also did his paintings here,
Massive works which generations have continued to revere.

Still to-day come modern artists to portray the buildings fair
And their pictures may be purchased on San Marco's famous
                                                            Square.

When the bell notes from the belfries and the campaniles chime
Still to-day we find Venetians elegantly killing time

In their gilded old palazzos, while the music in our ears
Is the distant band at Florians mixed with songs of gondoliers.

Thus the New World meets the Old World and the sentiments
expressed
Are melodiously mingled in my warm New England breast.

Felixstowe, or
The Last of Her Order

With one consuming roar along the shingle
    The long wave claws and rakes the pebbles down
To where its backwash and the next wave mingle,
    A mounting arch of water weedy-brown
Against the tide the off-shore breezes blow.
Oh wind and water, this is Felixstowe.

In winter when the sea winds chill and shriller
    Than those of summer, all their cold unload
Full on the gimcrack attic of the villa
    Where I am lodging off the Orwell Road,
I put my final shilling in the meter
And only make my loneliness completer.

In eighteen ninety-four when we were founded,
    Counting our Reverend Mother we were six,
How full of hope we were and prayer-surrounded
    "The Little Sisters of the Hanging Pyx".
We built our orphanage. We ran our school.
Now only I am left to keep the rule.

Here in the gardens of the Spa Pavilion
    Warm in the whisper of a summer sea,
The cushioned scabious, a deep vermilion,
    With white pins stuck in it, looks up at me

A sun-lit kingdom touched by butterflies
And so my memory of winter dies.

Across the grass the poplar shades grow longer
   And louder clang the waves along the coast.
The band packs up. The evening breeze is stronger
   And all the world goes home to tea and toast.
I hurry past a cakeshop's tempting scones
Bound for the red brick twilight of St. John's.

"Thou knowest my down sitting and mine uprising"
   Here where the white light burns with steady glow
Safe from the vain world's silly sympathizing,
   Safe with the Love that I was born to know,
Safe from the surging of the lonely sea
My heart finds rest, my heart finds rest in Thee.

Pershore Station,
or *A Liverish Journey First Class*

The train at Pershore station was waiting that Sunday night
Gas light on the platform, in my carriage electric light,
Gas light on frosty evergreens, electric on Empire wood,
The Victorian world and the present in a moment's
neighbourhood.
There was no one about but a conscript who was saying good-bye
to his love
On the windy weedy platform with the sprinkled stars above
When sudden the waiting stillness shook with the ancient spells
Of an older world than all our worlds in the sound of the
Pershore bells.
They were ringing them down for Evensong in the lighted
abbey near,
Sounds which had poured through apple boughs for seven
centuries here.
With Guilt, Remorse, Eternity the void within me fills
And I thought of her left behind me in the Herefordshire hills.
I remembered her defencelessness as I made my heart a stone
Till she wove her self-protection round and left me on my own.
And plunged in a deep self pity I dreamed of another wife
And lusted for freckled faces and lived a separate life.
One word would have made her love me, one word would have
made her turn
But the word I never murmured and now I am left to burn.
Evesham, Oxford and London. The carriage is new and smart.
I am cushioned and soft and heated with a deadweight in my
heart.

Hertfordshire

I had forgotten Hertfordshire,
  The large unwelcome fields of roots
Where with my knickerbockered sire
  I trudged in syndicated shoots;

And that unlucky day when I
  Fired by mistake into the ground
Under a Lionel Edwards sky
  And felt disapprobation round.

The slow drive home by motor-car,
  A heavy Rover Landaulette,
Through Welwyn, Hatfield, Potters Bar,
  Tweed and cigar smoke, gloom and wet:

"How many times must I explain
  The way a boy should hold a gun?"
I recollect my father's pain
  At such a milksop for a son.

And now I see these fields once more
  Clothed, thank the Lord, in summer green,
Pale corn waves rippling to a shore
  The shadowy cliffs of elm between,

Colour-washed cottages reed-thatched
  And weather-boarded water mills,

Flint churches, brick and plaster patched,
  On mildly undistinguished hills—

They still are there. But now the shire
  Suffers a devastating change,
Its gentle landscape strung with wire,
  Old places looking ill and strange.

One can't be sure where London ends,
  New towns have filled the fields of root
Where father and his business friends
  Drove in the Landaulette to shoot;

Tall concrete standards line the lane,
  Brick boxes glitter in the sun:
Far more would these have caused him pain
  Than my mishandling of a gun.

Lord Cozens Hardy

Oh Lord Cozens Hardy
  Your mausoleum is cold,
The dry brown grass is brittle
  And frozen hard the mould
And where those Grecian columns rise
  So white among the dark
Of yew trees and of hollies in
  That corner of the park
By Norfolk oaks surrounded
  Whose branches seem to talk,
I know, Lord Cozens Hardy,
  I would not like to walk.

And even in the summer,
  On a bright East-Anglian day
When round your Doric portico
  Your children's children play
There's a something in the stillness
  And our waiting eyes are drawn
From the butler and the footman
  Bringing tea out on the lawn,
From the little silver spirit lamp
  That burns so blue and still,
To the half-seen mausoleum
  In the oak trees on the hill.

But when, Lord Cozens Hardy,
   November stars are bright,
And the King's Head Inn at Letheringsett
   Is shutting for the night,
The villagers have told me
   That they do not like to pass
Near your curious mausoleum
   Moon-shadowed on the grass
For fear of seeing walking
   In the season of All Souls
That first Lord Cozens Hardy,
   The Master of the Rolls.

Variation on a Theme by Newbolt

The City will see him no more at important meetings
  In Renaissance board rooms by Edwin Cooper designed;
In his numerous clubs the politely jocular greetings
  Will be rather more solemn to-day with his death in mind.

Half mast from a first floor window, the Company's bunting
  Flops over Leadenhall Street in this wintry air
And his fellow directors, baulked of a good day's hunting
  Nod gloomily back to the gloomy commissionaire.

His death will be felt through the whole of the organization,
  In every branch of its vast managerial tree,
His brother-in-law we suppose will attend the cremation,
  A service will later be held in St. Katherine Cree.

But what of his guns?—he was always a generous giver.
  (Oh yes, of course, we will each of us send a wreath),
His yacht? and his shoot? and his beautiful reach of river?
  And all the clubs in his locker at Walton Heath?

I do not know, for my mind sees one thing only,
  A luxurious bedroom looking on miles of fir
From a Surrey height where his widow sits silent and lonely
  For the man whose love seemed wholly given to her.

Inevitable

First there was putting hot-water bottles to it,
    Then there was seeing what an osteopath could do,
Then trying drugs to coax the thing and woo it,
    Then came the time when he knew that he was through.

Now in his hospital bed I see him lying
    Limp on the pillows like a cast-off Teddy bear.
Is he too ill to know that he is dying?
    And, if he does know, does he really care?

Grey looks the ward with November's overcasting
    But his large eyes seem to see beyond the day;
Speech becomes sacred near silence everlasting
    Oh if I *must* speak, have I words to say?

In the past weeks we had talked about Variety,
    Vesta Victoria, Lew Lake and Wilkie Bard,
Horse-buses, hansoms, crimes in High Society—
    Although we knew his death was near, we fought against it
                                        hard.

Now from his remoteness in a stillness unaccountable
    He drags himself to earth again to say good-bye to me—
His final generosity when almost insurmountable
    The barriers and mountains he has crossed again must be.

N.W.5 & N.6

Red cliffs arise. And up them service lifts
Soar with the groceries to silver heights.
Lissenden Mansions. And my memory sifts
Lilies from lily-like electric lights
And Irish stew smells from the smell of prams
And roar of seas from roar of London trams.

Out of it all my memory carves the quiet
Of that dark privet hedge where pleasures breed,
There first, intent upon its leafy diet,
I watched the looping caterpillar feed
And saw it hanging in a gummy froth
Till, weeks on, from the chrysalis burst the moth.

I see black oak twigs outlined on the sky,
Red squirrels on the Burdett-Coutts estate.
I ask my nurse the question "Will I die?"
As bells from sad St. Anne's ring out so late,
"And if I do die, will I go to Heaven?"
Highgate at eventide. Nineteen-eleven.

"You will. I won't." From that cheap nursery-maid,
Sadist and puritan as now I see,
I first learned what it was to be afraid,
Forcibly fed when sprawled across her knee
Lock'd into cupboards, left alone all day,
"World without end." What fearsome words to pray.

"World without end." It was not what she'ld do
That frightened me so much as did her fear
And guilt at endlessness. I caught them too,
Hating to think of sphere succeeding sphere
Into eternity and God's dread will.
I caught her terror then. I have it still.

From the Great Western

These small West Country towns where year by year
Newly elected mayors oppose reforms
Their last year's Worships promised—down the roads
Large detached houses, Croydons of the West,
Blister in summer heat; striped awnings hang
Over front doors, and those geraniums,
Retired tradesmen love to cultivate,
Blaze in the gravel. From more furtive streets
Unmarried mothers leave for London. Girls
Who had such promise suddenly lose their looks.
Small businesses go bankrupt. Corners once
Familiar for a shuttered toll gate house
Are smoothed away to make amenities.
The copper beech, the bunchy sycamore
And churchyard limes are felled. Among their stumps
The almond tree shall flourish. Corn Exchange—
On with the Poultry Show! and Cemet'ry,
With your twin chapels, safely gather in
Church and dissent from small West Country towns
Where year by year,
Newly elected Mayors oppose reforms.

In the Public Gardens

In the Public Gardens,
> To the airs of Strauss,
Eingang we're in love again
> When *ausgang* we were *aus*.

The waltz was played, the songs were sung,
> The night resolved our fears;
From bunchy boughs the lime trees hung
> Their gold electroliers.

Among the loud Americans
> *Zwei Engländer* were we,
You so white and frail and pale
> And me so deeply me;

I bought for you a dark-red rose,
> I saw your grey-green eyes,
As high above the floodlights,
> The true moon sailed the skies.

In the Public Gardens,
> Ended things begin;
Ausgang we were out of love
> *Und eingang* we are in.

Preface to "High and Low"

MURRAY, you bid my plastic pen
A preface write. Well, here's one then.
Verse seems to me the shortest way
Of saying what one has to say,
A memorable means of dealing
With mood or person, place or feeling.
Anything extra that is given
Is taken as a gift from Heaven.

 The English language has such range,
Such rhymes and half-rhymes, rhythms strange,
And such variety of tone,
It is a music of its own.
With MILTON it has organ power
As loud as bells in Redcliffe tower;
It falls like winter crisp and light
On COWPER's Buckinghamshire night.
It can be gentle as a lake,
Where WORDSWORTH's oars a ripple make
Or rest with TENNYSON at ease
In sibilance of summer seas,
Or languorous as lilies grow,
When DOWSON's lamp is burning low—
For endless changes can be rung
On church-bells of the English tongue.
 MURRAY, your venerable door
Opened to BYRON, CRABBE and MOORE
And TOMMY CAMPBELL. How can I,

A buzzing insubstantial fly,
Compare with them? I do not try,
Pleased simply to be one who shares
An imprint that was also theirs,
And grateful to the people who
Have bought my verses hitherto.

Cornish Cliffs

Those moments, tasted once and never done,
Of long surf breaking in the mid-day sun.
A far-off blow-hole booming like a gun—

The seagulls plane and circle out of sight
Below this thirsty, thrift-encrusted height,
The veined sea-campion buds burst into white

And gorse turns tawny orange, seen beside
Pale drifts of primroses cascading wide
To where the slate falls sheer into the tide.

More than in gardened Surrey, nature spills
A wealth of heather, kidney-vetch and squills
Over these long-defended Cornish hills.

A gun-emplacement of the latest war
Looks older than the hill fort built before
Saxon or Norman headed for the shore.

And in the shadowless, unclouded glare
Deep blue above us fades to whiteness where
A misty sea-line meets the wash of air.

Nut-smell of gorse and honey-smell of ling
Waft out to sea the freshness of the spring
On sunny shallows, green and whispering.

The wideness which the lark-song gives the sky
Shrinks at the clang of sea-birds sailing by
Whose notes are tuned to days when seas are high.

From today's calm, the lane's enclosing green
Leads inland to a usual Cornish scene—
Slate cottages with sycamore between.

Small fields and tellymasts and wires and poles
With, as the everlasting ocean rolls,
Two chapels built for half a hundred souls.

Tregardock

A mist that from the moor arose
  In sea-fog wraps Port Isaac bay,
The moan of warning from Trevose
  Makes grimmer this October day.

Only the shore and cliffs are clear.
  Gigantic slithering shelves of slate
In waiting awfulness appear
  Like journalism full of hate.

On the steep path a bramble leaf
  Stands motionless and wet with dew,
The grass bends down, the bracken's brown,
  The grey-green gorse alone is new.

Cautious my sliding footsteps go
  To quarried rock and dripping cave;
The ocean, leaden-still below,
  Hardly has strength to lift a wave.

I watch it crisp into its height
  And flap exhausted on the beach,
The long surf menacing and white
  Hissing as far as it can reach.

The dunlin do not move, each bird
  Is stationary on the sand

As if a spirit in it heard
    The final end of sea and land.

And I on my volcano edge
    Exposed to ridicule and hate
Still do not dare to leap the ledge
    And smash to pieces on the slate.

By the Ninth Green, St. Enodoc

Dark of primaeval pine encircles me
With distant thunder of an angry sea
While wrack and resin scent alternately
    The air I breathe.

On slate compounded before man was made
The ocean ramparts roll their light and shade
Up to Bray Hill and, leaping to invade,
    Fall back and seethe.

A million years of unrelenting tide
Have smoothed the strata of the steep cliffside:
How long ago did rock with rock collide
    To shape these hills?

One day the mayfly's life, three weeks the cleg's,
The woodworm's four-year cycle bursts its eggs,
The flattened centipede lets loose its legs
    And stings and kills.

Hot life pulsating in this foreshore dry,
Damp life upshooting from the reed-beds high,
Under those barrows, dark against the sky,
    The Iron Age dead—

Why is it that a sunlit second sticks?
What force collects all this and seeks to fix
This fourth March morning nineteen sixty-six
    Deep in my head?

Winter Seascape

The sea runs back against itself
   With scarcely time for breaking wave
To cannonade a slatey shelf
   And thunder under in a cave

Before the next can fully burst.
   The headwind, blowing harder still,
Smooths it to what it was at first—
   A slowly rolling water-hill.

Against the breeze the breakers haste,
   Against the tide their ridges run
And all the sea's a dappled waste
   Criss-crossing underneath the sun.

Far down the beach the ripples drag
   Blown backward, rearing from the shore,
And wailing gull and shrieking shag
   Alone can pierce the ocean roar.

Unheard, a mongrel hound gives tongue,
   Unheard are shouts of little boys:
What chance has any inland lung
   Against this multi-water noise?

Here where the cliffs alone prevail
　　I stand exultant, neutral, free,
And from the cushion of the gale
　　Behold a huge consoling sea.

Old Friends

The sky widens to Cornwall. A sense of sea
   Hangs in the lichenous branches and still there's light.
The road from its tunnel of blackthorn rises free
      To a final height,

And over the west is glowing a mackerel sky
   Whose opal fleece has faded to purple pink.
In this hour of the late-lit, listening evening, why
      Do my spirits sink?

The tide is high and a sleepy Atlantic sends
   Exploring ripple on ripple down Polzeath shore,
And the gathering dark is full of the thought of friends
      I shall see no more.

Where is Anne Channel who loved this place the best,
   With her tense blue eyes and her shopping-bag falling apart,
And her racy gossip and nineteen-twenty zest,
      And warmth of heart?

Where's Roland, easing his most unwieldy car,
   With its load of golf-clubs, backwards into the lane?
Where's Kathleen Stokes with her Sealyhams? There's Doom Bar;
      Bray Hill shows plain;

For this is the turn, and the well-known trees draw near;
   On the road their pattern in moonlight fades and swells:

As the engine stops, from two miles off I hear
        St Minver bells.

What a host of stars in a wideness still and deep:
    What a host of souls, as a motor-bike whines away
And the silver snake of the estuary curls to sleep
        In Daymer Bay.

Are they one with the Celtic saints and the years between?
    Can they see the moonlit pools where ribbonweed drifts?
As I reach our hill, I am part of a sea unseen—
        And oppression lifts.

A Bay in Anglesey

The sleepy sound of a tea-time tide
Slaps at the rocks the sun has dried,

Too lazy, almost, to sink and lift
Round low peninsulas pink with thrift.

The water, enlarging shells and sand,
Grows greener emerald out from land

And brown over shadowy shelves below
The waving forests of seaweed show.

Here at my feet in the short cliff grass
Are shells, dried bladderwrack, broken glass,

Pale blue squills and yellow rock roses.
The next low ridge that we climb discloses

One more field for the sheep to graze
While, scarcely seen on this hottest of days,

Far to the eastward, over there,
Snowdon rises in pearl-grey air.

Multiple lark-song, whispering bents,
The thymy, turfy and salty scents

And filling in, brimming in, sparkling and free
The sweet susurration of incoming sea.

A Lament for Moira McCavendish

Through the midlands of Ireland I journeyed by diesel
    And bright in the sun shone the emerald plain;
Though loud sang the birds on the thorn-bush and teasel
    They could not be heard for the sound of the train.

The roll of the railway made musing creative:
    I thought of the colleen I soon was to see
With her wiry black hair and grey eyes of the native,
    Sweet Moira McCavendish, acushla machree.

Her brother's wee cabin stands distant from Tallow
    A league and a half, where the Blackwater flows,
And the musk and potato, the mint and the mallow
    Do grow there in beauty, along with the rose.

'Twas smoothly we raced through the open expansion
    Of rush-covered levels and gate-lodge and gate
And the ruined demesne and the windowless mansion
    Where once the oppressor had revelled in state.

At Castletownroche, as the prospect grew hillier,
    I saw the far mountains to Moira long-known
Till I came to the valley and townland familiar
    With the Protestant church standing locked and alone.

O vein of my heart! upon Tallow Road Station
    No face was to greet me, so freckled and white;

As the diesel slid out, leaving still desolation,
    The McCavendish ass-cart was nowhere in sight.

For a league and a half to the Blackwater river
    I tramped with my bundle her cabin to see
And herself by the fuchsias, her young lips a-quiver
    Half-smiling, half-weeping a welcome to me.

Och Moira McCavendish! the fangs of the creeper
    Have struck at the thatch and thrust open the door;
The couch in the garden grows ranker and deeper
    Than musk and potato which bloomed there before.

Flow on, you remorseless and salmon-full waters!
    What care I for prospects so silvery fair?
The heart in me's dead, like your sweetest of daughters,
    And I would that my spirit were lost on the air.

The Small Towns of Ireland

Public houses in Irish country towns are very often general merchants as well. You drink at a counter with bacon on it. Brooms and plastic dustpans hang from the ceiling. Loaves of new bread are stacked on top of fuse wire and, over all, there is a deep, delicious silence that can be found only in Ireland, in the midlands of Ireland in particular—the least touristed and profoundest part of that whole sad, beautiful country. Much that is native and traditional goes on, including the printing of ballads in metres derived from the Celts via Tom Moore. These ballads are called hedge poetry and their authors are the last descendants of the Gaelic bards. It was in just such a general shop as I have described that I might have found, pinned up among the notices for a local Feis, Gaelic football matches and Government proclamations, the following ballad, printed on emerald paper in a border of shamrocks.

The small towns of Ireland by bards are neglected,
    They stand there, all lonesome, on hilltop and plain.
The Protestant glebe house by beech trees protected
    Sits close to the gates of his Lordship's demesne.

But where is his Lordship, who once in a phaeton
    Drove out twixt his lodges and into the town?
Oh his tragic misfortunes I will not dilate on;
    His mansion's a ruin, his woods are cut down.

His impoverished descendant is dwelling in Ealing,
    His daughters must type for their bread and their board,
O'er the graves of his forebears the nettle is stealing
    And few will remember the sad Irish Lord.

Yet still stands the Mall where his agent resided,
  The doctor, attorney and such class of men.
The elegant fanlights and windows provided
  A Dublin-like look for the town's Upper Ten.

'Twas bravely they stood by the Protestant steeple
  As over the town rose their roof-trees afar.
Let us slowly descend to the part where the people
  Do mingle their ass-carts by Finnegan's bar.

I hear it once more, the soft sound of those voices,
  When fair day is filling with farmers the Square,
And the heart in my bosom delights and rejoices
  To think of the dealing and drinking done there.

I see thy grey granite, O grim House of Sessions!
  I think of the judges who sat there in state
And my mind travels back to our monster processions
  To honour the heroes of brave Ninety-Eight.

The barracks are burned where the Redcoats oppressed us,
  The gaol is broke open, our people are free.
Though Cromwell once cursed us, Saint Patrick has blessed
                                                      us—
  The merciless English have fled o'er the sea.

Look out where yon cabins grow smaller to smallest,
  Straw-thatched and one-storey and soon to come down,
To the prominent steeple, the newest and tallest,
  Of Saint Malachy's Catholic Church in our town:

The fine architécture, the wealth of mosaic,
  The various marbles on altars within—
To attempt a description were merely prosaic,
  So, asking your pardon, I will not begin.

O my small town of Ireland, the raindrops caress you,
  The sun sparkles bright on your field and your Square
As here on your bridge I salute you and bless you,
  Your murmuring waters and turf-scented air.

Ireland's Own

or

The Burial of Thomas Moore

In the churchyard of Bromham the yews intertwine
O'er a smooth granite cross of a Celtic design,
Looking quite out of place in surroundings like these
In a corner of Wilts 'twixt the chalk and the cheese.

I can but account you neglected and poor,
Dear bard of my boyhood, mellifluous Moore,
That far from the land which of all you loved best
In a village of England your bones should have rest.

I had rather they lay where the Blackwater glides
When the light of the evening doth burnish its tides
And St. Carthage Cathedral's meticulous spire
Is tipped like the Castle with sun-setting fire.

I had rather some gate-lodge of plaster and thatch
With slim pointed windows and porches to match
Had last seen your coffin drawn out on the road
From a great Irish house to its final abode.

Or maybe a rath with a round tower near
And the whispering Shannon delighting the ear
And the bog all around and the width of the sky
Is the place where your bones should deservedly lie.

The critics may scorn you and Hazlitt may carp
At the 'Musical Snuff-box' you made of the Harp;
The Regency drawing-rooms that thrilled with your song
Are not the true world to which now you belong.

No! the lough and the mountain, the ruins and rain
And purple-blue distances bound your demesne,
For the tunes to the elegant measures you trod
Have chords of deep longing for Ireland and God.

Great Central Railway
Sheffield Victoria to Banbury

'Unmitigated England'
  Came swinging down the line
That day the February sun
  Did crisp and crystal shine.
Dark red at Kirkby Bentinck stood
  A steeply gabled farm
'Mid ash trees and a sycamore
  In charismatic calm.
A village street—a manor house—
  A church—then, tally ho!
We pounded through a housing scheme
  With tellymasts a-row,
Where cars of parked executives
  Did regimented wait
Beside administrative blocks
  Within the factory gate.
She waved to us from Hucknall South
  As we hooted round a bend,
From a curtained front-window did
  The diesel driver's friend.
Through cuttings deep to Nottingham
  Precariously we wound;
The swallowing tunnel made the train
  Seem London's Underground.
Above the fields of Leicestershire
  On arches we were borne

And the rumble of the railway drowned
   The thunder of the Quorn;
And silver shone the steeples out
   Above the barren boughs;
Colts in a paddock ran from us
   But not the solid cows;
And quite where Rugby Central is
   Does only Rugby know.
We watched the empty platform wait
   And sadly saw it go.
By now the sun of afternoon
   Showed ridge and furrow shadows
And shallow unfamiliar lakes
   Stood shivering in the meadows.
Is Woodford church or Hinton church
   The one I ought to see?
Or were they both too much restored
   In 1883?
I do not know. Towards the west
   A trail of glory runs
And we leave the old Great Central line
   For Banbury and buns.

Matlock Bath

From Matlock Bath's half-timbered station
    I see the black dissenting spire—
Thin witness of a congregation,
    Stone emblem of a Handel choir;
In blest Bethesda's limpid pool
Comes treacling out of Sunday School.

By cool Siloam's shady rill—
    The sounds are sweet as strawberry jam:
I raise mine eyes unto the hill,
    The beetling HEIGHTS OF ABRAHAM;
The branchy trees are white with rime
In Matlock Bath this winter-time,

And from the whiteness, grey uprearing,
    Huge cliffs hang sunless ere they fall,
A tossed and stony ocean nearing
    The moment to o'erwhelm us all:
Eternal Father, strong to save,
How long wilt thou suspend the wave?

How long before the pleasant acres
    Of intersecting LOVERS' WALKS
Are rolled across by limestone breakers,
    Whole woodlands snapp'd like cabbage stalks?
O God, our help in ages past,
How long will SPEEDWELL CAVERN last?

In this dark dale I hear the thunder
  Of houses folding with the shocks,
The GRAND PAVILION buckling under
  The weight of the ROMANTIC ROCKS,
The hardest Blue John ash-trays seem
To melt away in thermal steam.

Deep in their Nonconformist setting
  The shivering children wait their doom—
The father's whip, the mother's petting
  In many a coffee-coloured room;
And attic bedrooms shriek with fright,
For dread of *Pilgrims of the Night*.

Perhaps it's this that makes me shiver
  As I ascend the slippery path
High, high above the sliding river
  And terraces of Matlock Bath:
A sense of doom, a dread to see
The *Rock of Ages cleft for me*.

An Edwardian Sunday
Broomhill, Sheffield

High dormers are rising
So sharp and surprising,
And ponticum edges
The driveways of gravel;
Stone houses from ledges
Look down on ravines.
The vision can travel
From gable to gable,
Italianate mansion
And turretted stable,
A sylvan expansion
So varied and jolly
Where laurel and holly
Commingle their greens.

Serene on a Sunday
The sun glitters hotly
O'er mills that on Monday
With engines will hum.
By tramway excursion
To Dore and to Totley
In search of diversion
The millworkers come;
But in our arboreta
The sounds are discreeter
Of shoes upon stone—

The worshippers wending
To welcoming chapel,
Companioned or lone;
And over a pew there
See loveliness lean,
As Eve shows her apple
Through rich bombazine:
What love is born new there
In blushing eighteen!

Your prospects will please her,
The iron-king's daughter,
Up here on Broomhill:
Strange Hallamshire, County
Of dearth and of bounty,
Of brown tumbling water
And furnace and mill.
Your own Ebenezer*
Looks down from his height
On back street and alley
And chemical valley
Laid out in the light;
On ugly and pretty
Where industry thrives
In this hill-shadowed city
Of razors and knives.

* The statue of Ebenezer Elliott (1781–1849) the 'Corn
Law Rhymer' outside the Mappin Gallery, Sheffield.

Lines written to Martyn Skinner before
his Departure from Oxfordshire in Search
of Quiet—1961

———————

Return, return to Ealing,
  Worn poet of the farm!
Regain your boyhood feeling
  Of uninvaded calm!
For there the leafy avenues
  Of lime and chestnut mix'd
Do widely wind, by art designed,
  The costly houses 'twixt.

No early morning tractors
  The thrush and blackbird drown,
No nuclear reactors
  Bulge huge below the down,
No youth upon his motor-bike
  His lust for power fulfils,
With dentist's drill intent to kill
  The silence of the hills.

In Ealing on a Sunday
  Bell-haunted quiet falls,
In Ealing on a Monday
  'Milk-o!' the milkman calls;
No lorries grind in bottom gear
  Up steep and narrow lanes,

Nor constant here offend the ear
  Low-flying aeroplanes.

Return, return to Ealing,
  Worn poet of the farm!
Regain your boyhood feeling
  Of uninvaded calm!
Where smoothly glides the bicycle
  And softly flows the Brent
And a gentle gale from Perivale
  Sends up the hayfield scent.

Uffington

Tonight we feel the muffled peal
   Hang on the village like a pall;
It overwhelms the towering elms—
   That death-reminding dying fall;
The very sky no longer high
   Comes down within the reach of all.
Imprisoned in a cage of sound
Even the trivial seems profound.

Anglo-Catholic Congresses

We, who remember the Faith, the grey-headed ones,
  Of those Anglo-Catholic Congresses swinging along,
Who heard the South Coast salvo of incense-guns
  And surged to the Albert Hall in our thousands strong
  With 'extreme' colonial bishops leading in song;

We, who remember, look back to the blossoming May-time
  On ghosts of servers and thurifers after Mass,
The slapping of backs, the flapping of cassocks, the play-time,
  A game of Grandmother's Steps on the vicarage grass—
  "Father, a little more sherry. I'll fill your glass."

We recall the triumph, that Sunday after Ascension,
  When our Protestant suffragan suffered himself to be coped—
The SYA and the Scheme for Church Extension—
  The new diocesan's not as 'sound' as we'd hoped,
  And Kensit threatens and has Sam Gurney poped?

Yet, under the Travers baroque, in a limewashed whiteness,
  The fiddle-back vestments a-glitter with morning rays,
Our Lady's image, in multiple-candled brightness,
  The bells and banners—those were the waking days
  When Faith was taught and fanned to a golden blaze.

In Willesden Churchyard

Come walk with me, my love, to Neasden Lane.
The chemicals from various factories
Have bitten deep into the Portland stone
And streaked the white Carrara of the graves
Of many a Pooter and his Caroline,
Long laid to rest among these dripping trees;
And that small heap of fast-decaying flowers
Marks Lupin Pooter lately gathered in;
And this, my love, is Laura Seymour's grave—
'So long the loyal counsellor and friend'
Of that Charles Reade whose coffin lies with hers.
Was she his mistress? Did he visit her
When coming down from Oxford by the coach?
Alighting at the turnpike, did he walk
These elmy lanes of Middlesex and climb
A stile or two across the dairy farms
Over to Harlesden at the wicket gate?
Then the soft rigours of his Fellowship
Were tenderly relaxed. The sun would send
Last golden streaks of mild October light
On tarred and weather-boarded barn and shed.
Blue bonfire smoke would hang among the trees;
And in the little stucco hermitage
Did Laura gently stroke her lover's head?
And did her Charles look up into her eyes
For loyal counsel there? I do not know.
Doubtless some pedant for his Ph.D.

Has ascertained the facts, or I myself
Might find them in the public libraries.
I only know that as we see her grave
My flesh, to dissolution nearer now
Than yours, which is so milky white and soft,
Frightens me, though the Blessed Sacrament
Not ten yards off in Willesden parish church
Glows with the present immanence of God.

The Commander

On a shining day of October we remembered you, Commander,
  When the trees were gold and still
And some of their boughs were green where the whip of the
                                        wind had missed them
  On this nippy Staffordshire hill.

A clean sky streamed through institutional windows
  As we heard the whirr of Time
Touching our Quaker silence, in builders' lorries departing
  For Newcastle-under-Lyme.

The proving words of the psalm you bequeathed to the gowned
                                        assembly
  On waiting silence broke,
'Lord, I am not high-minded . . .' In the youthful voice of the
                                        student
  Your own humility spoke.

I remembered our shared delight in architecture and nature
  As bicycling we went
By saffron-spotted palings to crumbling box-pewed churches
  Down hazel lanes in Kent.

I remembered on winter evenings, with wine and the family
                                        round you,
  Your reading Dickens aloud
And the laughs we used to have at your gift for administration,
  For you were never proud.

Sky and sun and the sea! the greatness of things was in you
    And thus you refrained your soul.
Let others fuss over academical detail,
    You saw people whole.

'Lord, I am not high-minded . . .' The final lesson you taught
                                                      me,
    When you bade the world good-bye,
Was humbly and calmly to trust in the soul's survival
    When my own hour comes to die.

Autumn 1964
(FOR KAREN)

Red apples hang like globes of light
    Against this pale November haze,
And now, although the mist is white,
    In half-an-hour a day of days
Will climb into its golden height
    And Sunday bells will ring its praise.

The sparkling flint, the darkling yew,
    The red brick, less intensely red
Than hawthorn berries bright with dew
    Or leaves of creeper still unshed,
The watery sky washed clean and new,
    Are all rejoicing with the dead.

The yellowing elm shows yet some green,
    The mellowing bells exultant sound:
Never have light and colour been
    So prodigally thrown around;
And in the bells the promise tells
    Of greater light where Love is found.

The Hon. Sec.

The flag that hung half-mast to-day
　　Seemed animate with being
As if it knew for whom it flew
　　And will no more be seeing.

He loved each corner of the links—
　　The stream at the eleventh,
The grey-green bents, the pale sea-pinks,
　　The prospect from the seventh;

To the ninth tee the uphill climb,
　　A grass and sandy stairway,
And at the top the scent of thyme
　　And long extent of fairway.

He knew how on a summer day
　　The sea's deep blue grew deeper,
How evening shadows over Bray
　　Made that round hill look steeper.

He knew the ocean mists that rose
　　And seemed for ever staying,
When moaned the foghorn from Trevose
　　And nobody was playing;

The flip of cards on winter eves,
　　The whisky and the scoring,

As trees outside were stripped of leaves
   And heavy seas were roaring.

He died when early April light
   Showed red his garden sally
And under pale green spears glowed white
   His lilies of the valley:

That garden where he used to stand
   And where the robin waited
To fly and perch upon his hand
   And feed till it was sated.

The Times would never have the space
   For Ned's discreet achievements;
The public prints are not the place
   For intimate bereavements.

A gentle guest, a willing host,
   Affection deeply planted—
It's strange that those we miss the most
   Are those we take for granted.

Monody on the Death of a Platonist Bank Clerk

This is the lamp where he first read Whitman
  Out of the library large and free.
Every quarter the bus to Kirkstall
  Stopped and waited, but on read he.

This was his room with books in plenty:
  Dusty, now I have raised the blind—
Fenimore Cooper, Ballantyne, Henty,
  Edward Carpenter wedged behind.

These are the walls adorned with portraits,
  Camera studies and Kodak snaps;
'Camp at Pevensey'—'Scouts at Cleethorpes'—
  There he is with the lads and chaps.

This is the friend, the best and greatest,
  Pure in his surplice, smiling, true—
The enlarged Photomaton—that's the latest,
  Next to the coloured one 'August Blue'.

These are his pipes. Ah! how he loved them,
  Puffed and petted them, after walks,
After tea and a frowst with crumpets,
  Puffed the smoke into serious talks.

All the lot of them, how they came to him—
    Tea and chinwag—gay young lives!
Somehow they were never the same to him
    When they married and brought their wives.

Good-bye

Some days before death
    When food's tasting sour on my tongue,
Cigarettes long abandoned,
    Disgusting now even champagne;
When I'm sweating a lot
    From the strain on a last bit of lung
And lust has gone out
    Leaving only the things of the brain;
More worthless than ever
    Will seem all the songs I have sung,
More harmless the prods of the prigs,
    Remoter the pain,
More futile the Lord Civil Servant
    As, rung upon rung,
He ascends by committees to roofs
    Far below on the plain.
But better down there in the battle
    Than here on the hill
With Judgement or nothingness waiting me,
    Lonely and chill.

Five o'Clock Shadow

This is the time of day when we in the Men's Ward
    Think "One more surge of the pain and I give up the fight,"
When he who struggles for breath can struggle less strongly:
    This is the time of day which is worse than night.

A haze of thunder hangs on the hospital rose-beds,
    A doctors' foursome out on the links is played,
Safe in her sitting-room Sister is putting her feet up:
    This is the time of day when we feel betrayed.

Below the windows, loads of loving relations
    Rev in the car park, changing gear at the bend,
Making for home and a nice big tea and the telly:
    "Well, we've done what we can. It can't be long till the end."

This is the time of day when the weight of bedclothes
    Is harder to bear than a sharp incision of steel.
The endless anonymous croak of a cheap transistor
    Intensifies the lonely terror I feel.

A Russell Flint

I could not speak for amazement at your beauty
    As you came down the Garrick stair,
Grey-green eyes like the turbulent Atlantic
    And floppy schoolgirl hair.

I could see you in a Sussex teashop,
    Dressed in peasant weave and brogues,
Turning over, as firelight shone on brassware,
    Last year's tea-stained *Vogues.*

I could see you as a large-eyed student,
    Frowning as you tried to learn,
Or, head flung back, the confident girl prefect,
    Thrillingly kind and stern.

I could not speak for amazement at your beauty;
    Yet, when you spoke to me,
You were calm and gentle as a rock pool
    Waiting, warm, for the sea.

Wave on wave, I plunged in them to meet you—
    In wave on wave I drown;
Calm rock pool, on the shore of my security
    Hold me when the tide goes down.

Perp. Revival i' the North

O, I wad gang tae Harrogate
   Tae a kirk by Temple Moore,
Wi' a tall choir and a lang nave
   And rush mats on the floor;
And Percy Dearmer chasubles
   And nae pews but chairs,
And there we'll sing the Sarum rite
   Tae English Hymnal airs.

It's a far cry frae Harrogate
   And mony a heathery mile
Tae a stane kirk wi' a wee spire
   And a verra wee south aisle.
The rhododendrons bloom wi'oot
   On ilka Simmer's day,
And it's there the Airl o' Feversham
   Wad hae his tenants pray;
For there's something in the painted roof
   And the mouldings round the door,
The braw bench and the plain font
   That tells o' Temple Moore.

Agricultural Caress

Keep me from Thelma's sister Pearl!
She puts my senses in a whirl,
Weakens my knees and keeps me waiting
Until my heart stops palpitating.

The debs may turn disdainful backs
On Pearl's uncouth mechanic slacks,
And outraged see the fire that lies
And smoulders in her long-lashed eyes.

Have they such weather-freckled features,
The smooth sophisticated creatures?
Ah, not to them such limbs belong,
Such animal movements sure and strong,

Such arms to take a man and press
In agricultural caress
His head to hers, and hold him there
Deep buried in her chestnut hair.

God shrive me from this morning lust
For supple farm girls: if you must,
Send the cold daughter of an earl—
But spare me Thelma's sister Pearl!

Narcissus

Yes, it was Bedford Park the vision came from—
    de Morgan lustre glowing round the hearth,
And that sweet flower which self-love takes its name from
    Nodding among the lilies in the garth,
And Arnold Dolmetsch touching the spinet,
And Mother, Chiswick's earliest suffragette.

I was a delicate boy—my parents' only—
    And highly strung. My father was in trade.
And how I loved, when Mother left me lonely,
    To watch old Martha spice the marmalade,
Or help with flower arrangements in the lobby
Before I went to find my playmate Bobby.

We'ld go for walks, we bosom boyfriends would
    (For Bobby's watching sisters drove us mad),
And when we just did nothing we were good,
    But when we touched each other we were bad.
I found this out when Mother said one day
She thought we were unwholesome in our play.

So Bobby and I were parted. Bobby dear,
    I didn't want my tea. I heard your sisters
Playing at hide-and-seek with you quite near
    As off the garden gate I picked the blisters.
Oh tell me, Mother, what I mustn't do—
Then, Bobby, I can play again with you.

For I know hide-and-seek's most secret places
  More than your sisters do. And you and I
Can scramble into them and leave no traces,
  Nothing above us but the twigs and sky,
Nothing below us but the leaf-mould chilly
Where we can warm and hug each other silly.

My Mother wouldn't tell me why she hated
  The things we did, and why they pained her so.
She said a fate far worse than death awaited
  People who did the things we didn't know,
And then she said I was her precious child,
And once there was a man called Oscar Wilde.

"Open your story book and find a tale
  Of ladyes fayre and deeds of derring-do,
Or good Sir Gawaine and the Holy Grail,
  Mother will read her boy a page or two
Before she goes, this Women's Suffrage Week,
To hear that clever Mrs Pankhurst speak.

Sleep with your hands above your head. That's right—
  And let no evil thoughts pollute the dark."
She rose, and lowered the incandescent light.
  I heard her footsteps die down Bedford Park.
Mother where are you? Bobby, Bobby, where?
I clung for safety to my teddy bear.

The Cockney Amorist

Oh when my love, my darling,
 You've left me here alone,
I'll walk the streets of London
 Which once seemed all our own.

The vast suburban churches
 Together we have found:
The ones which smelt of gaslight
 The ones in incense drown'd;
I'll use them now for praying in
 And not for looking round.

No more the Hackney Empire
 Shall find us in its stalls
When on the limelit crooner
 The thankful curtain falls,
And soft electric lamplight
 Reveals the gilded walls.

I will not go to Finsbury Park
 The putting course to see
Nor cross the crowded High Road
 To Williamsons' to tea,
For these and all the other things
 Were part of you and me.

I love you, oh my darling,
  And what I can't make out
Is why since you have left me
  I'm somehow still about.

Harvest Hymn

We spray the fields and scatter
    The poison on the ground
So that no wicked wild flowers
    Upon our farm be found.
We like whatever helps us
    To line our purse with pence;
The twenty-four-hour broiler-house
    And neat electric fence.

    All concrete sheds around us
        And Jaguars in the yard,
    The telly lounge and deep-freeze
        Are ours from working hard.

We fire the fields for harvest,
    The hedges swell the flame,
The oak trees and the cottages
    From which our fathers came.
We give no compensation,
    The earth is ours today,
And if we lose on arable,
    Then bungalows will pay.

    All concrete sheds . . . etc.

Meditation on the *A30*

A man on his own in a car
   Is revenging himself on his wife;
He opens the throttle and bubbles with dottle
   And puffs at his pitiful life.

"She's losing her looks very fast,
   She loses her temper all day;
That lorry won't let me get past,
   This Mini is blocking my way.

"Why can't you step on it and shift her!
   I can't go on crawling like this!
At breakfast she said that she wished I was dead—
   Thank heavens we don't have to kiss.

"I'd like a nice blonde on my knee
   And one who won't argue or nag.
Who dares to come hooting at *me*?
   I only give way to a Jag.

"You're barmy or plastered, I'll pass you, you bastard—
   I *will* overtake you. I *will*!"
As he clenches his pipe, his moment is ripe
   And the corner's accepting its kill.

Inexpensive Progress

Encase your legs in nylons,
Bestride your hills with pylons
　　O age without a soul;
Away with gentle willows
And all the elmy billows
　　That through your valleys roll.

Let's say good-bye to hedges
And roads with grassy edges
　　And winding country lanes;
Let all things travel faster
Where motor-car is master
　　Till only Speed remains.

Destroy the ancient inn-signs
But strew the roads with tin signs
　　'Keep Left,' 'M4,' 'Keep Out!'
Command, instruction, warning,
Repetitive adorning
　　The rockeried roundabout;

For every raw obscenity
Must have its small 'amenity,'
　　Its patch of shaven green,
And hoardings look a wonder
In banks of floribunda
　　With floodlights in between.

Leave no old village standing
Which could provide a landing
  For aeroplanes to roar,
But spare such cheap defacements
As huts with shattered casements
  Unlived-in since the war.

Let no provincial High Street
Which might be your or my street
  Look as it used to do,
But let the chain stores place here
Their miles of black glass facia
  And traffic thunder through.

And if there is some scenery,
Some unpretentious greenery,
  Surviving anywhere,
It does not need protecting
For soon we'll be erecting
  A Power Station there.

When all our roads are lighted
By concrete monsters sited
  Like gallows overhead,
Bathed in the yellow vomit
Each monster belches from it,
  We'll know that we are dead.

Mortality

———

The first-class brains of a senior civil servant
    Shiver and shatter and fall
As the steering column of his comfortable Humber
    Batters in the bony wall.
All those delicate little re-adjustments
    "On the one hand, if we proceed
With the *ad hoc* policy hitherto adapted
    To individual need . . .
On the other hand, too rigid an arrangement
    Might, of itself, perforce . . .
I would like to submit for the Minister's concurrence
    The following alternative course,
Subject to revision and reconsideration
    In the light our experience gains . . ."
And this had to happen at the corner where the by-pass
    Comes into Egham out of Staines.
That very near miss for an All Souls' Fellowship
    The recent compensation of a 'K'—
The first-class brains of a senior civil servant
    Are sweetbread on the road today.

Reproof Deserved
or
After the Lecture

When I saw the grapefruit drying, cherry in each centre lying,
  And a dozen guests expected at the table's polished oak,
Then I knew, my lecture finished, I'ld be feeling quite diminished
  Talking on, but unprotected, so that all my spirit broke.

"Have you read the last Charles Morgan?" "Are you writing for
                                                    the organ
  Which is published as a vital adjunct to our cultural groups?"
"This year some of us are learning all *The Lady's Not for
                                                    Burning*
  For a poetry recital we are giving to the troops."

"Mr Betjeman, I grovel before critics of the novel,
  Tell me, if I don't offend you, have you written one yourself?
You haven't? Then the one I wrote is (not that I expect a notice)
  Something I would like to send you, just for keeping on your
                                                    shelf."

"Betjeman, I bet your racket brings you in a pretty packet
  Raising the old lecture curtain, writing titbits here and there.
But, by Jove, your hair is thinner, since you came to us in Pinner,
  And you're fatter now, I'm certain. What you need is country
                                                    air."

This and that way conversation, till I turn in desperation
  To a kind face (can I doubt it?) mercifully mute so far.
"Oh," it says, "I missed the lecture, wasn't it on architecture?
  Do please tell me all about it, what you do and who you are."

Caprice

I sat only two tables off from the one I was sacked at,
　　　Just three years ago,
And here was another meringue like the one which I hacked at
　　　When pride was brought low
And the coffee arrived—the place which she had to use tact at
　　　For striking the blow.

"I'm making some changes next week in the organisation
　　　And though I admire
Your work for me, John, yet the need to increase circulation
　　　Means you must retire:
An outlook more global than yours is the qualification
　　　I really require."

Oh sickness of sudden betrayal! Oh purblind Creator!
　　　Oh friendship denied!
I stood on the pavement and wondered which loss was the
　　　　　　　　　　　　　　　　greater—
　　　The cash or the pride.
Explanations to make to subordinates, bills to pay later
　　　Churned up my inside.

I fell on my feet. But what of those others, worse treated,
　　　Your memory's ghosts,
In gloomy bed-sitters in Fulham, ill-fed and unheated,
　　　Applying for posts?
Do they haunt their successors and you as you sit here repleted
　　　With entrées and roasts?

Cricket Master
(AN INCIDENT)

My undergraduate eyes beholding,
    As I climbed your slope, Cat Hill:
Emerald chestnut fans unfolding,
    Symbols of my hope, Cat Hill,
What cared I for past disaster,
Applicant for cricket master,
Nothing much of cricket knowing,
Conscious but of money owing?
    Somehow I would cope, Cat Hill.

"The sort of man we want must be prepared
To take our first eleven. Many boys
From last year's team are with us. You will find
Their bowling's pretty good and they are keen."
"And so am I, Sir, very keen indeed."
Oh where's mid-on? And what is silly point?
Do six balls make an over? Help me, God!
"Of course you'll get some first-class cricket too;
The MCC send down an A team here."
My bluff had worked. I sought the common-room,
Of last term's pipe-smoke faintly redolent.
It waited empty with its worn arm-chairs
For senior bums to mine, when in there came
A fierce old eagle in whose piercing eye
I saw that instant-registered dislike
Of all unhealthy aesthetes such as me.

292

"I'm Winters—you're our other new recruit
And here's another new man—Barnstaple."
He introduced a thick Devonian.
"Let's go and have some practice in the nets.
You'd better go in first." With but one pad,
No gloves, and knees that knocked in utter fright,
Vainly I tried to fend the hail of balls
Hurled at my head by brutal Barnstaple
And at my shins by Winters. Nasty quiet
Followed my poor performance. When the sun
Had sunk behind the fringe of Hadley Wood
And Barnstaple and I were left alone
Among the ash-trays of the common-room,
He murmured in his soft West-country tones:
"D'you know what Winters told me, Betjeman?
He didn't think you'd ever held a bat."

The trusting boys returned. "We're jolly glad
You're on our side, Sir, in the trial match."
"But I'm no good at all." "Oh yes, you are."
When I was out first ball, they said "Bad luck!
You hadn't got your eye in." Still I see
Barnstaple's smile of undisguised contempt,
Still feel the sting of Winters' silent sneer.
Disgraced, demoted to the seventh game,
Even the boys had lost their faith in me.
God guards his aesthetes. If by chance these lines
Are read by one who in some common-room
Has had his bluff called, let him now take heart:
In every school there is a sacred place
More holy than the chapel. Ours was yours:
I mean, of course, the first-eleven pitch.

Here in the welcome break from morning work,
The heavier boys, of milk and biscuits full,
Sat on the roller while we others pushed
Its weighty cargo slowly up and down.
We searched the grass for weeds, caressed the turf,
Lay on our stomachs squinting down its length
To see that all was absolutely smooth.

    The prize-day neared. And, on the eve before,
We masters hung our college blazers out
In readiness for tomorrow. Matron made
A final survey of the boys' best clothes—
Clean shirts. Clean collars. "Rice, your jacket's torn.
Bring it to me this instant!" Supper done,
Barnstaple drove his round-nosed Morris out
And he and I and Vera Spencer-Clarke,
Our strong gymnasium mistress, squashed ourselves
Into the front and rattled to The Cock.

    Sweet bean-fields then were scenting Middlesex;
Narrow lanes led between the dairy-farms
To ponds reflecting weather-boarded inns.
There on the wooden bench outside The Cock
Sat Barnstaple, Miss Spencer-Clarke and I,
At last forgetful of tomorrow's dread
And gazing into sky-blue Hertfordshire.
Three pints for Barnstaple, three halves for me,
Sherry of course for Vera Spencer-Clarke.

    Pre-prize-day nerves? Or too much bitter beer?
What had that evening done to Barnstaple?
I only know that singing we returned;
The more we sang, the faster Barnstaple
Drove his old Morris, swerving down the drive

And in and out the rhododendron clumps,
Over the very playing-field itself,
And then—oh horror!—right across the pitch
Not once, but twice or thrice. The mark of tyres
Next day was noticed at the Parents' Match.
That settled Barnstaple and he was sacked,
While I survived him, lasting three more terms.

Shops and villas have invaded
    Your chestnut quiet there, Cat Hill.
Cricket field and pitch degraded,
    Nothing did they spare, Cat Hill.
Vera Spencer-Clarke is married
And the rest are dead and buried;
I am thirty summers older,
Richer, wickeder and colder,
    Fuller too of care, Cat Hill.

On Leaving Wantage 1972

I like the way these old brick garden walls
Unevenly run down to Letcombe Brook.
I like the mist of green about the elms
In earliest leaf-time. More intensely green
The duck-weed undulates; a mud-grey trout
Hovers and darts away at my approach.

    From rumpled beds on far-off new estates,
From houses over shops along the square,
From red-brick villas somewhat further out,
Ringers arrive, converging on the tower.
    Third Sunday after Easter. Public ways
Reek faintly yet of last night's fish and chips.
The plumes of smoke from upright chimney-pots
Denote the death of last week's Sunday press,
While this week's waits on many a step and sill
Unopened, folded, supplements and all.

    Suddenly on the unsuspecting air
The bells clash out. It seems a miracle
That leaf and flower should never even stir
In such great waves of medieval sound:
They ripple over roofs to fields and farms
So that 'the fellowship of Christ's religion'
Is roused to breakfast, church or sleep again.

    From this wide vale, where all our married lives
We two have lived, we now are whirled away

Momently clinging to the things we knew—
Friends, footpaths, hedges, house and animals—
Till, borne along like twigs and bits of straw,
We sink below the sliding stream of time.

On a Painting by Julius Olsson R.A.

———————

Over what bridge-fours has that luscious sea
    Shone sparkling from its frame of bronzéd gold
    Since waves of foaming opalescence roll'd
One warm spring morning, back in twenty-three,
All through the day, from breakfast-time till tea,
    When Julius Olsson, feeling rather cold,
    Packed up his easel and, contented, stroll'd
Back to St. Ives, its fisher-folk and quay.

Over what bridge-parties, cloche-hat, low waist,
    Has looked that seascape, once so highly-prized,
    From Lenygon-green walls, until, despised—
"It isn't art. It's only just a knack"—
    It fell from grace. Now, in a change of taste,
See Julius Olsson slowly strolling back.

Beaumaris
December 21, 1963

Low-shot light of a sharp December
  Shifting, lifted a morning haze:
Opening fans of smooth sea-water
  Touched in silence the tiny bays:
In bright Beaumaris the people waited—
  This was Laurelie's day of days.

At the northern end of the street a vista
  Of sunlit woodland; and south, a tower;
Across the water from Hansom's terrace,
  The glass'd reflection of Penmaenmawr:
High on her balcony Laurelie Williams
  Waved the shovel and shot the shower.

Down on us all fell heated ha'pence,
  Up to her all of us looked for more:
Laurelie Williams, Laurelie Williams—
  Lovelier now than ever before
With your straight black hair and your fresh complexion:
  Diamond-bright was the brooch you wore.

Life be kind to you, Laurelie Williams,
  With girlhood over and marriage begun:

Queuing for buses and rearing children,
   Washing the dishes and missing the fun,
May you still recall how you flung the coppers
   On bright Beaumaris in winter sun.

[It was a Christmas-tide custom at Beaumaris, Anglesey,
for the Queen of the Hunt Ball to throw heated halfpence
from a shovel to the crowd below.]

Hearts Together

How emerald the chalky depths
　　Below the Dancing Ledge!
We pulled the jelly-fishes up
　　And threw them in the hedge
That with its stones and sea-pink tufts
　　Ran to the high cliff edge.

And lucky was the jelly-fish
　　That melted in the sun
And poured its vitals on the turf
　　In self-effacing fun,
Like us who in each other's arms
　　Were seed and soul in one.

O rational the happy bathe
　　An hour before our tea,
When you were swimming breast-stroke, all
　　Along the rocking sea
And, in between the waves, explain'd
　　The Universe to me.

The Dorset sun stream'd on our limbs
　　And scorch'd our hinder parts:
We gazed into the pebble beach
　　And so discussed the arts,
O logical and happy we
　　Emancipated hearts.

Aldershot Crematorium

Between the swimming-pool and cricket-ground
   How straight the crematorium driveway lies!
And little puffs of smoke without a sound
   Show what we loved dissolving in the skies,
Dear hands and feet and laughter-lighted face
And silk that hinted at the body's grace.

But no-one seems to know quite what to say
   (Friends are so altered by the passing years):
"Well, anyhow, it's not so cold today"—
   And thus we try to dissipate our fears.
'*I am the Resurrection and the Life*':
Strong, deep and painful, doubt inserts the knife.

The Newest Bath Guide

Of all the gay places the world can afford,
By gentle and simple for pastime ador'd,
Fine balls, and fine concerts, fine buildings, and springs,
Fine walks, and fine views, and a thousand fine things
(Not to mention the sweet situation and air),
What place, my dear mother, with Bath can compare?
            Christopher Anstey: THE NEW BATH GUIDE, 1766

It is two hundred years since he got in his stride
And cantered away with *The New Bath Guide.*
His spondees and dactyls had quite a success,
And sev'ral editions were called from the press.
That guidebook consisted of letters in rhyme
On the follies and fashions of Bath at the time:
    I notice a quiver come over my pen
    As I think of the follies and fashions since then. . . .

Proud City of Bath with your crescents and squares,
Your hoary old Abbey and playbills and chairs,
Your plentiful chapels where preachers would preach
(And a different doctrine expounded in each),
Your gallant assemblies where squires took their daughters,
Your medicinal springs where their wives took the waters,
The terraces trim and the comely young wenches,
The cobbled back streets with their privies and stenches—
    How varied and human did Bath then appear
    As the roar of the Avon rolled up from the weir.

In those days, no doubt, there was not so much taste:
But now there's so much it has all run to waste
In working out methods of cutting down cost—
So that mouldings, proportion and texture are lost
In a uniform nothingness. (This I first find
In the terrible 'Tech' with its pointed behind.)
Now houses are 'units' and people are digits,
And Bath has been planned into quarters for midgets.
    Official designs are aggressively neuter,
    The Puritan work of an eyeless computer.

Goodbye to old Bath! We who loved you are sorry
They're carting you off by developer's lorry.

In Memory of George Whitby, Architect

Si monumentum requiris . . . the church in which we are sitting,
Its firm square ceiling supported by fluted Corinthian columns
In groups of three at the corners, its huge semi-circular windows
Lighting the elegant woodwork and plaster panels and gilding:
Look around you, behold the work of Nicholas Hawksmoor.

Si monumentum requiris . . . not far away and behind us
Rises the dome of Saint Paul's, around it a forest of steeples
In Portland stone and in lead, a human and cheerful collection,
Mostly by Christopher Wren, Nicholas Hawksmoor's master.
Si monumentum requiris . . . at the western gate of the City
Behold the Law's new fortress, ramparting over the Bailey
In cream-coloured clear-cut ashlar on grim granitic
                                            foundations—
But, like all good citizens, paying regard to its neighbours,
Florid baroque on one side, plain commercial the other.

This is your work, George Whitby, whose name to-day we
                                            remember:
From Donald McMorran and Dance to Wren and Nicholas
                                            Hawksmoor,
You stand in a long tradition; and we who are left salute you.

[Delivered at Saint Mary Woolnoth, 29 March 1973.]

Delectable Duchy

Where yonder villa hogs the sea
Was open cliff to you and me.
The many-coloured cara's fill
The salty marsh to Shilla Mill.
And, foreground to the hanging wood,
Are toilets where the cattle stood.
The mint and meadowsweet would scent
The brambly lane by which we went;
Now, as we near the ocean roar,
A smell of deep-fry haunts the shore.
In pools beyond the reach of tides
The Senior Service carton glides,
And on the sand the surf-line lisps
With wrappings of potato crisps.
The breakers bring with merry noise
Tribute of broken plastic toys
And lichened spears of blackthorn glitter
With harvest of the August litter.

Here in the late October light
See Cornwall, a pathetic sight,
Raddled and put upon and tired
And looking somewhat over-hired,
Remembering in the autumn air
The years when she was young and fair—
Those golden and unpeopled bays,
The shadowy cliffs and sheep-worn ways,

The white unpopulated surf,
The thyme- and mushroom-scented turf,
The slate-hung farms, the oil-lit chapels,
Thin elms and lemon-coloured apples—
Going and gone beyond recall
Now she is free for "One and All."*

One day a tidal wave will break
Before the breakfasters awake
And sweep the cara's out to sea,
The oil, the tar, and you and me,
And leave in windy criss-cross motion
A waste of undulating ocean
With, jutting out, a second Scilly,
The isles of Roughtor and Brown Willy.

* The motto of Cornwall.

The Costa Blanca
Two sonnets

SHE

The Costa Blanca! Skies without a stain!
Eric and I at almond-blossom time
Came here and fell in love with it. The climb
Under the pine trees, up the dusty lane
To Casa Kenilworth, brought back again
Our honeymoon, when I was in my prime.
Good-bye democracy and smoke and grime:
Eric retires next year. We're off to Spain!

We've got the perfect site beside the shore,
Owned by a charming Spaniard, Miguel,
Who says that he is quite prepared to sell
And build our Casa for us *and*, what's more,
Preposterously cheaply. We have found
Delightful English people living round.

HE (five years later)

Mind if I see your *Mail*? We used to share
Our *Telegraph* with people who've returned—
The lucky sods! I'll tell you what I've learned:
If you come out here put aside the fare
To England. *I'd* run like a bloody hare
If I'd a chance, and how we both have yearned
To see our Esher lawn. I think we've earned
A bit of what we had once over there.

That Dago caught the wife and me all right!
Here on this tideless, tourist-littered sea
We're stuck. You'd hate it too if you were me:
There's no piped water on the bloody site.
Our savings gone, we climb the stony path
Back to the house with scorpions in the bath.

Lenten Thoughts of a High Anglican

Isn't she lovely, 'the Mistress'?
  With her wide-apart grey-green eyes,
The droop of her lips and, when she smiles,
  Her glance of amused surprise?

How nonchalantly she wears her clothes,
  How expensive they are as well!
And the sound of her voice is as soft and deep
  As the Christ Church tenor bell.

But why do I call her 'the Mistress'
  Who know not her way of life?
Because she has more of a cared-for air
  Than many a legal wife.

How elegantly she swings along
  In the vapoury incense veil;
The angel choir must pause in song
  When she kneels at the altar rail.

The parson said that we shouldn't stare
  Around when we come to church,
Or the Unknown God we are seeking
  May forever elude our search.

But I hope the preacher will not think
  It unorthodox and odd
If I add that I glimpse in 'the Mistress'
  A hint of the Unknown God.

[This is about a lady I see on Sunday mornings in a London church.]

Executive

I am a young executive. No cuffs than mine are cleaner;
I have a Slimline brief-case and I use the firm's Cortina.
In every roadside hostelry from here to Burgess Hill
The *maîtres d'hôtel* all know me well and let me sign the bill.

You ask me what it is I do. Well actually, you know,
I'm partly a liaison man and partly P.R.O.
Essentially I integrate the current export drive
And basically I'm viable from ten o'clock till five.

For vital off-the-record work—that's talking transport-wise—
I've a scarlet Aston-Martin—and does she go? She flies!
Pedestrians and dogs and cats—we mark them down for
                                                slaughter.
I also own a speed-boat which has never touched the water.

She's built of fibre-glass, of course. I call her 'Mandy Jane'
After a bird I used to know—No soda, please, just plain—
And how did I acquire her? Well to tell you about that
And to put you in the picture I must wear my other hat.

I do some mild developing. The sort of place I need
Is a quiet country market town that's rather run to seed.
A luncheon and a drink or two, a little *savoir faire*—
I fix the Planning Officer, the Town Clerk and the Mayor.

And if some preservationist attempts to interfere
A 'dangerous structure' notice from the Borough Engineer
Will settle any buildings that are standing in our way—
The modern style, sir, with respect, has really come to stay.

Meditation on a Constable Picture

Go back in your mind to that Middlesex height
Whence Constable painted the breeze and the light
As down out of Hampstead descended the chaise
To the wide-spreading valley, half-hidden in haze:

The slums of St. Giles's, St. Mary'bone's farms,
And Chelsea's and Battersea's riverside charms,
The palace of Westminster, towers of the Abbey
And Mayfair so elegant, Soho so shabby,

The mansions where lilac hangs over brown brick,
The ceilings whose plaster is floral and thick,
The new stucco terraces facing the park,
The odorous alleyways, narrow and dark,

The hay barges sailing, the watermen rowing
On a Thames unembanked which was wide and slow-flowing,
The street-cries rebounding from pavements and walls
And, steeple-surrounded, the dome of St. Paul's.

No market nor High Street nor square was the same
In that cluster of villages, London by name.
Ere slabs are too tall and we Cockneys too few,
Let us keep what is left of the London we knew.

A Wembley Lad

To every ducal palace
  When days were old and slow,
Me and my sister Alice
  By charabanc would go.

My new position such is
  In halls of social fame
That many a duke and duchess
  I know by Christian name

Belvoir, Blenheim, Chatsworth,
  Luncheon, dinner, tea,
And stay the night—ah!—*that's* worth
  All the world to me.

And as for sister Alice
  She would not like it here:
She'd be nervous in a palace
  And call the duchess 'dear'.

So I'm off to the Bath Assembly
  With head and heart held high
But palaceless Alice in Wembley
  Knows how alone go I.

County

God save me from the Porkers,
  God save me from their sons,
Their noisy tweedy sisters
  Who follow with the guns,
The old and scheming mother,
  Their futures that she plann'd,
The ghastly younger brother
  Who married into land.

Their shots along the valley
  Draw blood out of the sky,
The wounded pheasants rally
  As hobnailed boots go by.
Where once the rabbit scampered
  The waiting copse is still
As Porker fat and pampered
  Comes puffing up the hill.

"A left and right! Well done, sir!
  They're falling in the road;
And here's your other gun, sir."
  "Don't talk. You're here to load."
He grabs his gun, not seeing
  A thing but birds in air,
And blows them out of being
  With self-indulgent stare.

Triumphant after shooting
   He still commands the scene,
His Land Rover comes hooting
   Beaters and dogs between.
Then dinner with a neighbour,
   It doesn't matter which,
Conservative or Labour,
   So long as he is rich.

A *faux-bonhomme* and dull as well,
   All pedigree and purse,
We must admit that, though he's hell,
   His womenfolk are worse.
Bright in their county gin sets
   They tug their ropes of pearls
And smooth their tailored twin-sets
   And drop the names of earls.

Loud talk of meets and marriages
   And tax-evasion's heard
In many first-class carriages
   While servants travel third.
"My dear, I have to spoil them too—
   Or who would do the chores?
Well, here we are at Waterloo,
   I'll drop you at the Stores."

God save me from the Porkers,
   The pathos of their lives,
The strange example that they set
   To new-rich farmers' wives

317

Glad to accept their bounty
And worship from afar,
And think of them as county—
County is what they are.

Greek Orthodox
To the Reverend T. P. Symonds

What did I see when first I went to Greece?
Shades of the Sixth across the Peloponnese.
Though clear the clean-cut Doric temple shone
Still droned the voice of Mr Gidney on;
"That ὅτι? Can we take its meaning here
Wholly as interrogative?" Edward Lear,
Show me the Greece of wrinkled olive boughs
Above red earth; thin goats, instead of cows,
Each with its bell; the shallow terraced soil;
The stone-built wayside shrine; the yellow oil;
The tiled and cross-shaped church, who knows how old
Its ashlar walls of honey-coloured gold?
Three centuries or ten? Of course, there'll be
The long meander off to find the key.

The domed interior swallows up the day.
Here, where to light a candle is to pray,
The candle flame shows up the almond eyes
Of local saints who view with no surprise
Their martyrdoms depicted upon walls
On which the filtered daylight faintly falls.
The flame shows up the cracked paint—sea-green blue
And red and gold, with grained wood showing through—
Of much-kissed ikons, dating from, perhaps,
The fourteenth century. There across the apse,

Ikon- and oleograph-adorned, is seen
The semblance of an English chancel screen.

"With *oleographs*?" you say. "Oh, what a pity!
Surely the diocese has some committee
Advising it on taste?" It is not so.
Thus vigorously does the old tree grow,
By persecution pruned, watered with blood,
Its living roots deep in pre-Christian mud,
It needs no bureaucratical protection.
It is its own perpetual resurrection.
Or take the galleon metaphor—it rides
Serenely over controversial tides
Triumphant to the Port of Heaven, its home,
With one sail missing—that's the Pope's in Rome.

Vicar, I hope it will not be a shock
To find this village has no 'eight o'clock'.
Those bells you heard at eight were being rung
For matins of a sort but matins sung.
Soon will another set of bells begin
And all the villagers come crowding in.
The painted boats rock empty by the quay
Feet crunch on gravel, faintly beats the sea.
From the domed church, as from the sky, look down
The Pantocrator's searching eyes of brown,
With one serene all-comprehending stare
On farmer, fisherman and millionaire.

Dilton Marsh Halt

Was it worth keeping the Halt open,
  We thought as we looked at the sky
Red through the spread of the cedar-tree,
  With the evening train gone by?

Yes, we said, for in summer the anglers use it,
  Two and sometimes three
Will bring their catches of rods and poles and perches
  To Westbury, home to tea.

There isn't a porter. The platform is made of sleepers.
  The guard of the last up-train puts out the light
And high over lorries and cattle the Halt unwinking
  Waits through the Wiltshire night.

O housewife safe in the comprehensive churning
  Of the Warminster launderette!
O husband down at the depot with car in car-park!
  The Halt is waiting yet.

And when all the horrible roads are finally done for,
  And there's no more petrol left in the world to burn,
Here to the Halt from Salisbury and from Bristol
  Steam trains will return.

Loneliness

The last year's leaves are on the beech:
    The twigs are black; the cold is dry;
To deeps beyond the deepest reach
    The Easter bells enlarge the sky.
Oh! ordered metal clatter-clang!
Is yours the song the angels sang?
You fill my heart with joy and grief—
Belief! Belief! And unbelief . . .
    And, though you tell me I shall die,
    You say not how or when or why.

Indifferent the finches sing,
    Unheeding roll the lorries past:
What misery will this year bring
    Now spring is in the air at last?
For, sure as blackthorn bursts to snow,
Cancer in some of us will grow,
The tasteful crematorium door
Shuts out for some the furnace roar;
    But church-bells open on the blast
    Our loneliness, so long and vast.

Back from Australia

Cocooned in Time, at this inhuman height,
    The packaged food tastes neutrally of clay.
    We never seem to catch the running day
But travel on in everlasting night
With all the chic accoutrements of flight:
    Lotions and essences in neat array
    And yet another plastic cup and tray.
"Thank you *so* much. Oh no, I'm quite all right."

At home in Cornwall hurrying autumn skies
    Leave Bray Hill barren, Stepper jutting bare,
        And hold the moon above the sea-wet sand.
The very last of late September dies
    In frosty silence and the hills declare
        How vast the sky is, looked at from the land.

The Manor House, Hale, near Liverpool

In early twilight I can hear
  A faintly-ticking clock,
While near and far and far and near
  Is Liverpool baroque.

And when the movement meets the hour
  To tell it, stroke by stroke,
"Rococo," says the pendulum,
  "Baroque, baroque, baroak."

Encrusted vases crowd the hall,
  Dark paintings grace the stairs
And from the wild wind's harp withal
  Sound soft Lancastrian airs.

On a bend sable three garbs or—
  Th'achievements hold my gaze;
Though fierce without the tempests roar
  The banner scarcely sways.

O'er Mersey mud and Mersey flood,
  Rust-red above the holly
How trimly rides the brick façade,
  As flimsy as a folly.

The Manor House, the Green, the church—
 From Runcorn to West Kirby
You will not find howe'er you search
 So sweet a *rus in urbe*.

Shattered Image

"... and that you did with said intent procure
the aforesaid Sidney Alexander Green
being at the time a minor. . . ." Aleco—
He always was just "Aleco" to me,
The shy turn of the head, the troubled eyes,
The freckled stubbiness, the curve of thigh,
Nape of the neck—my trusting Aleco.

Amateur typing by a constable
Filled in the gaps along official buff.

An after-door-chime silence. Strawberry pink
This leadless glaze and yet I can't be sick,
And strawberry pink the basin and the bath.
In bathrooms people often kill themselves.
And this new flat is such a good address—
One-seven Alvarez Cloister, Double-you-one,
(No need to put in Upper Berkeley Street):
Under-floor heating, pale green wall-to-wall,
Victoriana in the sitting-room.
Mother insisted on the powder-blue.

When Charlie got the maximum two years
He said the lack of privacy was the worst—
Having two others with you, boring talk,
Racing and football, and the dreadful stench
From that filled bucket all the bloody night.

Of course they found out why he was inside—
And that's a thing they never will forgive,
Touching the little children, better pooves
Or murderers, they said. I didn't touch—
Well not in the way that Charlie used to do—
". . . and that you did with said intent procure. . . ."
How many Tuinal have I got left?
Will twenty do it? But I mustn't try,
Especially now that I'm a Catholic.

"It is the thoughts, my son, that lead to acts
Which cry to heaven for vengeance.
Ye'll try to put those wicked thoughts away,
Ye're truly sorry for them, aren't ye now?
God in His mercy sent ye here to me.
But British justice—Oi can't help ye there.
Let me have word of where they're sending you.
Oi'll tell the Catholic chaplain. Holy Church
Never deserts her sons. Your penance now. . . ."

O Holy Mary! What will Mother say?
She takes the *Standard* and the *Daily Mail*.

Now let me see, let me have time to think.
What have I done that they could get me for?
Who could have talked? And when, and where . . .
                                          and what?
Look at it calmly. What can they really prove?
What is the worst that Aleco could have said?
And will they take his word against my own?
I'm only charged—the case unproven still;

I'm innocent until they've proved the charge.
They must have set a trap for him, the brutes.
Who could have set it? Not his brother Jim.
He came to Minehead with us in July.
The mother? No. She couldn't have. She's a pet.
As for the father—well, he doesn't count.
Never trust women, though. I'll ring up George.

"What rotten luck, what really rotten luck!
And if I could, you know I'd help you, Rex.
But frankly this is not a case for me.
I'm in another purlieu of the law,
Conveyancing. It's rather as if you asked
An obstetrician to do a dentist's job—
Not that we don't respect each other's skills.
I'll give you my advice for what it's worth
And that's, get hold of a solicitor.
Maybe your family man is not the one
To whom you'd really want to spill the beans.
Well, try another. Who did Charlie use?
It doesn't matter whether he got off
Or whether he didn't, Rex. The law's the law.
A lot depends upon the Magistrates.
They may dismiss the case. On the other hand
They may commit you, or you may be fined.
All sorts of things can happen . . . (That's the child—
Olivia's left me here to baby-sit.
It makes me hanker after bachelor days.)
So I must go. . . . Good luck—and keep in touch."

"Good God, not that, but this is serious.
Who says you've done it? Have they any proof?
Now look here, Rex, I've known you long enough,
Since we were kids in fact, and I will swear
You never could have done a thing like that,
Who's had the cheek—no, damned malicious spite—
To make this filthy charge? By God, old Rex,
Eileen and I have always looked to you
As someone, somehow, who was different.
I mean, you never fooled about with tarts.
I said to Eileen just the other night
'Some people don't need what we need, old girl.
Perhaps,' I said, 'if I'd not played around
I might have made the running—look at Rex,
Started from scratch, now top executive;
And look at me, still trailing on behind!
Of course it takes all sorts to make a world
And God knows *what* we do when we get pissed
But honestly I've never been so pissed
I couldn't tell a woman from a man.'
Look here old man, you've been so good to me—
Remember how we went to Ambleside
And slept the night on Dollywagon Pike?
I wouldn't have dared to do it on my own.
Remember camp at Camber, and your friend—
That funny chap so keen on railway trains?
And then the Major, I forget his name,
Who asked us to his house in Italy?

But look here Rex, d'you really mean to say
You did it stone-cold sober? Are you sure?

329

What was his age? Good God, man, let me think. . . .
We all have somewhere where we draw the line
And frankly I must draw the line at that.
I'll tell you one thing, Rex, I give my word
Eileen shall never hear of this from me.
I'd like a day or two to think it out.
Just now I simply feel inclined to puke.
I'm sorry I must go. No, let me pay."

"D'you like a slice of lemon with it? Good.
Look here, I'm awfully sorry about this.
Douglas has told me, and I thought it best
To have a private word with you myself.
You see, it's very awkward. Usually
I never interfere with private life.
Live and let live, and, well, your life's your own.
I'd never take a prudish line myself,
Although that sort of thing is not my taste—
But you're intelligent and civilized.
Now had you been the porter or a clerk
It wouldn't have mattered much. But then, you see
Our business is—well simply what it's called,
Public Relations. And our image counts
Not with our clients only, but beyond
In the hard world where men are selling things.
And with the sort of bloke we're dealing with,
Frankly, we can't afford the sort of slur
A case like yours brings with it.
I much appreciate your work for us,
Your contacts and the valuable accounts
That may have stayed with us because of you.

I know you'll understand me when I say
This isn't personal. I have to think
Of all your colleagues and our clients too.
We've got some tough competitors. I'll leave
The ball in your court now, and I suggest
Instead of letting me ask you to resign
You send a note to *me*, in which you say
That resignation is your own idea
And unconnected with your work for us—
Something quite neutral which will not reflect
Any discredit upon either side.
Good luck, goodbye. And would you, on your way
Please tell Miss Wood to bring me in my mail."

A Ballad of the Investiture 1969

The moon was in the Cambridge sky
    And bathed Great Court in silver light
When Hastings-Bass and Woods and I
    And quiet Elizabeth, tall and white,
With that sure clarity of mind
Which comes to those who've truly dined,

    Reluctant rose to say good-night;
And all of us were bathed the while
In the large moon of Harry's* smile.

Then, sir, you said what shook me through
    So that my courage almost fails:
"I want a poem out of you
    On my Investiture in Wales."
Leaving, you slightly raised your hand—
"And that," you said, "is a command."

    For years I wondered what to do
And now, at last, I've thought it better
To write a kind of rhyming letter.

Spring frocks, silk hats at morning's prime,
    One of a varied congregation
I glided out, at breakfast time,
    With Euston's Earl from Euston Station,

* The Reverend H. A. Williams, then Fellow and Dean of
Chapel of Trinity College, Cambridge, now a monk of the
Community of The Resurrection, Mirfield.

Through Willesden's bleak industrial parts,
Through Watford on to leafy Herts
    Bound for a single destination.
Warwicks and Staffs were soaked in rain;
So was the open Cheshire plain.

The railway crossed the river Dee
    Where Mary called the cattle home,
The wide marsh widened into sea,
    The wide sea whitened into foam.
The green Welsh hills came steeply down
To many a cara-circled town—
    Prestatyn, Rhyl—till here were we,
As mountains rose on either hand,
Awed strangers in a foreign land.

I can't forget the climbing street
    Below Caernarvon's castle wall,
The dragon flag, the tramp of feet,
    The gulls' perturbed, insistent call,
Bow-windowed house-fronts painted new,
Heads craning out to get a view,
    A mounting tension stilling all—
And, once within the castle gate,
The murmuring hush of those who wait.

Wet banners flap. The sea mist clears.
    Colours are backed by silver stone.
Moustached hereditary peers
    Are ranged in rows behind the throne.
With lifted sword the rites begin.

Earl Marshal leads the victims in.

    The Royal Family waits alone.
Now television cameras whirr
Like cats at last induced to purr.

You know those moments that there are
When, lonely under moon and star,
    You wait upon a beach?
Suddenly all Creation's near
And complicated things are clear,
    Eternity in reach!
So we who watch the action done—
A mother to her kneeling son
    The Crown of office giving—
Can hardly tell, so rapt our gaze
Whether but seconds pass or days
    Or in what age we're living.

You knelt a boy, you rose a man.
And thus your lonelier life began.

14 November, 1973

Hundreds of birds in the air
  And millions of leaves on the pavement,
And Westminster bells ringing on
  To palace and people outside—
And all for the words 'I will'
  To love's most willing enslavement.
All of our people rejoice
  With venturous bridegroom and bride.

Trumpets blare at the entrance,
  Multitudes crane and sway.
Glow, white lily in London,
  You are high in our hearts today!

A Mind's Journey to Diss

Dear Mary,
    Yes, it will be bliss
To go with you by train to Diss,
Your walking shoes upon your feet;
We'll meet, my sweet, at Liverpool Street.
That levellers we may be reckoned
Perhaps we'd better travel second;
Or, lest reporters on us burst,
Perhaps we'd better travel first.
Above the chimney-pots we'll go
Through Stepney, Stratford-atte-Bow
And out to where the Essex marsh
Is filled with houses new and harsh
Till, Witham pass'd, the landscape yields
On left and right to widening fields,
Flint church-towers sparkling in the light,
Black beams and weather-boarding white,
Cricket-bat willows silvery green
And elmy hills with brooks between,
Maltings and saltings, stack and quay
And, somewhere near, the grey North Sea;
Then further gentle undulations
With lonelier and less frequent stations,
Till in the dimmest place of all
The train slows down into a crawl
And stops in silence. . . . Where is this?
Dear Mary Wilson, this is Diss.

Fruit

Now with the threat growing still greater within me,
   The Church dead that was hopelessly over-restored,
The fruit picked from these yellowing Worcestershire orchards
   What is left to me, Lord?

To wait until next year's bloom at the end of the garden
   Foams to the Malvern Hills, like an inland sea,
And to know that its fruit, dropping in autumn stillness,
   May have outlived me.

Inland Waterway

He who by peaceful inland water steers
Bestirs himself when a new lock appears.
Slow swing the gates: slow sinks the water down;
This lower Stratford seems another town.
The meadows which the youthful Shakespeare knew
Are left behind, and, sliding into view,
Come reaches of the Avon, mile on mile,
Church, farm and mill and lover-leaned-on stile,
Till where the tower of Tewkesbury soars to heaven
Our homely Avon joins the haughty Severn.
Sweet is the fluting of the blackbird's note,
Sweet is the ripple from the narrow boat.

Your Majesty, our friend of many years,
Confirms a triumph now the moment nears:
The lock you have re-opened will set free
The heart of England to the open sea.

[Declaimed at the opening of the Upper Avon at Stratford
in the presence of the Queen Mother and Robert Aickman,
founder of the Inland Waterways Association, on 1st June,
1974.]

For Patrick, aetat: LXX*

How glad I am that I was bound apprentice
To Patrick's London of the 1920s.
Estranged from parents (as we all were then),
Let into Oxford and let out again,
Kind fortune led me, how I do not know,
To that Venetian flat-cum-studio
Where Patrick wrought his craft in Yeoman's Row.

For Patrick wrote and wrote. He wrote to live:
What cash he had left over he would give
To many friends, and friends of friends he knew,
So that the 'Yeo' to one great almshouse grew—
Not a teetotal almshouse, for I hear
The clink of glasses in my memory's ear,
The spurt of soda as the whisky rose
Bringing its heady scent to memory's nose
Along with smells one otherwise forgets:
Hairwash from Delhez, Turkish cigarettes,
The reek of Ronuk on a parquet floor
As parties came cascading through the door:
Elizabeth Ponsonby in leopard-skins
And Robert Byron and the Ruthven twins,
Ti Cholmondeley, Joan Eyres Monsell, Bridget Parsons,
And earls and baronets and squires and squarsons—
"Avis, it's *ages*! . . . Hamish, but its *aeons* . . ."
(Once more that record, the Savoy Orpheans).

* Patrick Balfour, 3rd Baron Kinross, b. 1904.

Leader in London's preservation lists
And least Wykehamical of Wykehamists:
Clan chief of Paddington's distinguished set,
Pray go on living to a hundred yet!

The Last Laugh

I made hay while the sun shone.
  My work sold.
Now, if the harvest is over
  And the world cold,
Give me the bonus of laughter
  As I lose hold.

1940

As I lay in the bath the air was filling with bells;
Over the steam of the window, out in the sun,
From the village below came hoarsely the patriot yells
And I knew that the next World War had at last begun.
As I lay in the bath I saw things clear in my head:
Ten to one they'd not bother to bomb us here,
Ten to one that they'd make for the barracks instead—
As I lay in the bath, I certainly saw things clear.
As I started to dry, came a humming of expectation;
Was it the enemy planes or was it young Jack
And the rest of the gang who have passed in their aviation
Setting across to Berlin to make an attack?
As the water gurgled away I put on a shirt,
I put on my trousers, and parted what's left of my hair,
And the humming above increased to a roaring spurt
And a shuddering thud drove all the bells from the air,
And a shuddering thud drove ev'rything else to silence.
There wasn't a sound, there wasn't a soul in the street,
There wasn't a wall to the house, there wasn't a staircase;
There was only the bathroom linoleum under my feet.
I called, as I always do, I called to Penelope,
I called to the strong with the petulant call of the weak;
There lay the head and the brown eyes dizzily open,
And the mouth apart but the tongue unable to speak;
There lay the nut-shaped head that I love for ever,
The thin little neck, the turned-up nose and the charms
Of pouting lips and lashes and circling eyebrows;

But where was the body? and where were the legs and arms?
And somewhere about I must seek in the broken building
Somewhere about they'll probably find my son.
Oh bountiful Gods of the air! Oh Science and Progress!
You great big wonderful world! Oh what have you done?

Interior Decorator

Eternal youth is in his eyes;
  Now he has freshened up his lips;
He slicks his hair and feigns surprise,
  Then glances at his fingertips.

'My dears, but yes, *of course* I know,
  Though why you think of asking *me*
I can't imagine, even though
  It rather *is* my cup of tea.

You see, my dears, I'm old—so old
  I'll *have* to give myself away—
So don't be flattering when you're told—
  But I was *sixty* yesterday.

And so, of course, I knew them *all*,
  And I was with them when they went
To Basil's marvellous *matelot* ball
  At Bedstead, somewhere down in Kent.

I was in decorating then,
  And Basil said the job was mine,
And, though I shouldn't say it, when
  I'd finished, it was just *divine*.

A *hideous* house, inside and out—
  And Basil's mother—well, not *quite*—

But still, I'll say for the old trout
    She paid my little bill all right.

I *stripped* the hideous painted wood,
    Stippled the corridors and halls,
And *pickled* everything I could,
    And *scumbled* nearly all the walls.

I put Red Ensigns on the seats
    And hung Blue Peters down their backs,
And on the beds, instead of sheets,
    Enormous pairs of Union Jacks.

My dears, just *everyone* was there—
    But oh, how *old* it makes me feel
When I recall that charming pair
    In *matelot* suits of *eau de nil*!

One was Kilcock, Clonbrassil's son,
    Who died in nineteen thirty-three
(God rest his soul!), the other one—
    Can you believe it—tiny *me*.

Bug Maxwell, Ropey, Rodney Park,
    Peter Beckhampton, Georges de Hem,
Maria Madeleine de Sark—
    I wonder what became of them?

Working in some department store—
    That was the last I heard of Bug.
Ropey was always such a bore,
    And didn't Rodney go to jug?

And Georges de Hem collaborated,
　　So that's the last we'll hear of him!
And Pete and I, though we're related,
　　Are out of touch, now he's so dim.

And what's become of poor Maria?
　　Patrick, I'd like another drink.'
He gazes sadly at the fire,
　　And solemnly pretends to think.

Eternal age is in his eyes;
　　They watch the countless parties pass,
And, as the conversation dies,
　　His consolation is the glass.

The Lift Man

In uniform behold me stand,
The lovely lift at my command.
   I press the button: Pop,
And down I go below the town;
The walls rise up as I go down
   And in the basement stop.

For weeks I've worked a morning shift
On this old Waygood-Otis lift.
   And goodness, don't I love
To press the knob that shuts the gate
When customers are shouting 'Wait!'
   And soar to floors above.

I see them from my iron cage,
Their faces looking up in rage,
   And then I call 'First floor!'
'Perfume and ladies' underwear!
'No sir, Up only. Use the stair.'
   And up again we soar.

The second floor for kiddie goods,
And kiddie-pantz and pixie-hoods,
   The third floor, restaurant:
And here the people always try
To find one going down, so I
   Am not the lift they want.

On the roof-garden floor alone
I wait for ages on my own
    High, high above the crowds.
O let them rage and let them ring,
For I am out of everything,
    Alone among the clouds.

[In 1956 John Betjeman wrote these lines, anonymously, for the late Gerard Hoffnung to recite.]

Archibald

The bear who sits above my bed
  A doleful bear he is to see;
From out his drooping pear-shaped head
  His woollen eyes look into me.
He has no mouth, but seems to say:
'They'll burn you on the Judgment Day.'

Those woollen eyes, the things they've seen
  Those flannel ears, the things they've heard—
Among horse-chestnut fans of green,
  The fluting of an April bird,
And quarrelling downstairs until
Doors slammed at Thirty One West Hill.

The dreaded evening keyhole scratch
  Announcing some return below,
The nursery landing's lifted latch,
  The punishment to undergo—
Still I could smooth those half-moon ears
And wet that forehead with my tears.

Whatever rush to catch a train,
  Whatever joy there was to share
Of sounding sea-board, rainbowed rain,
  Or seaweed-scented Cornish air,
Sharing the laughs, you still were there,
You ugly, unrepentant bear.

When nine, I hid you in a loft
  And dared not let you share my bed;
My father would have thought me soft,
  Or so at least my mother said.
She only then our secret knew,
And thus my guilty passion grew.

The bear who sits above my bed
  More agèd now he is to see,
His woollen eyes have thinner thread,
  But still he seems to say to me,
In double-doom notes, like a knell:
'You're half a century nearer Hell.'

Self-pity shrouds me in a mist,
  And drowns me in my self-esteem.
The freckled faces I have kissed
  Float by me in a guilty dream.
The only constant, sitting there,
Patient and hairless, is a bear.

And if an analyst one day
  Of school of Adler, Jung or Freud
Should take this agèd bear away,
  Then, oh my God, the dreadful void!
Its draughty darkness could but be
Eternity, Eternity.

The Retired Postal Clerk

Since the wife died the house seems lonely-like,
   It isn't quite the same place as before;
Ron's got the garage for his motor-bike—
   I didn't want the Morris any more.

Ron's wife's the trouble. When I said to her,
   'Why don't you come and settle here with Ron?'
She flat refused. You'd think she would prefer
   A bigger place, with mother being gone.

But not a bit of it: and all she said
   Was, 'What I want's a place to call my own'—
She meant that she could wait till I was dead;
   So here I am, just living all alone.

I sold the Morris out Benhilton way—
   I couldn't keep it in this summer weather—
That empty seat beside me all the day;
   Along the roads we used to go together

Out to Carshalton Beeches for a spin
   And back by Chislehurst and Bromley town,
Where Mum would have her lemon juice and gin
   And I would have a half of old and brown—
And those last months when she was really bad,
They were the only pleasures that she had.

Cheshire

Infirmaries by Aston Webb
  On ev'ry hill surmount the pines;
From two miles off you still can see
  Their terra-cotta Dutch designs,
And metalled roads bisect canals,
  And both are crossed by railway lines.

And here a copse of Douglas firs
  Protects the merchant on the links;
The timbered club-house is not yet
  As mediaeval as he thinks;
For miles around the villas rise
  In hard interminable pinks.

Oh spin with me on pylon wires
  You Chester, Northwich, Knutsford chaps!
Look down on muddy empty fields
  And empty sheds and foot-worn gaps,
And pipes, and recreation grounds,
  And then content yourselves with maps.

Advertising Pays

I sit in Claridge's from twelve till two
And simply do what other people do—
Meeting and greeting persons of renown,
And looking through the people who are down.
But not *all*, mind you! Some, who're down today
Next week may put a good thing in my way.
I'm Christian names with several Labour peers;
As for Conservatives—they're rather dears,
And, just in case, you see—well, *just in case* . . .
I give them my attention for a space.
Over a whisky watered down with ice
I specialize in being *very nice*.
   Why do I do it? Well, you see, I'm paid
By various representatives of Trade
For telling lies about the things they sell,
And writing lies about the things as well.
I understand the public, that is why
My entertainment costs are rather high:
Dining and wining is no light expense
If one's to know the men of influence.
As my old chief would say, Sir Wardour Street,
'Begin publicity with the *élite*;
Give them a glass or two of good champagne
And start a classy whispering campaign.
Then run your advertising in the press—
Start with the great, continue with the less.'
Sir Wardour, ah! he knew a thing or two:

He bought six hundred tons of government glue
And sold it all in tins as Irish stew.
And I have had my triumphs in my time:
Do you remember 'Inspirated Lime—
Sprinkle your roses with it, watch them grow
To twice their size in half an hour or so'?
Yes, that was mine. A client came to talk
About some crates of surplus blackboard chalk
That he'd been landed with. I told him plain,
'You won't sell that as blackboard chalk again.'
We both of us made thirty thousand clear:
The 'Inspirated' was my own idea.

   'Yoko' was mine, 'The Nectar of the Gods,
Prepared from Sterilized Laburnum Pods.'
Unluckily my client didn't know
Laburnum seeds were poisonous, and so . . .
Well, that was *his* affair, the silly mug;
I'm given to understand he's still in jug.

   Before the war, I started the campaign,
'If you can walk, why ever go by train?'
That was to sell a lot of surplus shoes—
And in the war, I faded from the news.

   Well now, of course, what with Sir Stafford Cripps,
And sending things to India in ships,
There's not so much to lie about as when
I started in the game in nineteen-ten.
So now I'm saying 'Advertise the Truth!'
And cashing in on Planning and on Youth.
Youth centres, youth discussion groups, youth teams—
The coupons and the permits come in streams!

354

Dumbleton Hall*

as by

HENRY WADSWORTH LONGFELLOW

——————

Not so far from Evesham's city on a woody hillside green
Stands an ancient stonebuilt mansion—nothing modern to be

seen,

Not a farmhouse, not a homestead, only trees on either hand
Billowing like heaps of cushions on the sofa of the land.
When the bells from that old belfry, that the monks in olden time
Built to God in sainted Evesham, hammer out the evening chime
Still I seem to see the pilgrims wending down the Chelt'nham

road

Stopping for a friendly parley at the Cock's old abode.
There perhaps goes William Shakespeare, he from Avon's grassy

side

In the creaking leather saddle on a morning horseback ride
Quaffing ale and eating oatcakes, countryman and poet he
Soon to be by printed pages bless'd with immortality.
There perhaps go rare Ben Jonson, Francis Beaumont, Fletcher,

Drake,

Jolly, bold Elizabethans pausing there their thirsts to slake,
Writing plays and shooting arrows, courting, fighting, one and all
Stopped, I deem, to steal some kisses from the daughter of the

Hall.

Time goes on into the present age of steam and gas and roar;
Still there stands that stonebuilt mansion as it stood in days of

yore.

*Built by Repton, 1837, in neo-Jacobean style.

Not a window has been altered, not a sculptured corbel head
But it looked on William Shakespeare decades, even centuries,
dead.

Those old pinnacles and turrets as in good Queen Bess's reign
Still jut out above the creeper, still the level lawns remain,
And within, upon the staircase, tapestries still catch the wind.
And there are tusks that Marco Polo may, perhaps, have brought
from Ind,
Quaint old lanterns light the carpets, quaint old carvings deck the
stair,

Sumptuous fabrics line the sofa such as Shakespeare used to wear;
And the heiress of the Cocks's still retains the name of Eyres,
With Sir Bolton standing by her still receives one on the stairs;
Best of all his lovely daughter welcomes every author-guest—
Newer Shakespeares, other Beaumonts with their Fletchers come
to rest:

Come to rest and to remember those romantic tales of old
That beside the blazing yule-log the Elizabethans told,
Come to steal, perhaps, some kisses just as Shakespeare did and
Drake—

Thus is kept thine ancient glory, Gothic Dumbleton, awake.

Thoughts in a Train

No doubt she is somebody's mistress,
   With that Greta Garbo hair,
As she sits, mascara-lidded,
   In the corner seat over there.

But why, if she's somebody's mistress,
   Is she travelling up in a Third?
Her luggage is leather, not plastic,
   Her jewelry rich and absurd.

'Oh I am nobody's mistress:
   The jewels I wear, you see,
Were, like this leather luggage,
   A present from Mummy to me.

'If you want to get on with the Government,
   You've got to be like it, I've heard;
So I've booked my suite in the Ritz Hotel
   and I'm travelling up in a Third.'

Shetland 1973

Fetlar is waiting. At its little quay
   Green seaweed stirs and ripples on the swell.
   The lone sham castle looks across at Yell,
And from the mainland hilltops you can see
Over to westward, glimmering distantly,
   The cliffs of Foula as the clouds dispel.
   Clear air, wide skies, crunch underfoot of shell—
The Viking kingdom waits what is to be.

Loud over Lerwick, seabirds wail and squawk,
   Portent of Shetland's fast approaching foes—
The briefcased oilmen with their wily talk;
   Soon we shall see, ranged all along the voes
Their hard-faced wives in ranch-type bungalows.

To the Crazy Gang

[Written to commemorate the last performance of the Crazy Gang in May 1962; John Betjeman presented copies of the poem to 'Monsewer' Eddie Gray, Jimmy Nervo, Jimmy Gold, Teddy Knox, Bud Flanagan, Charles Naughton and Jack Hylton.]

One Saturday night I sat in The London—
   The London Shoreditch—as peanuts cracked
With my tie askew and my waistcoat undone
   And sweating a lot as the house was packed.

The bar door swished when the bell was ringing
   And pipe smoke curled to the golden dome,
And Leo Dryden himself was singing
   Once more 'The Miner's Dream of Home'.

Oh, Saturday nights I've seen in plenty
   At the Bedford, Collins', South London, Met,
And I've laughed and wept since 1920
   At brilliant talent I can't forget.

But this is *the* Saturday night tremendous,
   This is the night with a parting pang,
This is the Saturday night to end us—
   We say goodbye to the Crazy Gang.

Goodbye old friends of the great tradition!
   From the serious thirties of slumps and tears
Into this age of nuclear fission
   You kept us laughing for thirty years.

Bud and Jimmy and Teddy you've done it,
     Monsewer, Charles Naughton and you, James Gold—
You've ridden a race and you've all of you won it
     And you've ended fresh as a two year old.

Goodbye old friends! and in skies above you
     Harry Tate, George Robey and Wilkie Bard
Are with us and watching—like us they love you—
     If there's clapping in heaven they're clapping hard.

Goodbye old friends! and now, Jack Hylton,
     I give you the greatest toast of all—
The toast of a rhymer, for I'm no Milton—
     But here's to London and Music Hall!

Kegans

On Paignton sands Hawaiian bands
  Play tunes across the sea
Like 'Home sweet home'; above the foam
  The Kegans call to me
As once again the Devon rain
  Upsets their picnic tea.

Black socks above gymnasium shoes,
  Grey bags above the socks
And golden sand on either hand
  And paper-littered rocks
And slot machines with Paris scenes
  And sharp electric shocks.

And bridge and golf and golf and bridge
  And travels in the car,
A large saloon with all aswoon
  From Reginald's cigar;
From three to four an A.A. tour
  And then the cinema.

We've left our hearts in Wimbledon
  Our feet are in the waves,
And when the rain comes down again
  We'll shelter in the caves,
And if we see impurity,
  Remember 'Jesus saves'.

Henley Regatta 1902

Underneath a light straw boater
In his pink Leander tie
Ev'ry ripple in the water caught the Captain in the eye.
O'er the plenitude of houseboats
Plop of punt-poles, creak of rowlocks,
Many a man of some distinction scanned the reach to Temple
Island

As a south wind fluttered by,
Till it shifted, westward drifting, strings of pennants house-boat
high,
Where unevenly the outline of the brick-warm town of Henley
Dominated by her church tower and the sheds of Brakspear's
Brewery

Lay beneath a summer sky.
Plash of sculls! And pink of ices!
And the inn-yards full of ostlers, and the barrels running dry,
And the baskets of geraniums
Swinging over river-gardens
Led us to the flowering heart of England's willow-cooled July.

1930 Commercial Style

['The Regency did not produce "gems" either in architecture or anything else'—Sir Reginald Blomfield (the architect of the New Lambeth Bridge, Regent Street and Carlton House Terrace) in *The Times*, December 14, 1932.]

How nice to watch the buildings go
From Regent Street to Savile Row.
How nice to know, despite it all,
We need not grumble when they fall;
For ain't the big new Quadrant lined
With facings 'Architect-designed'?
What has it got to do with us—
Mere cranks who like to make a fuss—
Because we get a little tired
Of ancient men, howe'er inspired,
Who since the century began
Have built in Frenchified Queen Anne?
Or just because we look askance
At England's Neo-Renaissance?
How nice to know that bare steel frame
Will soon look very much the same
As Greenwich: though three times as high—
A Christmas parcel for the sky,
All ugly function is not shown
When once it's wrapped in Portland stone.
That stucco in which Nash delighted
Is *false* and, like his times, benighted.
For how can Wren and Nash be call'd

As able as Sir Reginald?
And how could they, in their positions,
Have coped with modern changed conditions?
I hate to see the framework flanks
All bare behind the City banks;
I like to put, until it falls,
My capital in capitals.
How can we know, we carping fools,
Mysterious architectural rules?
And have we been to public schools?

Guilt

The clock is frozen in the tower,
    The thickening fog with sooty smell
Has blanketed the motor power
    Which turns the London streets to hell;
And footsteps with their lonely sound
Intensify the silence round.

I haven't hope. I haven't faith.
    I live two lives and sometimes three.
The lives I live make life a death
    For those who have to live with me.
Knowing the virtues that I lack,
I pat myself upon the back.

With breastplate of self-righteousness
    And shoes of smugness on my feet,
Before the urge in me grows less
    I hurry off to make retreat.
For somewhere, somewhere, burns a light
To lead me out into the night.

It glitters icy, thin and plain,
    And leads me down to Waterloo—
Into a warm electric train
    Which travels sorry Surrey through
Where, crystal-hung, the clumps of pine
Stand deadly still beside the line.

A Romance

'Twas at the Cecil-Samuels'
  In a sumptuous Holborn Hall,
Miss Dunlop and Diana Craig
  Went to a dinner-ball.
Soft as the heavy carpets
  Their eyes betrayed their souls,
As they gazed across the napery
  At well-selected Poles.

'Oh Captain Cecil-Samuel,
  I fear I'm dancing this
With Major Dobrezynski,
  And *he* knows how to kiss.
I like you very much indeed,
  And thank you all the same,
But I much prefer the Major
  With the long and funny name.'

Alas, the lush carnations!
  Each *most expensive* bloom
Was crushed against the Major
  As he whirled her round the room.
The chromium and the shaded lights
  They both began to spin
Like a glass of Lyons 'thirty-eight'
  Mixed in black-market gin.

'Oh Captain Cecil-Samuel,
    Miss Dunlop's very nice,
I know she'd like to dance with you,
    Her heart is made of ice.
My next fifteen are promised
    To the Pole that I adore,
But I like you very much indeed,
    As I have said before.'

The lights were switched to purple,
    The wine flowed on in waves,
And little jars of caviar
    Were handed round by slaves.
As Holborn Hall resounded
    To the throbbings of the band,
The Pole, he gave Diana Craig
    His castle and his hand.

'Oh Mrs Cecil-Samuel,
    It's been the greatest fun;
I'm sure that I've enjoyed it
    Far more than anyone . . .
I cannot quite express myself,
    I'm tied in lovers' knots;
But oh! I am so sorry
    About Carol's horrid spots.'

'Two thousand pounds it cost me,'
    Said the Captain to his mate,
'And there's our daughter Carol
    And she hasn't made a date.

I fear we made our guest-list
    Far too wide and vague
When we asked that cold Miss Dunlop
    And that fast Diana Craig.'

Advent 1955

The Advent wind begins to stir
With sea-like sounds in our Scotch fir,
It's dark at breakfast, dark at tea,
And in between we only see
Clouds hurrying across the sky
And rain-wet roads the wind blows dry
And branches bending to the gale
Against great skies all silver-pale.
The world seems travelling into space,
And travelling at a faster pace
Than in the leisured summer weather
When we and it sit out together,
For now we feel the world spin round
On some momentous journey bound—
Journey to what? to whom? to where?
The Advent bells call out 'Prepare,
Your world is journeying to the birth
Of God made Man for us on earth.'
  And how, in fact, do we prepare
For the great day that waits us there—
The twenty-fifth day of December,
The birth of Christ? For some it means
An interchange of hunting scenes
On coloured cards. And I remember
Last year I sent out twenty yards,
Laid end to end, of Christmas cards
To people that I scarcely know—

They'd sent a card to me, and so
I had to send one back. Oh dear!
Is this a form of Christmas cheer?
Or is it, which is less surprising,
My pride gone in for advertising?
The only cards that really count
Are that extremely small amount
From real friends who keep in touch
And are not rich but love us much.
Some ways indeed are very odd
By which we hail the birth of God.
We raise the price of things in shops,
We give plain boxes fancy tops
And lines which traders cannot sell
Thus parcell'd go extremely well.
We dole out bribes we call a present
To those to whom we must be pleasant
For business reasons. Our defence is
These bribes are charged against expenses
And bring relief in Income Tax.
Enough of these unworthy cracks!
'The time draws near the birth of Christ',
A present that cannot be priced
Given two thousand years ago.
Yet if God had not given so
He still would be a distant stranger
And not the Baby in the manger.

The Old Land Dog

AFTER HENRY NEWBOLT

———

Old General Artichoke lay bloated on his bed,
 Just like the Fighting Téméraire.
Twelve responsive daughters were gathered round his head
 And each of them was ten foot square.

Old General Artichoke he didn't want to die:
He never understood the truth and that perhaps was why
It wouldn't be correct to say he always told a lie.
 Womenfolk of England, oh beware!

'Fetch me down my rifle—it is hanging in the hall'
 Just like the Fighting Téméraire;
'Lydia, get my cartridge cases, twenty-four in all',
 And each of them is ten foot square.

'I'll tell you all in detail, girls, my every campaign
In Tuscany, Bolivia, Baluchistan and Spain;
And when I've finished telling you, I'll tell you all again;'
 Womenfolk of England, oh beware!

Old General Artichoke he's over eighty-two,
 Just like the Fighting Téméraire.
His daughters all make rush mats when they've nothing else to do,
 And each of them is ten foot square.

Now all ye pension'd army men from Tunbridge Wells to Perth,
Here's to General Artichoke, the purplest man on earth!
Give three loud cheers for Cheltenham, the city of his birth.
    Womenfolk of England, oh beware!

Before the Lecture

Secretary   Forgive me if, just for a moment, I
Give out our notices. Will members please
Note that next Sunday in the Free Thought Hall
The Peascod Players will do *Everyman*.
The play lasts seven hours, but with a break
For light refreshments when we can adjourn
To the Club Cocoa Fountain. And I trust
That *everyman*—and every *woman*, too!—
Will see this quaint old-world morality.

    Next week our lecturer is Putney Heath,
The celebrated publicist. He takes
A rather startling subject for his talk—
'Some aspects of the modern Cultural Drive
In Scandinavia', Bring your Kierkegaards,
Also your Kafkas. We in Edgbaston
Are not behindhand in these matters. Please
Send in your abstract art designs *at once*
To the Community Centre. And this year
The Art Committee asks me to point out
That no surrealist work will be allowed.
Last year, one lady member's canvas was,
To say the least, well—*most* unfortunate—
She mayn't have been aware of this herself;
She worked, no doubt, with her subconscious mind-
But there it was. So, if you please, this year
Pure abstract only. Thank you very much.

Lecturer   Ladies and gentlemen, I come to you
By kind permission of the D.I.A.,
The British Council, Min. of Ag. and Fish.,
The General Post Office, the L.M.S.,
The T.U.C., Unesco,
John Gloag and *Vogue*,
And Working Parties in the Board of Trade,
To tell you *how to beautify your homes*.

The Parochial Church Council

Last week a friend inquired of me,
'Oh, should I join our P.C.C.?'
I answered, rather priggishly,
'If you communicate, you can,
And want to help your clergyman.
Parochial Church Councils are
From Parish Councils different far.'
I said, 'And District Councils too
Have very different things to do,
For District Councils raise the rates
And have political debates.
If one side says "Preserve the Town",
The other side says "Pull it down!"
And Parish Councils try to make
The District Council keep awake
To local practical affairs—
Like village bus-shelter repairs.
Parish and Parliament and Queen,
A mighty structure thus is seen—
Endless committees in between.
And I suppose that it occurr'd
To someone as not quite absurd
To make our Church of England be
A similar democracy.
The Church Assembly's near the top,
Where people talk until they drop;
Next come Diocesan Committees,

Like Mayor and Aldermen in cities.
The equivalent to R.D.C's
Are ruri-decanal jamborees,
And at the root of all the tree
We find the homely P.C.C.
For P.C.C.'s were really made
To give your local vicar aid,
And I have always understood
That most of them are very good—
Where lay folk do what jobs they can
To help their church and clergyman.
But in small villages I've known
Of ones that make the vicar groan
And wish he could be left alone.
So just you come along with me
To a really wicked P.C.C.

    'Tis evening in the village school,
And perched upon an infant's stool
The village postmistress is sitting
Glancing at us above her knitting.
Like schoolchildren—but do not laugh—
Farmers in desks too small by half;
Prim ladies, brooding for a storm
Are ranged like infants, on a form.
We read the text that hangs above
In coloured letters "GOD is LOVE".
The Vicar takes the teacher's chair,
A dreadful tenseness fills the air.
"We will begin," he says, "with prayer".
We do. It doesn't make things better.
The Vicar reads the Bishop's letter—

"Diocesan this and quota that"—
He might be talking through his hat;
It is not what they've come about.
And now the devil's jumping out
For next we have the church accounts,
And as they're read, the tension mounts.
This Vicar has been forced to be
The Treasurer of his P.C.C.,
As no one else will volunteer
To do the hard work needed here.
"Well, Vicar, do I understand
Last year we had six pounds in hand?"
Says Farmer Pinch who's rich and round
And lord of ninety thousand pound,
"And this year you are three pound ten
In debt—and in the red again.
Now, Vicar, that is not the way
To make a parson's business pay.
You're losing cash. It's got to stop
Or you will have to shut up shop."
The tactless Vicar answers, "Sir,
Upon the church you cast a slur:
Church is not Trade"; "Then time it were,"
Says Farmer Pinch. And now Miss Right
Who has been spoiling for a fight—
Miss Right who thinks she's very Low
And cannot bring herself to go
To services where people kneel,
Miss Right who always makes you feel
You're in the wrong, and sulks at home
And says the Vicar's paid by Rome—

377

Cries "If the Vicar and his pals
Spent less on Popish fal-de-lals
Like altar candles and such frills
Perhaps we then could pay our bills."
The fight grows furious and thicker,
And what was meant to help the Vicar—
This democratic P.C.C.—
Seems just the opposite to me.
The meeting soon is charged with hate,
And turns the Devil's advocate:
Its members do not come to church.
Admittedly you'd have to search
A lot of villages to find
A P.C.C. that's so unkind,
But everywhere, just now and then,
The Devil tempts the best of men;
So if you join your P.C.C.
Be calm and full of charity'.

The Shires

Harmonious hydrangeas were concealing
    The bandsmen from the scarlet and the frills
Of the Corbets and the Heywood-Lonsdales wheeling
    Among the Heber-Percys and the Hills.

Then every name meant pink and brown and stables,
    And household servants getting up at five,
And window-boxes, turreting and gables,
    And gardeners raking gravel on the drive.

The morning-room with sun on pens and blotter,
    For recapitulations of the ball—
'What did Cousin Celia see in such a rotter?'
    'Did Jack propose to Olive after all?'

An Ecumenical Invitation

This is my tenth; his name is Damien—
Not Damien of Braganza, on whose day
My second youngest, Catherine, was born
(Antonia Fraser is her godmamma),
But Damien after Father Damien,
Whom Holy Church has just beatified.
But I forget, you're not a Catholic,
And this will seem too technical to you.
Still, never mind, there's whisky over there,
Gin, sherry—help yourself—no, not for me.

   Teresa, please take Damien away
I want to talk to Mr Betjeman.

   Well, tell me what you think of the reforms.
I understand that *you* have had some too,
Isn't *The Times* improved beyond belief?*
It's so much bigger than it used to be!
I never like that term 'non-Catholic'—
The word we used to use for Anglicans,
Though several of my really greatest friends
Were once non-Catholics—take Evelyn Waugh
(God rest his soul!) and Graham Sutherland;
And quite the sweetest girl I ever knew,
A district nurse, was once a Methodist—
But oh, so happy as a Catholic now.
Now, won't you give our churches back to us?

*William Rees-Mogg, a Roman Catholic, had become Editor of *The Times*.

Then you'll be Catholics too! I realise
It's somehow all mixed up with politics,
The Holy Father, though, will see to that;
What was I saying? England's heritage—
It *does* seem such a pity, doesn't it?
Those fine cathedrals crumbling to decay
Half empty, while our own, though brash and cheap,
Are always, always, crowded to the doors.

    But still I didn't ask you here for that,
I want to speak of something near my heart—
The Catholic League of Women Journalists.
I, for my sins, am President this year
And with ecumenism in the air
I thought—you'll know the Holy Father's said
That all the Christians in the world, the rank
Outsiders, I mean those outside our ranks,
As well as Catholics, must play their part,
And that was why I thought of asking you
To give us this year's annual address.
It's quite informal, only half an hour.

The Conversion of St. Paul

[In 1955 Mrs Margaret Knight, a humanist, caused a sensation by her broadcasts on BBC radio attacking Christianity. This was composed in reply to her arguments, and it was published in *The Listener* of February 10, 1955]

Now is the time when we recall
The sharp Conversion of St. Paul.
Converted! Turned the wrong way round—
A man who seemed till then quite sound,
Keen on religion—very keen—
No-one, it seems, had ever been
So keen on persecuting those
Who said that Christ was God and chose
To die for this absurd belief
As Christ had died beside the thief.
Then in a sudden blinding light
Paul knew that Christ was God all right—
And very promptly lost his sight.
Poor Paul! They led him by the hand
He who had been so high and grand
A helpless blunderer, fasting, waiting,
Three days inside himself debating
In physical blindness: 'As it's true
That Christ is God and died for you,
Remember all the things you did
To keep His gospel message hid.
Remember how you helped them even
To throw the stones that murdered Stephen.

And do you think that you are strong
Enough to own that you were wrong?'
They must have been an awful time,
Those three long days repenting crime
Till Ananias came and Paul
Received his sight, and more than all
His former strength, and was baptised.
Saint Paul is often criticised
By modern people who're annoyed
At his conversion, saying Freud
Explains it all. But they omit
The really vital point of it,
Which isn't *how* it was achieved
But what it was that Paul believed.
He knew as certainly as we
Know you are you and I am me
That Christ was all He claimed to be.
What is conversion? Turning round
From chaos to a love profound.
And chaos too is an abyss
In which the only life is this.
Such a belief is quite all right
If you are sure like Mrs. Knight
And think morality will do
For all the ills we're subject to.
But raise your eyes and see with Paul
An explanation of it all.
Injustice, cancer's cruel pain,
All suffering that seems in vain,
The vastness of the universe,
Creatures like centipedes and worse—

All part of an enormous plan
Which mortal eyes can never scan
And out of it came God to man.
Jesus is God and came to show
The world we live in here below
Is just an antechamber where
We for His Father's house prepare.
What is conversion? Not at all
For me the experience of St. Paul,
No blinding light, a fitful glow
Is all the light of faith I know
Which sometimes goes completely out
And leaves me plunging round in doubt
Until I will myself to go
And worship in God's house below—
My parish Church—and even there
I find distractions everywhere.

What is Conversion? Turning round
To gaze upon a love profound.
For some of us see Jesus plain
And never once look back again,
And some of us have seen and known
And turned and gone away alone,
But most of us turn slow to see
The figure hanging on a tree
And stumble on and blindly grope
Upheld by intermittent hope.
God grant before we die we all
May see the light as did St. Paul.

St Mary Magdalen, Old Fish Street Hill

On winter evenings I walk alone in the City
  When cobbles glisten with wet and it's foggy and still;
I am Rector's warden here. But more's the pity
  We haven't the Charity children now to fill
Our old west gallery front. Some new committee
  Has done away with them all. I beg your pardon,
  I omitted to tell you where I am Rector's warden—
At St Mary Magdalen's church, Old Fish Street Hill.

Unfortunately, the London Conflagration
  Of sixteen sixty-six was a moment when
The Roman style in general estimation
  Was held so high that our church was rebuilt by Wren.
It is just a box with a fanciful plaster ceiling
Devoid of a vestige of genuine Christian feeling,
  And our congregation is seldom more than ten.

Woman Driver

———

What joy awaits you from the station yard,
    Oh lithe-limbed lovely in the skiing pants?
What warm upholstery will hold those thighs?
    What tasselled lanes from Surrey into Hants
Will meet the rapture of those dark brown eyes?
What pedal feel the Dolcis pressing hard?
Yours, revved-up Mini-minor all her own——
Her passion's plaything and her body's throne.

The Ballad of George R. Sims*

It's an easy game, this reviewin'—the editor sends yer a book,
Yer puts it down on yer table and yer gives it a 'asty look,
An' then, Sir, yer writes about it as though yer 'ad read it all
                                       through,
And if ye're a pal o' the author yer gives it a good review.

But if the author's a wrong 'un—and *some* are, as I've 'eard tell—
Or if 'e's a stranger to yer, why then yer can give him 'ell.
So what would yer 'ave me do, Sir, to humour an editor's whims,
When I'm pally with Calder-Marshall, and never knew George R.
                                           Sims?

It is easy for you to deride me and brush me off with a laugh
And say 'Well, the answer's potty—yer review it just 'arf and
                                          'arf'—
For I fear I must change my tune, Sir, and pump the bellows of
                                          praise
And say that both 'alves are good, Sir, in utterly different ways.

I'm forgettin' my cockney lingo—for I lapse in my style now and
                                          then
As Sims used to do in his ballads when he wrote of the Upper
                                          Ten—
'Round in the sensuous galop the high-born maids are swung
Clasped in the arms of *roués* whose vice is on every tongue'.

*This was a verse review in the *New Statesman* (October 25, 1968) of a
selection of George R. Sims' Ballads introduced by Arthur Calder-Marshall.

'It was Christmas Day in the workhouse' is his best known line of
                                                                    all,
And this is his usual metre, which comes, as you may recall,
Through Tennyson, Gordon, Kipling and on to the Sergeants'
                                                              Mess,
A rhythm that's made to recite in, be it mufti or evening dress.

Now Arthur shows in his intro that George R. Sims was a bloke
Who didn't compose his ballads as a sort of caustic joke;
He cared about social justice but he didn't aim very high
Though he knew how to lay on the sobstuff and make his audience
                                                                 cry.

The village church on the back-drop is painted over for good,
The village concerts are done for where the Young Reciter stood,
The magic-lantern is broken and we laugh at the mission
                                                         hymns—
We laugh and we well might weep with the Ballads of George R.
                                                              Sims.

Civilized Woman

The women who walk down Oxford Street
Have bird-like faces and brick-like feet;
Floppity flop go 'tens' and 'elevens'
Of Eesiphit into D. H. Evans.
The women who walk down Oxford Street
Suffer a lot from nerves and heat,
But with Bovril, Tizer and Phospherine
They may all become what they might have been.
They gladly clatter with bag in hand
Out of the train from Metroland,
And gladly gape, when commerce calls,
At all the glory of plate-glass walls,
And gladly buy, till their bags are full,
'Milton' cleaner and 'Wolsey' wool,
'Shakespeare' cornflour, a 'Shelley' shirt,
'Brighto', 'Righto' and 'Moovyerdirt'.
Commerce pours on them gifts like rain;
Back in Metroland once again,
Wasn't it worth your weary feet—
The colourful bustle of Oxford Street?

To Stuart Piggott, 1975

Stuart, I sit here in a grateful haze
Recalling those spontaneous Berkshire days
In straw-thatched,

       chalk-built,

           pre-War

              Uffington

Before the March of Progress had begun,
When all the world seemed waiting to be won,
When evening air with mignonette was scented,
And 'picture-windows' had not been invented,
When shooting foxes still was thought unsporting,
And White Horse Hill was still the place for courting
When church was still the usual place for marriages
And carriage-lamps were only used for carriages.

  How pleased your parents were in their retirement
The garden and yourself their chief requirement.
Your father, now his teaching days were over,
Back in his native Berkshire lived in clover.
Your cheerful mother loyally concealed
Her inward hankering for Petersfield,
For Hampshire Downs were the first Downs you saw
And Heywood Sumner taught you there to draw.

  Under great elms which rustled overhead
By stile and foot-bridge village pathways led
To cottage gardens heavy with the flower

Of fruit and vegetables towards your tower,
St Mary, Uffington, famed now as then
The perfect Parker's Glossary specimen
Of purest Early English, tall and pale,
—To tourists the Cathedral of the Vale,
To us the church. I'm glad that I survive
To greet you, Stuart, now you're sixty-five.

Chelsea 1977

The street is bathed in winter sunset pink,
The air is redolent of kitchen sink,
Between the dog-mess heaps I pick my way
To watch the dying embers of the day
Glow over Chelsea, crimson load on load
All Brangwynesque across the long King's Road.
Deep in myself I feel a sense of doom,
Fearful of death I trudge towards the tomb.
The earth beneath my feet is hardly soil
But outstretched chicken-netting coil on coil
Covering cables, sewage-pipes and wires
While underneath burn hell's eternal fires.
Snap! crackle! pop! the kiddiz know the sound
And Satan stokes his furnace underground.

The Friends of the Cathedral

From *Poems in the Porch* 1954

At the end of our Cathedral
   Where people buy and sell
It says "Friends of the Cathedral",
   And I'm sure they wish it well.

Pehaps they gave the bookstall
   Of modernistic oak,
And the chairs for the assistants
   And the ashtrays for a smoke.

Is it they who range the marigolds
   In pots of art design
About "The Children's Corner",
   That very sacred shrine?

And do they hang the notices
   Off old crusader's toes?
And paint the cheeks of effigies
   That curious shade of rose?

Those things that look like wireless sets
   Suspended from each column,
Which bellow out the Litany
   Parsonically solemn—

Are these a present from the Friends?
  And if they are, how nice
That aided by their echo
  One can hear the service twice.

The hundred little bits of script
  Each framed in passe-partout
And nailed below the monuments,
  A clerical "Who's Who"—

Are they as well the work of Friends?
  And do they also choose
The chantry chapel curtains
  In dainty tea-shop blues?

The Friends of the Cathedral—
  Are they friendly with the Dean?
And if they do things on their own
  What does their friendship mean?

The Empty Pew

Written on Penelope Betjeman's admission to the Roman Catholic Church, 1948

In the perspective of Eternity
  The pain is nothing, now you go away
  Above the steaming thatch how silver-grey
Our chiming church tower, calling 'Come to me

My Sunday-sleeping villagers!' And she,
  Still half my life, kneels now with those who say
  'Take courage, daughter. Never cease to pray
God's grace will break him of his heresy.'

I, present with our Church of England few
  At the dear words of Consecration see
  The chalice lifted, hear the sanctus chime
And glance across to that deserted pew.
  In the Perspective of Eternity
  The pain is nothing – but, ah God, in Time.

SUMMONED BY BELLS

Author's Note to First Edition

Why is this account of some moments in the sheltered life of a middle-class youth not written in prose? The author has gone as near prose as he dare. He chose blank verse, for all but the more hilarious moments, because he found it best suited to brevity and the rapid changes of mood and subject.

He wishes to thank the Proprietors of *Punch* for permission to reprint the Edward James stanzas. He is particularly grateful to his friends John Hanbury Angus Sparrow and Thomas Edward Neil Driberg for going through the manuscript and proofs and making valuable suggestions which have almost always been adopted, and Cecil Roberts for his help. He wishes to thank Messrs. Mears & Stainbank for campanological advice.

I

Before MCMXIV

———————

Here on the southern slope of Highgate Hill
Red squirrels leap the hornbeams. Still I see
Twigs and serrated leaves against the sky.
The sunny silence was of Middlesex.
Once a Delaunay-Belleville crawling up
West Hill in bottom gear made such a noise
As drew me from my dream-world out to watch
That early motor-car attempt the steep.
But mostly it was footsteps, rustling leaves,
And blackbirds fluting over miles of Heath.

    Then Millfield Lane looked like a Constable
And all the grassy hillocks spoke of Keats.
Mysterious gravel drives to hidden wealth
Wound between laurels—mighty Caenwood Towers
And Grand Duke Michael's house and Holly Lodge.

    But what of us in our small villa row
Who gazed into the Burdett-Coutts estate?
I knew we were a lower, lesser world
Than that remote one of the carriage-folk
Who left their cedars and brown garden walls
In care of servants. I could also tell
That we were slightly richer than my friends,
The family next door: we owned a brougham
And they would envy us our holidays.
In fact it was the mother there who first
Made me aware of insecurity

399

When war was near: "Your name is German, John"—
But I had always thought that it was Dutch . . .
That tee-jay-ee, that fatal tee-jay-ee
Which I have watched the hesitating pens
Of Government clerks and cloakroom porters funk.
I asked my mother. "No," she said, "it's Dutch;
Thank God you're English on your mother's side."
O happy, happy Browns and Robinsons!

    Safe were those evenings of the pre-war world
When firelight shone on green linoleum;
I heard the church bells hollowing out the sky,
Deep beyond deep, like never-ending stars,
And turned to Archibald, my safe old bear,
Whose woollen eyes looked sad or glad at me,
Whose ample forehead I could wet with tears,
Whose half-moon ears received my confidence,
Who made me laugh, who never let me down.
I used to wait for hours to see him move,
Convinced that he could breathe. One dreadful day
They hid him from me as a punishment:
Sometimes the desolation of that loss
Comes back to me and I must go upstairs
To see him in the sawdust, so to speak,
Safe and returned to his idolator.

    Safe, in a world of trains and buttered toast
Where things inanimate could feel and think,
Deeply I loved thee, 31 West Hill!
At that hill's foot did London then begin,
With yellow horse-trams clopping past the planes
To grey-brick nonconformist Chetwynd Road
And on to Kentish Town and barking dogs

And costers' carts and crowded grocers' shops
And Daniels' store, the local Selfridge's,
The Bon Marché, the Electric Palace, slums
That thrilled me with their smells of poverty—
Till, safe once more, we gained the leafy slope
And buttered toast and 31 West Hill.
Here from my eyrie, as the sun went down,
I heard the old North London puff and shunt,
Glad that I did not live in Gospel Oak.

    "A diamond," "A heart," "No trumps," "Two spades"—
Happy and tense they played at Auction Bridge:
Two tables in the drawing-room for friends
From terra-cotta flats on Muswell Hill
And nearer Brookfield Mansions: cigarettes
And 'Votes for Women' ashtrays, mauve and green.
I watched the players, happy to be quiet
Till someone nice was dummy who would talk—
A talk soon drowned . . . "If you'd finessed my heart
And played your diamond . . ." "If I'd had the lead
I might have done." "Well, length is strength, you know."
"Not when your partner's sitting on the ace."
Did they, I wonder, leave us in a huff
After those hot post-mortems? All I knew
Were silks and bits of faintly scented fur
On ladies vaguely designated 'aunts'
Who came on second Thursdays to At Homes.

    The sunlit weeks between were full of maids:
Sarah, with orange wig and horsy teeth,
Was so bad-tempered that she scarcely spoke;
Maud was my hateful nurse who smelt of soap
And forced me to eat chewy bits of fish,

Thrusting me back to babyhood with threats
Of nappies, dummies and the feeding bottle.
She rubbed my face in messes I had made
And was the first to tell me about Hell,
Admitting she was going there herself.
· Sometimes, thank God, they left me all alone
In our small patch of garden in the front,
With clinker rockery and London Pride
And barren lawn and lumps of yellow clay
As mouldable as smelly Plasticine.
I used to turn the heavy stones to watch
The shiny red and waiting centipede
Which darted out of sight; the woodlouse slow
And flat; the other greyish-bluey kind
Which rolled into a ball till I was gone
Out of the gate to venture down the hill.
  "You're late for dinner, John." I feel again
That awful feeling, fear confused with thrill,
As I would be unbuttoned, bent across
Her starchy apron, screaming "Don't—Maud—don't!"
Till dissolution, bed and kindly fur
Of agèd, uncomplaining Archibald.

II

The Dawn of Guilt

My dear deaf father, how I loved him then
Before the years of our estrangement came!
The long calm walks on twilit evenings
Through Highgate New Town to the cinema:
The expeditions by North London trains
To dim forgotten stations, wooden shacks
On oil-lit flimsy platforms among fields
As yet unbuilt-on, deep in Middlesex . . .
We'd stand in dark antique shops while he talked,
Holding his deaf-appliance to his ear,
Lifting the ugly mouthpiece with a smile
Towards the flattered shopman. Most of all
I think my father loved me when we went
In early-morning pipe-smoke on the tram
Down to the Angel, visiting the Works.
"Fourth generation—yes, this is the boy."

The smell of sawdust still brings back to me
The rambling workshops high on Pentonville,
Built over gardens to White Lion Street,
Clicking with patents of the family firm
Founded in 1820. When you rang
The front-door bell a watchful packer pulled
A polished lever twenty yards away,
And this released the catch into a world
Of shining showrooms full of secret drawers

And Maharajahs' dressing-cases.

                             Hushed
Be thy green hilltop, handsome Highbury!
Stilled be the traffic roar of Upper Street!
Flash shop-fronts, masts and neon signs, drop off
The now-encumbered houses! O return,
Straw-smelling mornings, to old Islington!
A hint of them still hung about the Works
From the past days of our prosperity—
A hint of them in medals, photographs
And stockrooms heavy with the Tantalus
On which the family fortune had been made.
The Alexandra Palace patent lock,
The Betjemann device for hansom cabs,
Patents exhibited in '51,
Improvements on them shown in '62,
The Betjemann trolley used in coffee-rooms,
The inlaid brass, the figured rosewood box,
The yellow satinwood, the silverware—
What wealth the money from them once had brought
To fill the hot-house half-way up the stairs
With red begonias; what servants' halls;
What terrace houses and what carriage-drives!

   Bang through the packing-room! Then up a step:
"Be careful, Master John," old William called.
Over the silversmiths' uneven floor
I thought myself a fast electric train,
First stop the silver-plating shop (no time
To watch the locksmiths' and engravers' work):
For there in silence Buckland used to drop
Dull bits of metal into frothing tanks

And bring them out all gold or silver bright—
He'd turn a penny into half-a-crown.
Though he but seldom spoke, yet he and I
Worked there as one. He let me seem to work.
The cabinet-makers' shop, all belts and wheels
And whining saws, would thrill me with the scream
Of tortured wood, starting a blackened plank
Under the cruel plane and coming out
Sweet-scented, pink and smooth and richly grained;
While in a far-off shed, caressingly,
French-polishers, all whistling different tunes,
With reeking swabs would rub the coloured woods,
Bringing the figured surfaces to light;
Dark whirling walnut, deep and deeper brown,
And rare mahogany's pressed butterflies.
Beside the timber yard, a favourite hut
Encased the thumping heartbeat of the Works,
An old gas-engine smelling strong of oil.
Its mighty wheel revolved a leather belt
Which, turning lesser wheels and lesser belts,
Spread like a drawing by Heath Robinson
Through all the rambling length of wooden sheds.
    When lunch-time brought me hopes of ginger-beer
I'd meet my father's smile as there he stood
Among his clerks, with pens behind their ears,
In the stern silence of the counting-house;
And he, perhaps not ready to go out,
Would leave me to explore some upper rooms—
One full of ticking clocks, one full of books;
And once I found a dusty drawing-room,
Completely furnished, where long years ago

My great-grandfather lived above his work
Before he moved to sylvan Highbury.
But in the downstair showrooms I could find
No link between the finished articles
And all the clatter of the factory.
The Works in Birmingham, I knew, made glass;
The stoneworks in Torquay made other things . . .
But what did *we* do? This I did not know,
Nor ever wished to—to my father's grief.

    O Mappin, Webb, Asprey and Finnigan!
You polished persons on the retail side—
Old Mag Tags, Paulines and Old Westminsters—
Why did I never take to you? Why now
When, staying in a quiet country house,
I see an onyx ashtray of the firm,
Or in my bedroom, find the figured wood
Of my smooth-sliding dressing-table drawers
Has got a look about it of the Works,
Does my mind flinch so?

                              Partly it is guilt:
'Following in Father's footsteps' was the theme
Of all my early childhood. With what pride
He introduced me to old gentlemen,
Pin-striped commercial travellers of the firm
And tall proprietors of Bond Street shops.
With joy he showed me old George Betjeman's book.
(He was a one-'n' man before the craze
For all things German tacked another 'n'):
'December eighteen seven. Twelve and six—
For helping brother William with his desk.'
Uninteresting then it seemed to me,

Uninteresting still. Slow walks we took
On sunny afternoons to great-great-aunts
In tall Italianate houses: Aberdeen Park,
Hillmarton Road and upper Pooter-land,
Short gravel drives to steepish flights of steps
And stained-glass windows in a purple hall,
A drawing-room with stands of potted plants,
Lace curtains screening other plants beyond.
"Fourth generation—yes, this is the boy."

   Partly my guilt is letting down the men—
William our coachman who, turned chauffeur, still
Longed for his mare and feared the motor-car
Which he would hiss at, polishing its sides;
Bradshaw and Pettit of the lathe and plane;
Fieldhouse and Lovely, and the old and bent
With wire-framed spectacles and aproned knees;
The young apprentices old custom called,
Indentures done, to passing-out parade
Down a long alley formed among the men
Beating on bits of metal. How they all
Trusted that I would fill my father's place!
"The Guv'nor's looking for you, Master John . . ."
"Well now, my boy, I want your solemn word
To carry on the firm when I am gone:
Fourth generation, John—they'll look to you.
They're artist-craftsmen to their fingertips . . .
Go on creating beauty!"
                                        What is beauty?
Here, where I write, the green Atlantic bursts
In cannonades of white along Pentire.
There's beauty here. There's beauty in the slate

And granite smoothed by centuries of sea,
And washed to life as rain and spray bring out
Contrasting strata higher up the cliff,
But none to me in polished wood and stone
Tortured by Father's craftsmen into shapes
To shine in Asprey's showrooms under glass,
A Maharajah's eyeful.

               For myself,
I knew as soon as I could read and write
That I must be a poet. Even today,
When all the way from Cambridge comes a wind
To blow the lamps out every time they're lit,
I know that I must light mine up again.

    My first attraction was to tripping lines;
Internal rhyming, as in Shelley's 'Cloud',
Seemed then perfection. 'O'er' and 'ere' and 'e'en'
Were words I liked to use. My father smiled:
"And how's our budding bard? Let what you write
Be funny, John, and be original."
Secretly proud, I showed off merrily.
But certain as the stars above the twigs
And deeply fearful as the pealing bells
And everlasting as the racing surf
Blown back upon itself in Polzeath Bay,
My urge was to encase in rhythm and rhyme
The things I saw and felt (I could not *think*).

    And so, at sunset, off to Hampstead Heath
I went with pencil and with writing-pad
And stood tip-toe upon a little hill,
Awaiting inspiration from the sky.
"Look! there's a poet!", people might exclaim

On footpaths near. The muse inspired my pen:
The sunset tipped with gold St. Michael's church,
Shouts of boys bathing came from Highgate Ponds,
The elms that hid the houses of the great
Rustled with mystery, and dirt-grey sheep
Grazed in the foreground; but the lines of verse
Came out like parodies of *A & M.*

   The gap between my feelings and my skill
Was so immense, I wonder I went on.
A stretch of heather seen at Haslemere
And 'Up the airy mountain' (Allingham)
Merged in the magic of my Highgate pen:

> When the moors are pink with heather
>   When the sky's as blue as the sea,
> Marching all together
>   Come fairy folk so wee.

My goodness me! It seemed perfection then—
The brilliance of the rhymes A B, A B!
The vastness and the daintiness combined!
The second verse was rather less inspired:

> Some in green and some in red
>   And some with a violet plume,
> And a little cap on each tiny head
>   Watching the bright white moon.

I copied out the lines into a book,
A leather-bound one given me for verse
And stamped with my initials. There it stood
On the first page, that poem—a reproach.
In later years I falsified the date

To make it seem that I was only seven,
Not eight, when these weak stanzas were composed.

   The gap from feeling to accomplishment!
In Highgate days that gap was yawning wide,
But awe and mystery were everywhere,
Most in the purple dark of thin St. Anne's:
Down Fitzroy Park what unimagined depths
Of glade led on to haunts of Robin Hood
(Never a real favourite of mine).
A special Tube train carried Archibald
Northward to Merton, south to Millfield Lane.
A silver blight that made my blood run cold
Hung on a grey house by the cemetery—
So that for years I only liked red brick.
The turrets on the chapel for the dead
And Holly Village with its prickly roofs
Against the sky were terrifying shapes.
"Dong!" went the distant cemetery bell
And chilled for good the east side of the hill
And all things east of me. But in the west
Were health and sunshine, bumps on Hampstead Heath,
Friends, comfort, railways, brandy-balls and grass;
And west of westward, somewhere, Cornwall lay.

   Once when my father took me to the Tate
We stood enraptured by 'The Hopeless Dawn',
The picture first to move me. Twenty times,
They told me, had Frank Bramley watched the flame
Expiring in its candlestick before
He put it down on canvas. Guttering there,
It symbolized the young wife's dying hope
And the old mother's—gazing out to sea:

The meal upon the table lay prepared
But no good man to eat it: through the panes,
An angry sea below the early light
Tossed merciless, as I had seen the waves
In splendid thunder over Greenaway
Send driftwood shooting up the beach as though
Great planks were light as paper. "Put it down!
Translate the picture into verse, my boy,
And here's your opening—

> Through the humble cottage window
> Streams the early dawn."

The lines my father gave me sounded well;
But how continue them? How make a rhyme?

> O'er the tossing bay of Findow
> In the mournful morn.

With rising hopes I sought a gazetteer—
Findochty, Findon, Finglas, Finistère—
Alas! no Findow . . . and the poem died.
   Atlantic rollers bursting in my ears,
And pealing church-bells and the puff of trains,
The sight of sailing clouds, the smell of grass—
Were always calling out to me for words.
I caught at them and missed and missed again.
"Catch hold," my father said, "catch hold like this!",
Trying to teach me how to carpenter,
"Not *that* way, boy! When will you ever learn?"—
I dug the chisel deep into my hand.
"Shoot!" said my father, helping with my gun
And aiming at the rabbit—"Quick, boy, fire!"

411

But I had not released the safety-catch.
I was a poet. That was why I failed.
My faith in this chimera brought an end
To all my father's hopes. In later years,
Now old and ill, he asked me once again
To carry on the firm, I still refused.
And now when I behold, fresh-published, new,
A further volume of my verse, I see
His kind grey eyes look woundedly at mine,
I see his workmen seeking other jobs,
And that red granite obelisk that marks
The family grave in Highgate Cemetery
Points an accusing finger to the sky.

III
Highgate

O Peggy Purey-Cust, how pure you were:
My first and purest love, Miss Purey-Cust!
Satchel on back I hurried up West Hill
To catch you on your morning walk to school,
Your nanny with you and your golden hair
Streaming like sunlight. Strict deportment made
You hold yourself erect and every step
Bounced up and down as though you walked on springs.
Your ice-blue eyes, your lashes long and light,
Your sweetly freckled face and turned-up nose
So haunted me that all my loves since then
Have had a look of Peggy Purey-Cust.
Along the Grove, what happy, happy steps
Under the limes I took to Byron House,
And blob-work, weaving, carpentry and art,
Walking with you; and with what joy returned.
Wendy you were to me in *Peter Pan*,
The Little Match Girl in Hans Andersen—
But I would rescue you before you died.
And once you asked me to your house to tea:
It seemed a palace after 31—
The lofty entrance hall, the flights of stairs,
The huge expanse of sunny drawing-room,
Looking for miles across the chimney-pots
To spired St. Pancras and the dome of Paul's;
And there your mother from a sofa smiled.

After that tea I called and called again,
But Peggy was not in. She was away;
She wasn't well. *House of the Sleeping Winds*,
My favourite book with whirling art-nouveau
And Walter Crane-ish colour plates, I brought
To cheer her sick-bed. It was taken in.
Weeks passed and passed . . . and then it was returned.
Oh gone for ever, Peggy Purey-Cust!

   And at that happy school in Byron House
Only one harbinger of future woe
Came to me in those far, sun-gilded days—
Gold with the hair of Peggy Purey-Cust—
Two other boys (my rivals, I suppose)
Came suddenly round a corner, caught my arms
And one, a treacherous, stocky little Scot,
Winded me with a punch and "Want some more?"
He grunted when I couldn't speak for pain.
Why did he do it? Why that other boy,
Who hitherto had been a friend of mine,
Was his accomplice I could not divine,
Nor ever have done. But those fatal two
Continued with me to another school—
Avernus by the side of Highgate Hill.

   Let those who have such memories recollect
Their sinking dread of going back to school.
I well remember mine. I see again
The great headmaster's study lined with books
Where somewhere, in a corner, there were canes.
He wrapped his gown, the great headmaster did,
About himself, chucked off his mortar-board
And, leaning back, said: "Let's see what you know,

How many half-crowns are there in a pound?"
I didn't know. I couldn't even guess.
My poor fond father, hearing nothing, smiled;
The gold clock ticked; the waiting furniture
Shone like a colour plate by H. M. Brock . . .
No answer—and the great headmaster frown'd;
But let me in to Highgate Junior School.

In late September, in the conker time,
When Poperinghe and Zillebeke and Mons
Boomed with five-nines, large sepia gravures
Of French, Smith-Dorrien and Haig were given
Gratis with each half-pound of Brooke Bond tea.
A neighbour's son had just been killed at Ypres;
Another had been wounded. *Rainbow* came
On Wednesdays—with the pranks of Tiger Tim,
And Bonnie Bluebell and her magic gloves.
'Your Country needs you!' serious Kitchener
Commanded from the posters. Up West Hill
I walked red-capped and jacketed to school,
A new boy much too early: school at nine,
And here I was outside at half-past eight.
I see the asphalt slope and smell again
The sluggish, sour, inadequate latrines.
I watch the shrubbery shake as, leaping out,
Come my two enemies of Byron House,
But now red-capped and jacketed like me:

> "Betjeman's a German spy—
> Shoot him down and let him die:
> Betjeman's a German spy,
> A German spy, a German spy."

They danced around me and their merry shouts
Brought other merry newcomers to see.

    Walking from school is a consummate art:
Which routes to follow to avoid the gangs,
Which paths to find that lead, circuitous,
To leafy squirrel haunts and plopping ponds,
For dreams of Archibald and Tiger Tim;
Which hiding-place is safe, and when it is;
What time to leave to dodge the enemy.
I only once was trapped. I knew the trap—
I heard it in their tones: "Walk back with us."
I knew they weren't my friends; but that soft voice
Wheedled me from my route to cold Swain's Lane.
There in a holly bush they threw me down,
Pulled off my shorts, and laughed and ran away;
And, as I struggled up, I saw grey brick,
The cemetery railings and the tombs.

    See the rich elms careering down the hill—
Full billows rolling into Holloway;
In the tall classroom hear again the drone
Of multiplication tables chanted out;
Recall how Kelly stood us in a ring:
"Three sevens, then add eight, and take away
Twelve; what's the answer?" Hesitation then
Meant shaking by the shoulders till we cried.
Deal out again the dog-eared poetry books
Where Hemans, Campbell, Longfellow and Scott
Mixed their dim lights with Edgar Allan Poe
(Who 'died of dissipation', said the notes).
"And what is dissipation, please, Miss Long?"
Its dreadfulness so pleased me that I learned

'The Bells' by heart, but all the time preferred
'Casabianca' and 'The Hesperus'
As poetry, and Campbell's 'Soldier's Dream'.
I couldn't see why Shakespeare was admired;
I thought myself as good as Campbell now
And very nearly up to Longfellow;
And so I bound my verse into a book,
The Best of Betjeman, and handed it
To one who, I was told, liked poetry—
The American master, Mr. Eliot.
That dear good man, with Prufrock in his head
And Sweeney waiting to be agonized,
I wonder what he thought? He never says
When now we meet, across the port and cheese.
He looks the same as then, long, lean and pale,
Still with the slow deliberating speech
And enigmatic answers. At the time
A boy called Jelly said "He thinks they're bad"—
But he himself is still too kind to say.

IV
Cornwall in Childhood

Come, Hygiene, goddess of the growing boy,
I here salute thee in Sanatogen!
Anaemic girls need Virol, but for me
Be Scott's Emulsion, rusks, and Mellin's Food,
Cod-liver oil and malt, and for my neck
Wright's Coal Tar Soap, Euthymol for my teeth.
Come, friends of Hygiene, Electricity
And those young twins, Free Thought and clean Fresh Air:
Attend the long express from Waterloo
That takes us down to Cornwall. Tea-time shows
The small fields waiting, every blackthorn hedge
Straining inland before the south-west gale.
The emptying train, wind in the ventilators,
Puffs out of Egloskerry to Tresméer
Through minty meadows, under bearded trees
And hills upon whose sides the clinging farms
Hold Bible Christians. Can it really be
That this same carriage came from Waterloo?
On Wadebridge station what a breath of sea
Scented the Camel valley! Cornish air,
Soft Cornish rains, and silence after steam . . .
As out of Derry's stable came the brake
To drag us up those long, familiar hills,
Past haunted woods and oil-lit farms and on
To far Trebetherick by the sounding sea.

    Oh what a host of questions in me rose:

Were spring tides here or neap? And who was down?
Had Mr. Rosevear built himself a house?
Was there another wreck upon Doom Bar?
The carriage lamps lit up the pennywort
And fennel in the hedges of the lane;
Huge slugs were crawling over slabs of slate;
Then, safe in bed, I watched the long-legg'd fly
With red transparent body tap the walls
And fizzle in the candle flame and drag
Its poisonous-looking abdomen away
To somewhere out of sight and out of mind,
While through the open window came the roar
Of full Atlantic rollers on the beach.

    Then before breakfast down toward the sea
I ran alone, monarch of miles of sand,
Its shining stretches satin-smooth and vein'd.
I felt beneath bare feet the lugworm casts
And walked where only gulls and oyster-catchers
Had stepped before me to the water's edge.
The morning tide flowed in to welcome me,
The fan-shaped scallop shells, the backs of crabs,
The bits of driftwood worn to reptile shapes,
The heaps of bladder-wrack the tide had left
(Which, lifted up, sent sandhoppers to leap
In hundreds round me) answered "Welcome back!"
Along the links and under cold Bray Hill
Fresh water pattered from an iris marsh
And drowned the golf-balls on its stealthy way
Over the slates in which the elvers hid,
And spread across the beach. I used to stand,
A speculative water engineer—

Here I would plan a dam and there a sluice
And thus divert the stream, creating lakes,
A chain of locks descending to the sea.
Inland I saw, above the tamarisks,
From various villas morning breakfast smoke
Which warned me then of mine; so up the lane
I wandered home contented, full of plans,
Pulling a length of pink convolvulus
Whose blossoms, almost as I picked them, died.

    Bright as the morning sea those early days!
Though there were tears, and sand thrown in my eyes,
And punishments and smells of mackintosh,
Long barefoot climbs to fetch the morning milk,
Terrors from hissing geese and angry shouts,
Slammed doors and waitings and a sense of dread,
Still warm as shallow sea-pools in the sun
And welcoming to me the girls and boys.

    Wet rocks on which our bathing dresses dried;
Small coves, deserted in our later years
For more adventurous inlets down the coast:
Paralysis when climbing up the cliff—
Too steep to reach the top, too far to fall,
Tumbling to death in seething surf below,
A ledge just wide enough to lodge one's foot,
A sea-pink clump the only thing to clutch,
Cold wave-worn slate so mercilessly smooth
And no one near and evening coming on—
Till Ralph arrived: "Now put your left foot here.
Give us your hand" . . . and back across the years
I swing to safety with old friends again.
Small seem they now, those once tremendous cliffs,

Diminished now those joy-enclosing bays.

    Sweet were the afternoons of treasure-hunts.
We searched in pairs and lifted after showers
The diamond-sparkling sprays of tamarisk:
Their pendent raindrops would release themselves
And soak our shirt-sleeves. Then upon the links
Under a tee-box lay a baffling clue:
A foursome puffing past the sunlit hedge
With rattling golf bags; all the singing grass
Busy with crickets and blue butterflies;
The burnet moths, the unresponsive sheep
Seemed maddeningly indifferent to our plight . . .
"Oh, hurry up, man: why, we're third from last."
And in the Oakleys' garden after tea
Of splits and cream under old apple boughs,
With high tide offering prospects of a bathe,
The winners had their prizes. Once I won—
But that was an unfortunate affair:
My mother set the clues and I, the host,
Knew well the likely workings of her mind.

    Do you remember, Joan, the awkward time
When we were non-co-operative at sports,
Refusing to be organized in heats?
And when at last we were, and had to race
Out to low-tide line and then back again,
A chocolate biscuit was the only prize?
I laughed. Miss Tunstall sent me home to bed.
You laughed, but not so loudly, and escaped.

    That was the summer Audrey, Joc and I
And all the rest of us were full of hope:
"Miss Usher's coming." Who Miss Usher was,

And why she should be coming, no one asked.
She came, a woman of the open air,
Swarthy and in Girl Guide-y sort of clothes:
How nice she was to Audrey and to Joc,
How *very* nice to Biddy and to Joan . . .
But somehow, somehow, not so nice to me.
"I *love* Miss Usher," Audrey said. "Don't you?"
"Oh yes," I answered. "So do I," said Joc
"We vote Miss Usher topping. Itchicoo!"
What was it I had done? Made too much noise?
Increased Miss Tunstall's headache? Disobeyed?
After Miss Usher had gone home to Frant,
Miss Tunstall took me quietly to the hedge:
"Now shall I tell you what Miss Usher said
About you, John?" "Oh please, Miss Tunstall, do!"
"She said you were a common little boy."

    Childhood is measured out by sounds and smells
And sights, before the dark of reason grows.
Ears! Hear again the wild sou'westers whine!
Three days on end would the September gale
Slam at our bungalows; three days on end
Rattling cheap doors and making tempers short.
It mattered not, for then enormous waves
House-high rolled thunderous on Greenaway,
Flinging up spume and shingle to the cliffs.
Unmoved amid the foam, the cormorant
Watched from its peak. In all the roar and swirl
The still and small things gained significance.
Somehow the freckled cowrie would survive
And prawns hang waiting in their watery woods;
Deep in the noise there was a core of peace;

Deep in my heart a warm security.

Nose! Smell again the early morning smells:
Congealing bacon and my father's pipe;
The after-breakfast freshness out of doors
Where sun had dried the heavy dew and freed
Acres of thyme to scent the links and lawns;
The rotten apples on our shady path
Where blowflies settled upon squashy heaps,
Intent and gorging; at the garden gate
Reek of Solignum on the wooden fence;
Mint round the spring, and fennel in the lane,
And honeysuckle wafted from the hedge;
The Lynams' cess-pool like a body-blow;
Then, clean, medicinal and cold—the sea.
"Breathe in the ozone, John. It's iodine."
But which is iodine and which is drains?
Salt and hot sun on rubber water-wings . . .
Home to the luncheon smell of Irish stew
And washing-up stench from the kitchen sink
Because the sump is blocked. The afternoons
Brought coconut smell of gorse; at Mably's farm
Sweet scent of drying cowdung; then the moist
Exhaling of the earth in Shilla woods—
First earth encountered after days of sand.
Evening brought back the gummy smell of toys
And fishy stink of glue and Stickphast paste,
And sleep inside the laundriness of sheets.

Eyes! See again the rock-face in the lane,
Years before tarmac and the motor-car.
Across the estuary Stepper Point
Stands, still unquarried, black against the sun;

On its Atlantic face the cliffs fall sheer.
Look down into the weed world of the lawn—
The devil's-coach-horse beetle hurries through,
Lifting its tail up as I bar the way
To further flowery jungles.
                                    See once more
The Padstow ferry, worked by oar and sail,
Her outboard engine always going wrong,
Ascend the slippery quay's up-ended slate,
The sea-weed hanging from the harbour wall.
Hot was the pavement under, as I gazed
At lanterns, brass, rope and ships' compasses
In the marine-store window on the quay.
The shoe-shop in the square was cool and dark.
The Misses Quintrell, fancy stationers,
Had most to show me—dialect tales in verse
Published in Truro (Netherton and Worth)
And model lighthouses of serpentine.
Climb the steep hill to where that belt of elm
Circles the town and church tower, reached by lanes
Whose ferny ramparts shelter toadflax flowers
And periwinkles. See hydrangeas bloom
In warm back-gardens full of fuchsia bells.
To the returning ferry soon draws near
Our own low bank of sand-dunes; then the walk
Over a mile of quicksand evening-cold.
   It all is there, excitement for the eyes,
Imagined ghosts on unfrequented roads
Gated and winding up through broom and gorse
Out of the parish, on to who knows where?
What pleasure, as the oil-lamp sparkled gold

On cut-glass tumblers and the flip of cards,
To feel protected from the night outside:
Safe Cornish holidays before the storm!

V

Private School

———————

Percival Mandeville, the perfect boy,
Was all a schoolmaster could wish to see—
Upright and honourable, good at games,
Well-built, blue-eyed; a sense of leadership
Lifted him head and shoulders from the crowd.
His work was good. His written answers, made
In a round, tidy and decided hand,
Pleased the examiners. His open smile
Enchanted others. He could also frown
On anything unsporting, mean or base,
Unworthy of the spirit of the school
And what it stood for. Oh the dreadful hour
When once upon a time he frowned on me!
Just what had happened I cannot recall—
Maybe some bullying in the dormitory;
But well I recollect his warning words:
"I'll fight you, Betjeman, you swine, for that,
Behind the bike shed before morning school."
So all the previous night I spewed with fear.
I could not box: I greatly dreaded pain.
A recollection of the winding punch
Jack Drayton once delivered, blows and boots
Upon the bum at Highgate Junior School,
All multiplied by X from Mandeville,
Emptied my bladder. Silent in the dorm
I cleaned my teeth and clambered into bed.

Thin seemed pyjamas and inadequate
The regulation blankets once so warm.
"What's up?" "Oh, nothing." I expect they knew . . .
And, in the morning, cornflakes, bread and tea,
Cook's Farm Eggs and a spoon of marmalade,
Which heralded the North and Hillard hours
Of Latin composition, brought the post.
Breakfast and letters! Then it was a flash
Of hope, escape and inspiration came:
Invent a letter of bad news from home.
I hung my head and tried to look as though,
By keeping such a brave stiff upper lip
And just not blubbing, I was noble too.
I sought out Mandeville. "I say," I said,
"I'm frightfully sorry I can't fight today.
I've just received some rotten news from home:
My mater's very ill." No need for more—
His arm was round my shoulder comforting:
"All right, old chap. Of course I understand."

　　Before the hymn the Skipper would announce
The latest names of those who'd lost their lives
For King and Country and the Dragon School.
Sometimes his gruff old voice was full of tears
When a particular favourite had been killed.
Then we would hear the nickname of the boy,
'Pongo' or 'Podge', and how he'd played 3Q
For Oxford and, if only he had lived,
He might have played for England—which he did,
But in a grimmer game against the Hun.
And then we'd all look solemn, knowing well
There'd be no extra holiday today.

427

And we were told we each must do our bit,
And so we knitted shapeless gloves from string
For men in mine-sweepers, and on the map
We stuck the Allied flags along the Somme;
Visited wounded soldiers; learned by heart
Those patriotic lines of Oxenham

> What can a little chap do
> For his country and for you—

"He can boil his head in the stew",
We added, for the trenches and the guns
Meant less to us than bicycles and gangs
And marzipan and what there was for prep.

   Take me, my Centaur bike, down Linton Road,
Gliding by newly planted almond trees
Where the young dons with wives in tussore clad
Were building in the morning of their lives
Houses for future Dragons. Rest an arm
Upon the post of the allotment path,
Then dare the slope! We choked in our own dust,
The narrowness of the footpath made our speed
Seem swift as light. May-bush and elm flashed by,
Allotment holders turning round to stare,
Potatoes in their hands. Speed-wobble! Help!
And, with the Sturmey-Archer three-speed gear
Safely in bottom, resting from the race
We pedalled round the new-mown meadow-grass
By Marston Ferry with its punt and chain.
   Show me thy road, Crick, in the early spring:
Laurel and privet and laburnum ropes

And gabled-gothic houses gathered round
Thy mothering spire, St. Philip and St. James.
Here by the low brick semi-private walls
Bicycling past a trotting butcher's-cart,
I glimpsed, behind lace curtains, silver hair
Of sundry old Professors. Here were friends
Of Ruskin, Newman, Pattison and Froude
Among their books and plants and photographs
In comfortable twilight. But for me,
Less academic, red-brick Chalfont Road
Meant great-aunt Wilkins, tea and buttered toast.

    Ronald Hughes Wright, come with me once again
Bicycling off to churches in the town:
St. Andrew's first, with neo-Norman apse,
St. Old's—distinctly Evangelical—
And, Lower still, St. Ebbe's, which smelt of gas.
In New Inn Hall Street dare the double doors,
Partitions and red baize till stands revealed
Peter-le-Bailey's Irish gothic nave.

    St. Giles' had still a proper fair-ground air,
For Oxford once had been a Cotswold town
Standing in water meadows of the Thames:
The cattle moaned in pens on Gloucester Green;
In George Street there were country cottages;
And thy weak Dec., St. George-the-Martyr's church,
Prepared us for our final port of call—
St. Aloysius of the Church of Rome.
Its incense, reliquaries, brass and lights
Made all seem plain and trivial back at school.

    One lucky afternoon in Chaundy's shop
I bought a book with tipped-in colour plates—

'City of Dreaming Spires' or some such name—
Soft late-Victorian water-colours framed
Against brown paper pages. Thus it was
'Sunset in Worcester Gardens' meant for me
Such beauty in that black and shallow pool
That even today, when from the ilex tree
I see its shining length, I fail to hear
The all-too-near and omnipresent train.
The Founder's Tower in Magdalen still seems drowned
In red Virginia creeper, and The High
Has but one horse-tram down its famous length,
While a gowned Doctor of Divinity
Enters the porch of Univ.; Christ Church stairs
(A single column supporting the intricate roof),
Wallflowers upon the ruined city wall,
Wistaria-mantled buildings in St. John's—
All that was crumbling, picturesque and quaint
Informed my taste and sent me biking off,
Escaped from games, for Architecture bound.

    Can words express the unexampled thrill
I first enjoyed in Norm., E.E. and Dec.?
Norm., crude and round and strong and primitive,
E.E., so lofty, pointed, fine and pure,
And Dec. the high perfection of it all,
Flowingly curvilinear, from which
The Perp. showed such a 'lamentable decline'.
Who knew what undiscovered glories hung
Waiting in locked-up churches—vaulting shafts,
Pillar-piscinas, floreated caps.,
Squints, squinches, low side windows, quoins and groins—

Till I had roused the Vicar, found the key,
And made a quick inspection of the church?
Then, full of my discovery returned,
Hot from my bicycle to Gerald Haynes.

   Much do I owe this formidable man
(Harrow and Keble): from his shambling height
Over his spectacles he nodded down.
We called him 'Tortoise'. From his lower lip
Invariably hung a cigarette.
A gym-shoe in his hand, he stood about
Waiting for misdemeanours—then he'd pounce:
"Who's talking here?" The dormitory quailed.
"Who's talking?" Then, though innocent myself,
A schoolboy hero to the dorm at last,
Bravely I answered, "Please, sir, it was me."
"All right. Bend over." A resounding three
From the strong gym-shoe brought a gulp of pain.
"I liked the way you took that beating, John.
Reckon yourself henceforth a gentleman."
Were those the words that made me follow him,
Waiting for hours in churches while he fixed
His huge plate camera up and, a black cloth
Over his bald head, photographed the font?
Was that the reason why the pale grey slides
Of tympana, scratch dials and Norfolk screens
So pleased me at his lectures? I think not:
Rather his kindness and his power to share
Joys of his own, churches and botany,
With those of us whose tastes he could inform.
He motor-bicycled his life away,

Looking for orchids in the Wytham Woods,
And Early English in Northamptonshire.
He was the giver: ours it was to take.

The bindweed hung in leafy loops
    O'er half a hundred hawthorn caves,
For Godstow bound, the white road wound
    In swirls of dust and narrow shaves,
And we were biking, Red Sea troops,
    Between the high cow-parsley waves.

Port Meadow's level green grew near
    With Wytham Woods and Cumnor Hurst:
I clicked my Sturmey-Archer gear
    And pedalled till I nearly burst—
And, king of speed, attained the lead
    And got to gushing Godstow first.

The skiffs were moored above the lock,
    They bumped each other side to side:
I boarded one and made her rock—
    "Shut up, you fool," a master cried.
By reed and rush and alder-bush
    See soon our long procession glide.

There is a world of water weed
    Seen only from a shallow boat:
Deep forests of the bladed reed
    Whose wolves are rats of slimy coat,
Whose yellow lily-blossoms need
    Broad leaves to keep themselves afloat.

A heaving world, half-land, half-flood;
    It rose and sank as ripples rolled,
The hideous larva from the mud
    Clung to a reed with patient hold,
Waiting to break its sheath and make
    An aeroplane of green and gold.

The picnic and the orchid hunt,
    On Oxey mead the rounders played,
The belly-floppers from the punt,
    The echoes that our shouting made:
The rowing back, relaxed and slack,
    The shipping oars in Godstow shade . . .

Once more we biked beside the hedge—
    And darker seemed the hawthorn caves
And lonelier looked the water's edge,
    And we were sad returning slaves
To bell and rule and smell of school,
    Beyond the high cow-parsley waves.

VI
London

When I returned from school I found we'd moved:
"53 Church Street. Yes, the slummy end"—
A little laugh accompanied the joke,
For we were Chelsea now and we had friends
Whose friends had friends who knew Augustus John:
We liked bold colour schemes—orange and black—
And clever daring plays about divorce
At the St. Martin's. Oh, our lives were changed!
Ladies with pearls and hyphenated names
Supplanted simpler aunts from Muswell Hill:
A brand-new car and brand-new chauffeur came
To carry off my father to the Works.
                  Old Hannah Wallis left:
For years she'd listened to me reading verse;
Tons, if you added them, of buttered toast
Had she and I consumed through all the days
In happy Highgate. Now her dear old face,
Black bonnet, sniffs and comfortable self
Were gone to Tottenham where her daughter lived.
   What is it first breeds insecurity?
Perhaps a change of house? I missed the climb
By garden walls and fences where a stick,
Dragged on the palings, clattered to my steps.
I missed the smell of trodden leaves and grass,
Millfield and Merton Lanes and sheep-worn tracks
Under the hawthorns west of Highgate ponds.

I missed the trams, the few North London trains,
The frequent Underground to Kentish Town.
Here in a district only served by bus,
Here on an urban level by the Thames—
I never really liked the Chelsea house.
"It's simply sweet, Bess," visitors exclaimed,
Depositing their wraps and settling down
To a nice rubber. "So artistic, too."
To me the house was poky, dark and cramped,
Haunted by quarrels and the ground-floor ghost.
I'd slam behind me our green garden door—
Well do I recollect that bounding thrill!—
And hare to Cheyne Gardens—free! free! free!—
By Lawrence Street and Upper Cheyne Row,
Safe to the tall red house of Ronnie Wright.

    Great was my joy with London at my feet—
All London mine, five shillings in my hand
And not expected back till after tea!
Great was our joy, Ronald Hughes Wright's and mine,
To travel by the Underground all day
Between the rush hours, so that very soon
There was no station, north to Finsbury Park,
To Barking eastwards, Clapham Common south,
No temporary platform in the west
Among the Actons and the Ealings, where
We had not once alighted. Metroland
Beckoned us out to lanes in beechy Bucks—
Goldschmidt and Howland (in a wooden hut
Beside the station): 'Most attractive sites
Ripe for development'; Charrington's for coal;
And not far off the neo-Tudor shops.

We knew the different railways by their smells.
The City and South reeked like a changing-room;
Its orange engines and old rolling-stock,
Its narrow platforms, undulating tracks,
Seemed even then historic. Next in age,
The Central London, with its cut-glass shades
On draughty stations, had an ozone smell—
Not seaweed-scented ozone from the sea
But something chemical from Birmingham.
When, in a pause between the stations, quiet
Descended on the carriage we would talk
Loud gibberish in angry argument,
Pretending to be foreign.
                                    Then I found
Second-hand bookshops in the Essex Road,
Stacked high with powdery leather flaked and dry,
Gilt letters on red labels—*Mason's Works*
(But volume II is missing), Young's *Night Thoughts*,
Falconer's *Shipwreck* and *The Grave* by Blair,
A row of Scott, for certain incomplete,
And always somewhere Barber's *Isle of Wight*;
The antiquarian works that no one reads—
Church Bells of Nottingham, Baptismal Fonts
('Scarce, 2s. 6d., a few plates slightly foxed').
Once on a stall in Farringdon Road I found
An atlas folio of great lithographs,
Views of Ionian Isles, flyleaf inscribed
By Edward Lear—and bought it for a bob.
Perhaps one day I'll find a 'first' of Keats,
Wedged between Goldsmith and *The Law of Torts*;
Perhaps—but that was not the reason why

Untidy bookshops gave me such delight.
It was the smell of books, the plates in them,
Tooled leather, marbled paper, gilded edge,
The armorial book-plate of some country squire,
From whose tall library windows spread his park
On which this polished spine may once have looked,
From whose twin candlesticks may once have shone
Soft beams upon the spacious title-page.
Forgotten poets, parsons with a taste
For picturesque descriptions of a hill
Or ruin in the parish, pleased me much;
But steel engravings pleased me most of all—
Volumes of London views or Liverpool,
Or Edinburgh, 'The Athens of the North'.
I read the prose descriptions, gazed and gazed
Deep in the plates, and heard again the roll
Of market-carts on cobbles, coach-doors slammed
Outside the posting inn; with couples walked
Toward the pillared entrance of the church
'Lately erected from designs by Smirke';
And sauntered in some newly planted square.
Outside the bookshop, treasure in my hands,
I scarcely saw the trams or heard the bus
Or noticed modern London: I was back
With George the Fourth, post-horns, street-cries and bells.
"More books," my mother sighed as I returned;
My father, handing to me half-a-crown,
Said, "If you must buy books, then buy the best."

    All silvery on frosty Sunday nights
Were City steeples white against the stars.
And narrowly the chasms wound between

Italianate counting-houses, Roman banks,
To this church and to that. Huge office-doors,
Their granite thresholds worn by weekday feet
(Now far away in slippered ease at Penge),
Stood locked. St. Botolph this, St. Mary that
Alone shone out resplendent in the dark.
I used to stand by intersecting lanes
Among the silent offices, and wait,
Choosing which bell to follow: not a peal,
For that meant somewhere active; not St. Paul's,
For that was too well-known. I liked things dim—
Some lazy Rector living in Bexhill
Who most unwillingly on Sunday came
To take the statutory services.
A single bell would tinkle down a lane:
My echoing steps would track the source of sound—
A cassocked verger, bell-rope in his hands,
Called me to high box pews, to cedar wood
(Like incense where no incense ever burned),
To ticking gallery-clock, and charity bench,
And free seats for the poor, and altar-piece—
Gilded Commandment boards—and sword-rests made
For long-discarded aldermanic pomp.
A hidden organist sent reedy notes
To flute around the plasterwork. I stood,
And from the sea of pews a single head
With cherries nodding on a black straw hat
Rose in a neighbouring pew. The caretaker?
Or the sole resident parishioner?
And so once more, as for three hundred years,
This carven wood, these grey memorial'd walls

Heard once again the Book of Common Prayer,
While somewhere at the back the verger, now
Turned Parish Clerk, would rumble out "Amen."
'Twas not, I think, a conscious search for God
That brought me to these dim forgotten fanes.
Largely it was a longing for the past,
With a slight sense of something unfulfilled;
And yet another feeling drew me there,
A sense of guilt increasing with the years—
"When I am dead you will be sorry, John"—
Here I could pray my mother would not die.
Thus were my London Sundays incomplete
If unaccompanied by Evening Prayer.
How trivial used to seem the Underground,
How worldly looked the over-lighted west,
How different and smug and wise I felt
When from the east I made my journey home!

VII
Marlborough

Luxuriating backwards in the bath,
I swish the warmer water round my legs
Towards my shoulders, and the waves of heat
Bring those five years of Marlborough through to me,
In comfortable retrospect: 'Thank God
I'll never have to go through them again.'
As with my toes I reach towards the tap
And turn it to a trickle, stealing warm
About my tender person, comes a voice,
An inner voice that calls, 'Be fair! be fair!
It was not quite as awful as you think.'
In steam like this the changing-room was bathed;
Pink bodies splashed hot water on themselves
After the wonderful release from games,
When Atherton would lead the songs we sang.
I see the tall Memorial Reading Room,
Which smelt of boots and socks and water-pipes,
Its deaf invigilator on his throne—
"*Do you tickle your arse with a feather, Mr. Purdick?*"
"*What?*"
"*Particularly nasty weather, Mr. Purdick!*"
"*Oh.*"

    And, as the water cools, the Marlborough terms
Form into seasons. Winter starts us off,
Lasting two years, for we were new boys twice—
Once in a junior, then a senior house.

Spring has its love and summer has its art:
It is the winter that remains with me,
Black as our college suits, as cold and thin.
    Doom! Shivering doom! Clutching a leather grip
Containing things for the first night of term—
House-slippers, sponge-bag, pyjams, Common Prayer,
My health certificate, photographs of home
(Where were my bike, my playbox and my trunk?)—
I walked with strangers down the hill to school.
The town's first gaslights twinkled in the cold.
Deserted by the coaches, poorly served
By railway, Marlborough was a lonely place;
The old Bath Road, in chalky whiteness, raised
Occasional clouds of dust as motors passed.
    Those few who read Dean Farrar's *Eric* now
Read merely for a laugh; yet still for me
That mawkish and oh-so-melodious book
Holds one great truth—through every page there runs
The schoolboy sense of an impending doom
Which goes with rows of desks and clanging bells.
It filters down from God, to Master's Lodge,
Through housemasters and prefects to the fags.
    Doom! Shivering doom! Inexorable bells
To early school, to chapel, school again:
Compulsory constipation, hurried meals
Bulked out with Whipped Cream Walnuts from the town.
At first there was the dread of breaking rules—
"Betjeman, you know that new boys mustn't show
Their hair below the peak of college caps:
Stand still and have your face slapped." "Sorry, Jones."
The dread of beatings! Dread of being late!

And, greatest dread of all, the dread of games!
    "The centre and the mainspring of your lives,
The inspiration for your work and sport,
The corporate life of this great public school
Spring from its glorious chapel. Day by day
You come to worship in its noble walls,
Hallowed by half a century of prayer."
The Old Marlburian bishop thundered on
When all I worshipped were the athletes, ranged
In the pews opposite. "Be pure," he cried,
And, for a moment, stilled the sea of coughs.
"Do nothing that would make your mother blush
If she could see you. When the Tempter comes
Spurn him and God will lift you from the mire."
Oh, who is God? O tell me, who is God?
Perhaps He hides behind the reredos . . .
Give me a God whom I can touch and see.
The bishop was more right than he could know,
For safe in G. F. Bodley's greens and browns,
Safe in the surge of undogmatic hymns,
The Chapel *was* the centre of my life—
The only place where I could be alone.

    There was a building known as Upper School
(Abolished now, thank God, and all its ways),
An eighteen-fifty warehouse smelling strong
Of bat-oil, biscuits, sweat and rotten fruit.
The corporate life of which the bishop spoke,
At any rate among the junior boys,
Went on within its echoing whitewashed walls.
    Great were the ranks and privileges there:
Four captains ruled, selected for their brawn

And skill at games; and how we reverenced them!
Twelve friends they chose as brawny as themselves.
'Big Fire' we called them; lording it they sat
In huge armchairs beside the warming flames
Or played at indoor hockey in the space
Reserved for them. The rest of us would sit
Crowded on benches round another grate.

   Before the master came for evening prep
The captains entered at official pace
And, walking down the alley-way of desks,
Beat on their level lids with supple canes.
This was the sign for new boys to arise,
To pick up paper, apple-cores and darts
And fill huge baskets with the muck they found;
Then, wiping hands upon grey handkerchiefs
And trousers, settle down to Latin prose.

   Upper School captains had the power to beat:
Maximum six strokes, usually three.
My frequent crime was far too many books,
So that my desk lid would not shut at all:
"Come to Big Fire then, Betjeman, after prep."
I tried to concentrate on delicate points—
Ut, whether final or consecutive?
(Oh happy private-school days when I knew!)—
While all the time I thought of pain to come.
Swift after prep all raced towards 'Big Fire',
Giving the captain space to swing his cane:
"*One*," they would shout and downward came the blow;
"*Two*" (rather louder); then, exultant, "*Three!*"
And some in ecstasy would bellow "*Four.*"
These casual beatings brought us no disgrace,

443

Rather a kind of glory. In the dorm,
Comparing bruises, other boys could show
Far worse ones that the beaks and prefects made.
    No, Upper School's most terrible disgrace
Involved a very different sort of pain.
Our discontents and enmities arose
Somewhere about the seventh week of term:
The holidays too far off to count the days
Till our release, the weeks behind, a blank.
"Haven't you heard?" said D. C. Wilkinson.
"Angus is to be basketed tonight."
Why Angus . . . ? Never mind. The victim's found.
Perhaps he sported coloured socks too soon,
Perhaps he smarmed his hair with scented oil,
Perhaps he was 'immoral' or a thief.
We did not mind the cause: for Angus now
The game was up. His friends deserted him,
And after his disgrace they'd stay away
For fear of being basketed themselves.
"*By* the boys, *for* the boys. The boys know best.
Leave it to them to pick the rotters out
With that rough justice decent schoolboys know."
And at the end of term the victim left—
Never to wear an old Marlburian tie.
    In quieter tones we asked in Hall that night
Neighbours to pass the marge; the piles of bread
Lay in uneaten slices with the jam.
Too thrilled to eat we raced across the court
Under the frosty stars to Upper School.
Elaborately easy at his desk
Sat Angus, glancing through *The Autocar*.

444

Fellows walked past him trying to make it look
As if they didn't know his coming fate,
Though the boy's body called "Unclean! Unclean!"
And all of us felt goody-goody-good,
Nice wholesome boys who never sinned at all.
At ten to seven 'Big Fire' came marching in
Unsmiling, while the captains stayed outside
(For this was 'unofficial'). Twelve to one:
What chance had Angus? They surrounded him,
Pulled off his coat and trousers, socks and shoes
And, wretched in his shirt, they hoisted him
Into the huge waste-paper basket; then
Poured ink and treacle on his head. With ropes
They strung the basket up among the beams,
And as he soared I only saw his eyes
Look through the slats at us who watched below.
Seven. "It's prep." They let the basket down
And Angus struggled out. "Left! Right! Left! Right!"
We stamped and called as, stained and pale, he strode
Down the long alley-way between the desks,
Holding his trousers, coat and pointed shoes.
"You're for it next," said H. J. Anderson.
"I'm not." "You are. I've heard." So all that term
And three terms afterwards I crept about,
Avoiding public gaze. I kept my books
Down in the basement where the boot-hole was
And by its fishtail gas-jet nursed my fear.

The smell of trodden leaves beside the Kennet,
    On Sunday walks, with Swinburne in my brain,
November showers upon the chalk dust, when it
    Would turn to streaming milk in Manton Lane
And coming back to feel one's footsteps drag
At smells of burning toast and cries of "Fag!".

The after-light that hangs along the hedges,
    On sunward sides of them when sun is down,
The sprinkled lights about the borough's edges,
    The pale green gas-lamps winking in the town,
The waiting elm-boughs black against the blue
Which still to westward held a silver hue—

Alone beside the fives-courts pacing, pacing,
    Waiting for God knows what. O stars above!
My clothes clung tight to me, my heart was racing:
    Perhaps what I was waiting for was love!
And what is love? And wherefore is its shape
To do with legs and arms and waist and nape?

First tremulous desires in Autumn stillness—
    Grey eyes, lips laughing at another's joke,
A nose, a cowlick—a delightful illness
    That put me off my food and off my stroke.
Here, 'twixt the church tower and the chapel spire
Rang sad and deep the bells of my desire.

Desire for what? I think I can explain.
The boys I worshipped did not notice me:
The boys who noticed me I did not like . . .
And life was easier in terms of jokes
And gossip, chattered with contemporaries—

And then there came my final summer term.

    "Coming down town?" I had not thought of him,
Though for four years we'd struggled up the school
In the same house. He was a noisy boy,
One of a gang so mad on motor-cars
That I, the aesthete, hardly noticed him.
Why should he want to go down town with me?
Perhaps because his friends had parents down,
Perhaps because we both were on our own—
But off we walked to Stratton, Sons & Mead
Down the hot High Street. "Can't think why we pay
Threepence at Knapton's for a water ice
When Ducks' is tuppence. There's a Frazer-Nash.
Gosh, what an engine! Did you hear her rev?"
Returning with sardines and sausages,
We found the College empty—free till six—
All Wiltshire winking in the summer sun.

    We changed and bicycled to Silbury
By burnt-up hawthorn edged again with white
From chalk dust whirled by Fords and Lancias
Scorching to Bath. Up Seven Barrows Hill
We overtook a six-ton Sentinel,
Our bike chains creaking with the strain. The heat
Cooled into green below the waiting elms
That rampart round sepulchral Avebury.
And gliding through the Winterbournes was peace:
Calm as canoeing were those winding lanes
Of meadowsweet and umbelliferae.

    He took the lead and raced for Hackpen Hill,
Up, up and up and waited at the top.
He sat among the harebells in his shorts,

Hugging his knees till I caught up with him.
A lock of hair kept falling on his face;
He pushed it back and, looking past me, said:
"Why do you always go about with Black?"
"I haven't thought. I'm used to him, you know."
"I never liked the fellow." Here was love
Too deep for words or touch. The golden downs
Looked over elm tops islanded in mist,
And short grass twinkled with blue butterflies.
Henceforward Marlborough shone.

                            I used to sketch
Under the tutelage of Mr. Hughes,
Who taught us art and let us speak our minds—
And now how lovely seemed the light and shade
On cob and thatch of Wiltshire cottages.
When trout waved lazy in the clear chalk streams,
Glory was in me as I tried to paint
The stretch of meadow and the line of downs,
Putting in buttercups in bright gamboge,
Ultramarine and cobalt for the sky,
With blotting-paper, while the page was wet,
For cloud effects. The eighteenth-century front
Of Ramsbury Manor, solid on its slope,
With subtly curving drive towards the lake,
Calm and trout-plopping in surrounding trees,
Defied my brush. What matter?—poetry
Poured from my pen to keep the ecstasy.
Those were the days when Huxley's *Antic Hay*
Shocked our conventions, when from month to month
I rushed to buy *The London Mercury*,
And moved from Austin Dobson on to Pope.

What joy abounded when the shadows raced
From Rockley to Old Eagle over grass
Faster than I could run! I was released
Into Swinburnian stanzas with the wind.
I felt so strong that I could leap a brook,
So clever, I could master anything;
For Marlborough now was home and beautiful.
Then on the final morning of the term,
Wearing his going-away suit, which had lain
Pressed by his mattress all the previous night,
He came and handed me an envelope
And went without a word. Inside I found
The usual smiling farewell photograph.

VIII
Cornwall in Adolescence

———————

The Arrol-Johnston spun him down to Slough—
Cornwall the object of the early start
And Newbury a foretaste of the goal,
With Trust House lunch and double Scotch at two.
The golf bag shifted as she took the hill
And set a-swing a dangling metal case
That held a piece of sponge for cleaning balls—
A dozen Silver Kings with bramble marks
To sail the fairway, chip upon the green,
And tittup straight and true into the hole.
A smell of leather and of Harris tweed;
The gun-case in the back: Okehampton-wards,
Through broad red Devon: there's a field of roots,
A covey and an orchard and a farm.
"It's getting dark, Bates, switch the headlights on."
Here, in his deafness and his loneliness,
My father's sad grey eyes in gathering dusk
Saw Roughtor and Brown Willy hide the view
Of that bold coast-line where he was not born—
Not born but would he had been, would he had
More right than just the price of them to wear
Those tweeds and leather leggings! "Hurry, Bates."
'His Gibson Girl, his white, his good queen Bess
Straw-hatted bicycling down Surrey lanes . . .
Her welcome for him coming home from work . . .
That early flat, electrically lit,

Red silk and leather in the dining-room,
Beads round the drawing-room electrolier . . .
Singing in bed, to make the youngster laugh,
Tosti's "Goodbye", Lord Henry's "Echo Song"—
And windy walks on Sunday to the Heath,
While dogs were barking round the White Stone pond . . .'
These were the years when love gave way to fear.
I feared my father, loved my mother more,
And just because of this would criticize,
In my own mind, the artless things she said.
    "Dr. Macmillan, who's so good and cheap,
Says I will tire my kidneys if I stoop,
And oh, I *do* love gardening, for now
My garden is the last thing I have left.
You'll help me with the weeding, won't you, John?
He says my teeth are what is wrong, the roots
Have been attacked by dangerous bacilli
Which breed impurities through all my blood,
And this inflames my kidneys. Mrs. Bent
Had just the same (but not, of course, so bad);
She nearly died, poor thing, till Captain Bent
Insisted she should have them out at once.
But mine are ossified into my gums—
No dentist could extract them. Listen, John . . ."
Poor mother, walking bravely on the lawn,
Her body one huge toothache! Would she die?
And if she died could I forgive myself?
"Besides there's what we pay in bills for you.
We've sent you to a most expensive school,
And John, oh John, you've disappointed us.
Your father said to me the other day

How much he wished you were like other boys.
He says that you should earn your keep by now,
By working at the bench. I did my best
To make him give you just another chance."

   Her wit, her gaiety, the jokes we shared,
The love for her that waited underneath,
I kept in check; and as the motor sped
At thirty-five through Shepton on to Wells
Bearing its chauffeur-driven bogey-man,
Down here in Cornwall I would run away
And leave her as we let the tension mount
Through all the Cornish summer afternoon;
   "See how the wind has knocked the rambler down
And damaged my gloxinias. Thank you, Maud.
And now if you will find my spectacles,
And put the ashtray there. That's better. Ah . . .
'Peace, perfect peace.' My pain is nearly gone.
Yes, thank you, Maud. Is everything prepared?
He should be here by dinner. Keep it hot.
Put the potatoes on to boil in time:
You know he's very angry if they're hard.
And put some water in his dressing-room—
The white enamel jug below the stairs—
You know he's very angry if there's none.
And put the drinks out on the silver tray,
And see the whiskey is decanted, Maud:
You know he's very angry if it's not.
And let me know when Master John is back.
Oh, what it is to run a country house!
Certainly not a holiday for me.
The constant worry simply knocks me up;

Our dear old Doctor Blaber used to say,
'Bessie, I fear, is rather delicate.'
What would he say, then, if he saw me now—
Twenty-five years without a holiday,
Housekeeping for a husband and a son?
Five-thirty! Two more hours of quiet bliss!
From this verandah I can see the world
And be at one with Nature. Think Good Thoughts,
And merge myself into the Infinite.
There's Ethel Harden coming up the lane,
I expect she's been to Padstow . . . Oh, how kind!
She promised she would bring me back some wool.
If only John were kind to me like that . . .
Who are those vulgar people on the links—
So out of touch with all the beauty here?
If only Ernest were more sensitive . . .
But never mind. Think Good Thoughts, Bess, cheer up,
And saturate your soul with loveliness.
Knowledge is Power—breathe deeply—Power is Life,
God is the Source of Infinite Resolve,
Ill-health is Evil, therefore Health is God.
I'll think of all the nice things in the world:
A cup of tea, a sunny afternoon,
A snooze, a cigarette, this comfy chair,
A book, *The Education of Eric Lane*—
Now that reminds me. Coo-ee! Jonathan!
Maud! Can you come a moment? Maud! . . . Ah, Maud,
I cannot move, I am too comfortable:
I really should have sent for Master John,
But he is out—my book—the sitting-room—
And—if you're not too busy—bring it here . . .

The one from Boots's with the marker in—
Stephen McKenna, such a clever man . . .
Not there? It must be in my bedroom then.
Ah! *Thank* you . . . If the kettle's on the boil,
Just fill this bottle for me once again.
Where was I? 'And when Cynthia saw his face,
So proudly sensitive, the easy way
He wore those old, albeit well-cut, tweeds
With all the breeding that was Eric Lane,
And saw the twinkle in his blue-grey eyes,
She knew, instinctively, she was forgiven.' "

    A motor broke the spell and that was that;
And here was home, and here the gate, and there
The Arrol-Johnston crawling down the lane.
    And on the morning after burst the storm:
"How often have I said the bacon's cold?
Confound it, Bess! Confound! When will they learn?"
Bang! Boom! His big fists set the cups a-dance,
The willow-pattern shivered on the shelves,
His coat-sleeve swept an ash-tray to the floor . . .
"Just down for breakfast, sir? You're good enough
To honour us by coming down at ten!
Don't fidget, boy. Attention when I speak!
As I was saying—now I look at you—
Bone-lazy, like my eldest brother Jack,
A rotten, low, deceitful little snob.
Yes, I'm in trade and proud of it, I am!"
Black waves of hate went racing round the room;
My gorge was stuck with undigested toast.
And did this woman once adore this man?
And did he love her for her form and face?

I drew my arm across my eyes to hide
The horror in them at the wicked thoughts.
"My boy, it's no good sulking. Listen here.
You'll go to Bates and order me the car,
You'll caddy for me on the morning round,
This afternoon you'll help me dig for bait,
You'll weed the lawn and, when you've finished that,
I'll find another job for you to do.
I'll keep you at it as I've kept myself—
I'll have obedience! Yes, by God, I will!"
"You damn well won't! I'm going out to-day!"
I darted for the door. My father rose.
My saintly mother, on her serious face
A regal look of dignified reproach—
"They both are in the wrong"—now seized her chance:
She waved an arm and dropped her cigarette.
"Come back!" she cried, and heard her cry ring out
As rang the martyred wife's or mother's cry
In many a Temple Thurston she had read,
Or Philip Gibbs: "He *is* your father, John!"
I scraped my wrist along the unstained oak
And slammed the door against my father's weight—
And ran like mad and ran like mad and ran . . .
"I'm free! I'm free!" The open air was warm
And heavy with the scent of flowering mint,
And beetles waved on bending leagues of grass,
And all the baking countryside was kind.

    Dear lanes of Cornwall! With a one-inch map,
A bicycle and well-worn *Little Guide*,
Those were the years I used to ride for miles
To far-off churches. One of them that year

So worked on me that, if my life was changed,
I owe it to St. Ervan and his priest
In their small hollow deep in sycamores.
The time was tea-time, calm free-wheeling time,
When from slashed tree-tops in the combe below
I heard a bell-note floating to the sun;
It gave significance to lichened stone
And large red admirals with outspread wings
Basking on buddleia. So, coasting down
In the cool shade of interlacing boughs,
I found St. Ervan's partly ruined church.
Its bearded Rector, holding in one hand
A gong-stick, in the other hand a book,
Struck, while he read, a heavy-sounding bell,
Hung from an elm bough by the churchyard gate.
"Better come in. It's time for Evensong."

   There wasn't much to see, there wasn't much
The *Little Guide* could say about the church.
Holy and small and heavily restored,
It held me for the length of Evensong,
Said rapidly among discoloured walls,
Impatient of my diffident response.
"Better come in and have a cup of tea."
The Rectory was large, uncarpeted;
Books and oil-lamps and papers were about;
The study's pale green walls were mapped with damp;
The pitch-pine doors and window-frames were cracked;
Loose noisy tiles along the passages
Led to a waste of barely furnished rooms:
Clearly the Rector lived here all alone.

   He talked of poetry and Cornish saints;

He kept an apiary and a cow;
He asked me which church service I liked best—
I told him Evensong . . . "And I suppose
You think religion's mostly singing hymns
And feeling warm and comfortable inside?"
And he was right: most certainly I did.
"Borrow this book and come to tea again."
With Arthur Machen's *Secret Glory* stuffed
Into my blazer pocket, up the hill
On to St. Merryn, down to Padstow Quay
In time for the last ferry back to Rock,
I bicycled—and found Trebetherick
A worldly contrast with my afternoon.

    I would not care to read that book again.
It so exactly mingled with the mood
Of those impressionable years, that now
I might be disillusioned. There were laughs
At public schools, at chapel services,
At masters who were still 'big boys at heart'—
While all the time the author's hero knew
A Secret Glory in the hills of Wales:
Caverns of light revealed the Holy Grail
Exhaling gold upon the mountain-tops;
At "Holy! Holy! Holy!" in the Mass
King Brychan's sainted children crowded round,
And past and present were enwrapped in one.

    In quest of mystical experience
I knelt in darkness at St. Enodoc;
I visited our local Holy Well,
Whereto the native Cornish still resort
For cures for whooping-cough, and drop bent pins

Into its peaty water . . . Not a sign:
No mystical experience was vouchsafed:
The maidenhair just trembled in the wind
And everything looked as it always looked . . .
But somewhere, somewhere underneath the dunes,
Somewhere among the cairns or in the caves
The Celtic saints would come to me, the ledge
Of time we walk on, like a thin cliff-path
High in the mist, would show the precipice.
   An only child, deliciously apart,
Misunderstood and not like other boys,
Deep, dark and pitiful I saw myself
In my mind's mirror, every step I took
A fascinating study to the world.
Box-wallahs, doctors, schoolmasters and dons,
The other parents of the holidays,
Seemed easier to deal with than my own.
In bungalows, with relics of the East
Spared from their London houses, they reclined
On sofas and with happy faces watched
Their bouncing young ones in the drawing-room
Roll up the carpet ready for a dance.
The jingle tinkled in the entrance-hall,
Japanese lanterns lit the sandy paths;
Over the tamarisks the summer night
Heard Melville Gideon on the gramophone.
   And one there was of all the adults there
Who took me at my reckoning of myself—
Aunt Elsie, aunt of normal Scottish boys,
Adopted aunt of lone abnormal me:
She understood us all, she treated us

With reason, waiting while we choked with rage.
"Aunt Elsie, surely I could have the car?"
The eucalyptus shivered in the drive,
The stars were out above the garage roof,
Night-scented stock and white tobacco plant
Gave way to petrol scent and came again.
A rival, changing gear along the lane,
Alone disturbed the wide September night.
"Come in, John, and I'll tell you why you can't."
And there, among the water-colours, screens,
Thick carpets, Whistler books and porcelain,
There, in that more-than-summer residence,
She would explain that I was still a boy.

    'Was still a boy?' Then what, by God, was this—
This tender, humble, unrequited love
For Biddy Walsham? What the worshipping
That put me off my supper, fixed my hair
Thick with Anzora for the dance tonight?
The Talbot-Darracq, with its leather seats
And Biddy in beside me! I could show
Double-declutching to perfection now.
What though the Stokeses were a field away?
Biddy would scream with laughter as I'd charge
Up the steep corner of Coolgrena drive,
And slip from top to second, down to first,
And almost seem to ram the bungalow,
And swirl around the terraced plateau, brake—
Then switch the headlights off and we would wait
While the recovering engine ticked to quiet
In comfortable darkness. If my hand
By accident should touch her hand, perhaps

The love in me would race along to her
On the electron principle, perhaps . . . ?
"So surely, John, it's sensible to walk?"

IX

The Opening World

———————

Balkan Sobranies in a wooden box,
The college arms upon the lid; Tokay
And sherry in the cupboard; on the shelves
The University Statutes bound in blue,
Crome Yellow, *Prancing Nigger*, Blunden, Keats.
My walls were painted Bursar's apple-green;
My wide-sashed windows looked across the grass
To tower and hall and lines of pinnacles.
The wind among the elms, the echoing stairs,
The quarters, chimed across the quiet quad
From Magdalen tower and neighbouring turret-clocks,
Gave eighteenth-century splendour to my state.
Privacy after years of public school;
Dignity after years of none at all—
First college rooms, a kingdom of my own:
What words of mine can tell my gratitude?

   No wonder, looking back, I never worked.
Too pleased with life, swept in the social round,
I soon left Old Marlburians behind.
(As one more solemn of our number said:
"Spiritually I was at Eton, John.")
I cut tutorials with wild excuse,
For life was luncheons, luncheons all the way—
And evenings dining with the Georgeoisie.
Open, swing doors, upon the lighted 'George'
And whiff of *vol-au-vent*! Behold the band

461

Sawing away at gems from *Chu Chin Chow*,
As Harold Acton and the punkahs wave:
"My dears, I want to rush into the fields
And slap raw meat with lilies."
But as the laughs grew long and loud I heard
The more insistent inner voice of guilt:
"Stop!" cried my mother from her bed of pain.
I heard my father in his factory say:
"Fourth generation, John, they look to you."

   "Harry Strathspey is coming if he can
After he's dined at Blenheim. Hamish says
That Ben has got twelve dozen Bollinger."
"And Sandy's going as a matelot."
"I will not have that Mr. Mackworth Price;
Graham will be so furious if he's asked—
We do *not* want another ghastly brawl" . . .
"Well, don't ask Graham, then." "I simply must."
"The hearties say they're going to break it up."
"Oh no, they're not. I've settled *them* all right,
I've bribed the Boat Club with a cask of beer."
Moon after parties: moon on Magdalen Tower,
And shadow on the place for climbing in . . .
Noise, then the great, deep silences again.

   Silk-dressing-gowned, to Sunday-morning bells,
Long after breakfast had been cleared in Hall,
I wandered to my lavender-scented bath;
Then, with a loosely knotted shantung tie
And hair well soaked in Delhez' Genêt d'Or,
Strolled to the Eastgate. Oxford marmalade
And a thin volume by Lowes Dickinson
But half-engaged my thoughts till Sunday calm

Led me by crumbling walls and echoing lanes,
Past college chapels with their organ-groan
And churches stacked with bicycles outside,
To worship at High Mass in Pusey House.

    Those were the days when that divine baroque
Transformed our English altars and our ways.
Fiddle-back chasuble in mid-Lent pink
Scandalized Rome and Protestants alike:
"Why do you try to ape the Holy See?"
"Why do you sojourn in a halfway house?"
And if these doubts had ever troubled me
(Praise God, they don't) I would have made the move.
What seemed to me a greater question then
Tugged and still tugs: Is Christ the Son of God?
Despite my frequent lapses into lust,
Despite hypocrisy, revenge and hate,
I learned at Pusey House the Catholic faith.
Friends of those days, now patient parish priests,
By worldly standards you have not 'got on'
Who knelt with me as Oxford sunlight streamed
On some colonial bishop's broidered cope.
Some know for all their lives that Christ is God,
Some start upon that arduous love affair
In clouds of doubt and argument; and some
(My closest friends) seem not to want His love—
And why this is I wish to God I knew.
As at the Dragon School, so still for me
The steps to truth were made by sculptured stone,
Stained glass and vestments, holy-water stoups,
Incense and crossings of myself—the things
That hearty middle-stumpers most despise

As 'all the inessentials of the Faith'.

　　What cranking-up of round-nosed Morrises
Among the bicycles of broad St. Giles'!
What mist of buds about the guardian elms
Before St. John's! What sense of joys to come
As opposite the Randolph's Gothic pile
We bought the Sunday newspapers and rush'd
Down Beaumont Street to Number 38
And Colonel Kolkhorst's Sunday-morning rout!

　　　　　　D'ye ken Kolkhorst in his artful parlour,
　　　　　　Handing out the drink at his Sunday morning gala?
　　　　　　Some get sherry and some Marsala—
　　　　　　　　With his arts and his crafts in the morning!

The over-crowded room was lit by gas
And smelt of mice and chicken soup and dogs.
Among the knick-knacks stood a photograph
Of that most precious Oxford essayist,
Upon whose margin Osbert Lancaster
Wrote 'Alma Pater' in his sloping hand.
George Alfred Kolkhorst, you whom nothing shocked,
Who never once betrayed a confidence,
No one believed you really were a don
Till Gerard Irvine (now a parish priest)
Went to your lecture on *Le Cid* and clapped.
You swept towards him, gowned, and turned him out.
I see the lines of laughter in your face,
I see you pouring sherry—round your neck
A lump of sugar hanging on a thread
'To sweeten conversation': to your ear
A trumpet held 'for catching good remarks'.

An earlier generation called you 'G'ug':
We called you 'Colonel' just because you were,
Though tall, so little like one. Round your room
The rhyming folklore grew luxuriant:

> G'uggery G'uggery Nunc,
> Your room is all cluttered with junk:
> Candles, bamboonery,
> Plush and saloonery—
> Please pack it up in a trunk.*

You loved the laughter at your own expense:

> That's the wise G'ug, he says each thing twice over,
> Lest you should think he never could recapture
> That first fine *careful* rapture:†

How trivial and silly now they look
Set up in type, acknowledgments and all,
Those rhymes that rocked the room in Beaumont Street,
Preposterous as th' apostrophe in Gug,
Dear private giggles of a private world!
Alan Pryce-Jones came in a bathing-dress
And, seated at your low harmonium,
Struck up the Kolkhorst Sunday-morning hymn:
"There's a home for Colonel Kolkhorst"—final verse
ff with all the stops out:—

> There Bignose plays the organ
>   And the pansies all sing flat,
> But G'ug's no ear for music,
>   He never notices that.

* Words by Rev. Colin Gill, Rector of St. Magnus-the-Martyr, City of London.
† Words by R. Browning and J. D. K. Lloyd, F.S.A.

> The stairs are never smelly,
>> The dogs are well-behaved
> And the Colonel makes his *bons mots*
>> To an audience of the saved.*

Perhaps you do. Perhaps you stand up there,
Waiting with sherry among other friends
Already come, till we rush up the stairs.
   Oxford May mornings! When the prunus bloomed
We'd drive to Sunday lunch at Sezincote:
First steps in learning how to be a guest,
First wood-smoke-scented luxury of life
In the large ambience of a country house.
Heavy with hawthorn scent were Cotswold lanes,
Golden the church towers standing in the sun,
And Gordon Russell with his arts and crafts,
Somewhere beyond in Broadway. Down the drive,
Under the early yellow leaves of oaks;
One lodge is Tudor, one in Indian style.
The bridge, the waterfall, the Temple Pool—
And there they burst on us, the onion domes,
Chajjahs and *chattris* made of amber stone:
'Home of the Oaks', exotic Sezincote!
Stately and strange it stood, the Nabob's house,
Indian without and coolest Greek within,
Looking from Gloucestershire to Oxfordshire;
And, by supremest landscape-gardener's art,
The lake below the eastward slope of grass
Was made to seem a mighty river-reach

---

* Words by A. Midlane (1825–1909), Osbert Lancaster and J. Betjeman.

Curving along to Chipping Norton's hills.

    Crackle of gravel! in the entrance-hall
Boot-jacks and mattocks, hunting mackintosh,
And whips and sticks and barometric clock
Were Colonel Dugdale's; but a sheaf of bast
And gardening-basket told us of his wife.
"Camilla Russell—Bridget King-Tenison—
And Major Attlee—Patsy Rivington—
Shall we go in? I think it's rather late."

    Dear Mrs. Dugdale, mother of us all,
In trailing and Edwardian-looking dress,
A Sargent portrait in your elegance,
Sweet confidante in every tale of woe!
She and her son and we were on the Left,
But Colonel Dugdale was Conservative.
From one end of the butler-tended board
The Colonel's eyes looked out towards the hills,
While at the other end our hostess heard
Political and undergraduate chat.
"Oh, Ethel," loudly Colonel Dugdale's voice
Boomed sudden down the table, "that manure—
I've had it shifted to the strawberry-beds."
"Yes, Arthur . . . Major Attlee, as you said,
Seventeen million of the poor Chinese
Eat less than half a calory a week?"

        How proud beneath the swelling dome
           I sang Lord Ullin's daughter
        At Mrs. Dugdale's grand At Home
           To Lady Horsbrugh-Porter.

So Sezincote became a second home.

    The love between those seeming opposites,
Colonel and Mrs. Dugdale, warmed their guests.
The paddock where the Colonel's favourite mare,
His tried companion of the '14 war,
Grazed in retirement—what is in it now?
New owners wander to the Temple Pool
Where Mrs. Dugdale snipped exotic shrubs
With secateurs as on and on I talked.
The onion dome which listened all the time
To water filling after-tennis baths,
To water splashing over limestone rock
Under the primulas and thin bamboo,
The cottages and lanes and woods and paths
Are all so full of voices from the past
I do not dare return.

    At six o'clock from Bourton-on-the-Hill
The bells rang out above the clumps of oak;
A lighter peal from Longborough lingered on;
Moreton-in-Marsh came echoing from the vale . . .
So gently broke the triple waves of sound
On a still evening of enormous light
That, when they ceased, I almost seemed to hear
From open church-doors village voluntaries
A mile and more away.

                It's time to go.
Dinner with Maurice Bowra sharp at eight—
High up in Wadham's hospitable quad:
The Gilbert Spencers and the Campbell Gray
Bright in the inner room; the brown and green
Of rows and rows of Greek and Latin texts;

The learning lightly worn; the grand contempt
For pedants, traitors and pretentiousness.
A dozen oysters and a dryish hock;
Claret and *tournedos*; a *bombe surprise* . . .
The fusillade of phrases ("I'm a man
More dined against than dining") rattled out
In that incisive voice and chucked away
To be re-used in envious common-rooms
By imitation Maurices. I learned,
If learn I could, how not to be a bore,
And merciless was his remark that touched
The tender spot if one were showing off.
Within those rooms I met my friends for life.
True values there were handed on a plate
As easily as sprouts and aubergines:
"A very able man." "But what's he like?"
"I've told you. He's a very able man."
Administrators, professorial chairs
In subjects such as Civics, and the cad
Out for himself, pretending to be kind—
He summed them up in scathing epigram,
Occasionally shouting out the truth
In forceful nineteen-fourteen army slang;
And as the evening mellowed into port,
He read us poems. There I learned to love
That lord of landscape, Alfred Tennyson;
There first heard Thomas Hardy's poetry,
Master of metre, local as his lanes,
The one expressive village fatalist.
Yeats he would chant in deep sonórous voice;
Bring Rudyard Kipling—then so out-of-date—

To his full stature; show that wisdom was
Not memory-tests (as I had long supposed),
Not 'first-class brains' and swotting for exams,
But humble love for what we sought and knew.
King of a kingdom underneath the stars,
I wandered back to Magdalen, certain then,
As now, that Maurice Bowra's company
Taught me far more than all my tutors did.

    Come, Michael Arthur Stratford Dugdale, rise,
        And Lionel Geoffrey Perry. It is ten.
    Binsey to Cowley, Oxford open lies.
        They breakfasted at eight, the college men
    In college blazers clad and college ties
        Who will be pouring out of lectures when
            Eleven strikes,
    For morning coffee at 'The Super' bound,
        And stack their bikes
    St. Mary Mag's Tractarian walls around.

    Rise! we ourselves are pledged to drink with Ben.
        John Edward Bowle
        Will bring his soul
    And even Mr. Bryson may be coming.
    Rise from your beds! The hawthorn trees are humming
    With insects down the length of Banbury Road,
        The water splashes over Medley Weir.
        The freckled undergraduettes appear,
    Handle-bar baskets heavy with the load
        Of books on Middle English. Up! Away!
    We're lunching at the Liberal Club today
        Where, though the credit's good, the food is poor.
            And should a single Liberal dare

To show his hunted features there
We'll freeze him with a stony stare
That drives him to the door.

New College calls us with her Wykehamists,
Old home of essays, gowns and lecture lists,
Where Sparrow, with his cowlick lock of hair
And schoolboy looks,
Stands a young contrast to his antique books
On walls, floor, table, window-seats and chair.

What time magnolia's bursting into bloom
By Balliol's brain-grey wall,
See clever satyr sprawl
And well-bred faun
Round 'Sligger' in his deck-chair on the lawn.
Deep in their books they are, yet notice whom
They will, with cheerful shout across the grass
For peer and Isis Idol as they pass,
While Sandy Lindsay from his lodge looks down
Dreaming of Adult Education where
The pottery chimneys flare
On lost potential firsts in some less favoured town.

We'll thread the hurrying Corn and George Street crowds
To the unlovely entrance of the OUDS
And hear
How Harman Grisewood, in the tones which thrill
His audience in *Lear*,
Orders a postcard and a penny stamp;
While Emlyn Williams, palm to either ear,
Struggles to learn a part,
And in the next-door room is heard the tramp

And 'rhubarb, rhubarb' as the crowd rehearse
   A one-act play in verse,
Written by someone who is wedded still
   To Gordon Bottomley and Celtic Art.

And does an unimportant don
In Pembroke College linger on,
   With sported oak, alone?
Do nearby bells of low St. Ebbe's
   Ring all unnoticed there?
Can only climbing ivy see
That he for weeks has ceased to be,
While hungry spiders spin their webs
   Between his desk and chair,
Where he is sitting very still
With all Eternity to kill?
How empty, creeper-grown and odd
Seems lonely Pembroke's second quad!
   Still, when I see it, do I wonder why
   That college so polite and shy
Should have more character than Queen's
   Or Univ. splendid in The High.

Friends, we will let our final visit be
   Oxford's epitome:
   The place they call The House
   That shelters A. L. Rowse,
Where the unnoticed canons and their wives
   Live safe North Oxford lives
While peer and peasant tread the sculptured stair
   The festal light to share
   Of Christ Church hall.
Let the obscure cathedral's organ note

Out, out into the starry darkness float
O'er my friend Auden and the clever men,
Running like mad to miss the upper ten
Who burst from 'Peck' in Bullingdonian brawl,
    Jostling some pale-faced victim, you or me.
        I tell you, Brian Howard,
        'Fore God, I am no coward—
    But the triumphant Philistines I see,
And hear a helpless body splash in muddy Mercury.

With sports Bugattis roaring in my ears,
    With 'Blackbirds' bursting from my gramophone,
Lunching with poets, dining late with peers,
    I felt that I had come into my own.

What *was* my own? Large parts of it were jest.
    Recall the music room in Holywell,
The nice North Oxford audience, velvet-dress'd,
    Waiting a treat whose title promised well:

HOMAGE TO BEETHOVEN the posters show.
    'Words: Thomas Driberg. Music: Archie Browne'.
Good wives of Heads of Houses, do you know
    For what it is you've given your half-crown?

What was 'my own'? I partly liked to shock—
    But strawberry-coloured trousers soon made way
For shirts by Hawes and Curtis, hats by Lock,
    And suits for which my father had to pay.

What was my own? Week after sunny week
    I climbed, still keeping in, I thought, with God,
Until I reached what seemed to me the peak—
    The leisured set in Canterbury Quad.

The sun that shines on Edward James
    Shines also down on me:
It's strange that two such simple names
    Should spell such mystery.
The air he breathes, I breathe it too—
But where's he now? What does he do?

On tapestries from Brussels looms
    The low late-'20s sunlight falls
In those black-ceilinged Oxford rooms
    And on their silver-panelled walls;
ARS LONGA VITA BREVIS EST
Was painted round them—not in jest.

And who in those days thought it odd
    To liven breakfast with champagne
And watch, in Canterbury Quad,
    Pale undergraduates in the rain?
For, while we ate Virginia hams,
Contemporaries passed exams.

Tutorials and dons there were,
    And tests and teams and toughs and games—
But these were neither here nor there
    To such as me and Edward James:
We swung the incense-smoke about
To drive the smells of breakfast out,

And talked of Eliot and Wilde
    And Sachie's *Southern Baroque Art*,
While all the time our darling child,
    The poem we had learned by heart
(And wrote last night) must be recited,
Whether or not it were invited.

At William Morris how we laughed,
    And hairy tweeds and knitted ties:
Pub poets who from tankards quaff'd
    Glared up at us with angry eyes—
For, Regency before our time,
We first found Cheltenham sublime.

Ah, how the trivial would enchant!
    On our Botanic Gardens walk
We touched the tender Sensitive Plant
    And saw the fronds enfold the stalk
At each light blow our fingers dealt—
So very like ourselves, we felt.

But in the end they sent me down
    From that sweet hothouse world of bells
And crumbling walls of golden-brown
    And dotty peers and incense-smells
And dinners at the George and hock
And Wytham Woods and Godstow Lock.

Failed in Divinity! Oh count the hours
Spent on my knees in Cowley, Pusey House,
St. Barnabas', St. Mary Mag's, St. Paul's,
Revering chasubles and copes and albs!
Consider what I knew of 'High' and 'Low' . . .
Failed in Divinity! O, towers and spires!
Could no one help? Was nothing to be done?
No. No one. Nothing. Mercilessly calm,
The Cherwell carried under Magdalen Bridge
Its leisured puntfuls of the fortunate
Who next term and the next would still come back.
Could no one help? I'd seen myself a don,

Reading old poets in the library,
Attending chapel in an M.A. gown
And sipping vintage port by candlelight.
I sought my tutor in his arid room,
Who told me, "You'd have only got a Third."
I wandered into Blackwell's, where my bill
Was so enormous that it wasn't paid
Till ten years later, from the small estate
My father left. Not even dusty shelves
Of folios of architectural plates
Could comfort me. Outside, the sunny Broad,
The mouldering busts round the Sheldonian,
The hard Victorian front of Exeter,
The little colleges that front the Turl,
The lean acacia tree in Trinity,
Stood strong and confident, outlasting me.

I called on Ava. He was packing up
For Ireland, for the scintillating lake,
His gate-lodge, woods and winding avenue
Around the limestone walls of Clandeboye.
"Cheer up! You're looking like a soul in hell.
Here's some Amontillado." As I drank,
Already I could hear my father's voice.
"My boy, henceforward your allowance stops:
You'll copy me, who with my strong right arm
Alone have got myself the victory."
"Your father's right, John; you must earn your keep."
Pentonville Road! How could I go by tram
In suit from Savile Row and Charvet tie?
How could I, after Canterbury Quad,

My peers and country houses and my jokes,
Talk about samples, invoices and stock?

Ah, welcome door, Gabbitas Thring & Co.'s
Scholastic agency in Sackville Street!
"The Principal will see you." "No degree?
There is, perhaps, a temporary post
As cricket master for the coming term
At Gerrard's Cross. Fill in this form and give
Qualifications—testimonials
Will help—and if you are accepted, please
Pay our commission promptly. Well, good day!"

> The sun that shone on Edward James
>   Shone also down on me—
> A prep-school master teaching Games,
>   Maths, French, Divinity.
> Harsh hand-bells harried me from sleep
> For thirty pounds a term and keep.
>
> And he continued friendly still,
>   And wrote his verses out with care
> On vellum with a coloured quill,
>   And published them in volumes rare
> Of hand-made paper bound up fine . . .
> And then, by Jove, he published mine!
>
> They tell me he's in Mexico,
>   They will not give me his address;
> But if he sees this book he'll know
>   I do not value him the less.
> For Art is long and Life must end,
> My earlier publisher and friend.

CRICKET MASTER
(*An Incident*)

My undergraduate eyes beholding,
    As I climbed your slope, Cat Hill:
Emerald chestnut fans unfolding,
    Symbols of my hope, Cat Hill.
What cared I for past disaster,
Applicant for cricket master,
Nothing much of cricket knowing,
Conscious but of money owing?
    Somehow I would cope, Cat Hill.

"The sort of man we want must be prepared
To take our first eleven. Many boys
From last year's team are with us. You will find
Their bowling's pretty good and they are keen."
"And so am I, Sir, very keen indeed."
Oh where's mid-on? And what is silly point?
Do six balls make an over? Help me, God!
"Of course you'll get some first-class cricket too;
The MCC send down an A team here."
My bluff had worked. I sought the common-room,
Of last term's pipe-smoke faintly redolent.
It waited empty with its worn arm-chairs
For senior bums to mine, when in there came
A fierce old eagle in whose piercing eye
I saw that instant-registered dislike
Of all unhealthy aesthetes such as me.
"I'm Winters—you're our other new recruit
And here's another new man—Barnstaple."

478

He introduced a thick Devonian.
"Let's go and have some practice in the nets.
You'd better go in first." With but one pad,
No gloves, and knees that knocked in utter fright,
Vainly I tried to fend the hail of balls
Hurled at my head by brutal Barnstaple
And at my shins by Winters. Nasty quiet
Followed my poor performance. When the sun
Had sunk behind the fringe of Hadley Wood
And Barnstaple and I were left alone
Among the ash-trays of the common-room,
He murmured in his soft West-country tones:
"D'you know what Winters told me, Betjeman?
He didn't think you'd ever held a bat."

    The trusting boys returned. "We're jolly glad
You're on our side, Sir, in the trial match."
"But I'm no good at all." "Oh yes, you are."
When I was out first ball, they said "Bad luck!
You hadn't got your eye in." Still I see
Barnstaple's smile of undisguised contempt,
Still feel the sting of Winters' silent sneer.
Disgraced, demoted to the seventh game,
Even the boys had lost their faith in me.
God guards his aesthetes. If by chance these lines
Are read by one who in some common-room
Has had his bluff called, let him now take heart:
In every school there is a sacred place
More holy than the chapel. Ours was yours:
I mean, of course, the first-eleven pitch.
Here in the welcome break from morning work,
The heavier boys, of milk and biscuits full,

Sat on the roller while we others pushed
Its weighty cargo slowly up and down.
We searched the grass for weeds, caressed the turf,
Lay on our stomachs squinting down its length
To see that all was absolutely smooth.

    The prize-day neared. And, on the eve before,
We masters hung our college blazers out
In readiness for tomorrow. Matron made
A final survey of the boys' best clothes—
Clean shirts. Clean collars. "Rice, your jacket's torn.
Bring it to me this instant!" Supper done,
Barnstaple drove his round-nosed Morris out
And he and I and Vera Spencer-Clarke,
Our strong gymnasium mistress, squashed ourselves
Into the front and rattled to The Cock.

    Sweet bean-fields then were scenting Middlesex;
Narrow lanes led between the dairy-farms
To ponds reflecting weather-boarded inns.
There on the wooden bench outside The Cock
Sat Barnstaple, Miss Spencer-Clarke and I,
At last forgetful of tomorrow's dread
And gazing into sky-blue Hertfordshire.
Three pints for Barnstaple, three halves for me,
Sherry of course for Vera Spencer-Clarke.

    Pre-prize-day nerves? Or too much bitter beer?
What had that evening done to Barnstaple?
I only know that singing we returned;
The more we sang, the faster Barnstaple
Drove his old Morris, swerving down the drive
And in and out the rhododendron clumps,
Over the very playing-field itself,

And then—oh horror!—right across the pitch
Not once, but twice or thrice. The mark of tyres
Next day was noticed at the Parents' Match.
That settled Barnstaple and he was sacked,
While I survived him, lasting three more terms.

> Shops and villas have invaded
>   Your chestnut quiet there, Cat Hill.
> Cricket field and pitch degraded,
>   Nothing did they spare, Cat Hill.
> Vera Spencer-Clarke is married
> And the rest are dead and buried;
> I am thirty summers older,
> Richer, wickeder and colder,
>   Fuller too of care, Cat Hill.

481

INDEX OF FIRST LINES

Index of First Lines

485

INDEX OF PLACES

Index of Places

Pevensey, Sussex 273
Pinner, Middlesex 169, 219, 289
Plush, Dorset 31
Plymouth, Devon 115
Polegate, Sussex 176
Polzeath, Cornwall 245, 408
Pontefract, West Yorkshire 155
Poole, Dorset 145
Poperinghe, Belgium 415
Port Isaac, Cornwall 239
Potters Bar, Hertfordshire 225
Prestatyn, Clwyd 333
Preston, Lancashire 128
Purbeck, Dorset 145

Ramsbury, Wiltshire 448
Ramsey (Rumsaa), Isle of Man 65
Rhyl, Clwyd 333
Rime Intrinsica, Dorset 31
Rock, Cornwall 137, 457
Rockley, Wiltshire 449
Rome, Italy 210, 320, 377, 463
Roscommon, County, Ireland 198
Rough Tor, Cornwall 307, 450
Rugby, Warwickshire 257
Runcorn, Cheshire 325
Rutland 145

St. Enodoc, Cornwall 53, 113, 135, 241,
    271, 457
St. Ervan, Cornwall 456–7
St. Ives, Cornwall 298
St. Merryn, Cornwall 457
Salisbury, Wiltshire 321
Scandinavia, 373
Scotland 358, 372, 437, 458
Severn, River 42, 338
Sezincote, Gloucestershire 466–8
Shanghai, China 137
Shannon, River, Ireland 254
Sheffield, South Yorkshire 256, 260
Shepton Mallet, Somerset 452
Shetland 358
Shilla, Cornwall 52, 306, 423
Shropshire 42
Shroton, Dorset 31
Silbury, Wiltshire 447
Slough, Berkshire 20, 450

Snaefell, Isle of Man 65
Snowdon, Wales 247
Solihull, West Midlands 128
Somerset 89, 145, 328, 452
Somme, River, France 428
Spain 308, 371
Speedwell Cavern, Derbyshire 258
Staffordshire 268, 333
Staines, Surrey 288
Stepper, Cornwall 135, 323, 423
Stinsford, Dorset 36
Stratford-atte-Bow, Essex 336
Stratford-upon-Avon, Warwickshire
    338
Sturminster Newton, Dorset 31
Sudan 194
Suffolk 222, 336
Surrey 10, 23, 45, 88, 200, 211, 229,
    237, 288, 308, 351, 365, 386, 409,
    450
Sussex 145, 175, 277, 312, 329, 422,
    438
Swindon, Wiltshire 109, 128
Switzerland 201

Tallow, County Waterford, Ireland
    249
Tewkesbury, Gloucestershire 338
Thame, Oxfordshire 120
Thames, River 84, 216, 314, 362, 429,
    435
Thanet, Kent 12
Togoland 74
Torquay, Devon 145, 406
Trebetherick, Cornwall 52, 418, 457
Tregardock, Cornwall 239
Trenain, Cornwall 136
Trent, River 144
Tresmeer, Cornwall 418
Trevose, Cornwall 239, 271
Tristernagh, County Westmeath,
    Ireland 67
Truro, Cornwall 424
Tunbridge Wells, Kent 214, 372
Tuscany, Italy 371

Uffington, Oxfordshire 264, 391
United States of America 190, 221